THE KOREAN WAR

Paul M. Edwards

The Greenwood Press "Daily Life Through History" Series

American Soldiers' Lives
David S. Heidler and Jeanne T. Heidler, Series Editors

GREENWOOD PRESS
Westport, Connecticut • London

Library of Congress Cataloging-in-Publication Data

Edwards, Paul M.
   The Korean War / Paul M. Edwards.
      p.cm.—(The Greenwood Press "Daily life through history" series, ISSN 1080-4749)
   Includes bibliographical references and index.
   ISBN 0-313-33248-7 (alk. paper)
   1. Korean War, 1950–1953. 2. Korean War, 1950–1953—Participation, American.
   3. United States—Armed Forces—History. I. Title. II. Series.
   DS918.E362 2006
   951.904'2373—dc22   2006015360

British Library Cataloguing in Publication Data is available.

Library of Congress Catalog Card Number: 2006015360
ISBN: 0-313-33248-7
ISSN: 1080-4749

First published in 2006

Greenwood Press, 88 Post Road West, Westport, CT 06881
An imprint of Greenwood Publishing Group, Inc.
www.greenwood.com

Printed in the United States of America

The paper used in this book complies with the
Permanent Paper Standard issued by the National
Information Standards Organization (Z39.48-1984).

10 9 8 7 6 5 4 3 2 1

This volume is affectionately dedicated to the vivacious Carolynn Jean Edwards, wife, mother, grandmother, great-grandmother, and delightful companion for more than half-a-century.

CONTENTS

SERIES FOREWORD

More than once during the military campaigns undertaken by American armies, leaders in both civilian and martial roles have been prompted to ask in admiration, "Where do such people come from?" The question, of course, was both rhetorical and in earnest: the one because they knew that such people hailed from the coasts and the heartland, from small hamlets and sprawling cities, from expansive prairies and breezy lakeshores. They were as varied as the land they represented, as complex as the diversity of their faiths and ethnic identities, all nonetheless defined by the overarching identity of "American," made more emphatic by their transformation into "American soldiers."

They knew and we know where they came from. On the other hand, the question for anyone who knows the tedium, indignity, discomfort, and peril of military service in wartime is more aptly framed, "Why did they come at all?"

In the volumes of this series, accomplished scholars of the American military answer that question, and more. By depicting the daily routines of soldiers at war, they reveal the gritty heroism of those who conquered the drudgery of routine and courageously faced the terrors of combat. With impeccable research and a deep understanding of the people who move through these grandly conceived stories—for war, as Tolstoy has shown us, is the most grandly conceived and complex story of all—these books take us to the heart of great armies engaged in enormous undertakings. Bad food, disease, haphazardly treated wounds, and chronic longing for loved ones form part of these stories, for those are the universal afflictions of soldiers. Punctuating long stretches of loneliness and monotony were interludes of horrific violence that scarred every soldier, even those who escaped physical injury. And insidious wounds could fester because of ugly customs and ingrained prejudices: for too long a span, soldiers who happened to be minorities suffered galling injustices at the hands of those they served, often giving for cause and comrades what Lincoln called "the last full measure of devotion," despite unfair indignities and undeserved ignominy. And sadly, it is true that protracted or unpopular wars could send veterans returning to a country indifferent about their sacrifices, sometimes hostile to the cause for which they fought, and begrudging even marginal compensation to their spouses and orphans. But quiet courage, wry humor, tangible camaraderie, and implacable pride are parts of these stories as well, ably conveyed by these gifted writers who have managed to turn the pages that follow into vivid snapshots of accomplishment, sacrifice, and triumph.

Until recently the American soldier has usually been a citizen called to duty in times of extraordinary crisis. The volunteer army of this latest generation, though, has created a remarkable hybrid in the current American soldier, a professional who nevertheless upholds the traditions of American citizens who happen to be in uniform to do a tough job. It is a noble tradition that ennobles all who have honored it. And more often than not, they who have served have managed small miracles of fortitude and resolve.

Walter Lord's *Incredible Victory* recounts the story of Mike Brazier, the rear-seat man on a torpedo plane from the carrier *Yorktown* in the Battle of Midway. He and pilot Wilhelm Esders were among that stoic cadre of fliers who attacked Japanese carriers, knowing that their fuel was insufficient for the distance to and from their targets. Having made their run under heavy enemy fire, Esders finally had to ditch the spent and damaged plane miles short of the *Yorktown* in the rolling Pacific. He then discovered that Brazier had been shot to pieces. Despite his grave wounds, Brazier had managed to change the coils in the radio to help guide the plane back toward the *Yorktown*. In the life raft as he died, Mike Brazier never complained. He talked of his family and how hard it had been to leave them, but he did not complain. Instead he apologized that he could not be of more help.

In the great, roiling cauldron of the Second World War, here was the archetype of the American soldier: uncomplaining while dying far from home in the middle of nowhere, worried at the last that he had not done his part.

Where do such people come from?

We invite you to read on, and find out.

David S. Heidler and Jeanne T. Heidler
Series Editors

PREFACE

If I owned both hell and Korea, I'd live in hell and rent out Korea.

—Theodore H. Smith
(paraphrase of William T. Sherman)

Memory is an elusive thing, and no two men or women who served during the Korean War will retain identical memories of their experiences. Each life was different, each experience unique, though there are some shared memories: the adjustment to military service, the bumpy roads choked with dust that suddenly turned into thick heavy mud, the waiting, the uniformity, and the discipline. The men and women who fought would remember the long hours on guard duty in the cold and the rain against an enemy who came from every side. Men would recall the sweat that made mud on their faces and the cold that formed icicles on a week's growth of beard. Individually, they would remember preparation for patrols, blackened faces, grenades fastened to the cartridge belts, the final cigarette, sweating out the start. Strong among the memories would be the patrols, the stealth while moving across rice paddies and rocky hillsides, the apprehension and keyed-up nerves. They'd recollect the first cool smoke at the end of patrol, the flack vests, rubber mattresses, sleeping bags, the weight of the Browning Automatic Rifle, the soupy communication trenches, and the thousands of hills that always seemed to go up. And they remembered the marching, the physical education, retreats and sick call, and flying twenties and loneliness.

Collectively, they share the name *Korean War Veteran* and, as such, have in common a significant role in one of the great moments in history. Many of these veterans believe they have been forgotten and their war is identified, even among military historians, as

"The Forgotten War." These veterans are not whiners; in fact, they are often reluctant to speak, but they sometimes feel that their own service, and that of the military in Korea, has been misunderstood and unnecessarily discounted. Unfortunately, this is at least partially true.

HISTORICAL SIGNIFICANCE OF THE KOREAN WAR

Somehow, the historical significance of the Korean War has not been properly acknowledged, nor have the events that occurred there received the attention they rightly deserve. It is perhaps more accurate to say that those who fought in this terrible war have been ignored rather than forgotten, a situation that arises more from ignorance than any discredit. It is not so much that Americans do not care about this event, nor about the men and women on whose shoulders it fell, but rather that the war came at a difficult time for America. It came at a time when the memories of the heroic efforts during World War II were still most vivid. It is also true that the character of the Korean War was such that it required an adjustment for those used to a different, perhaps more simple, time.

This series, *American Soldiers' Lives,* comprises nine volumes about the American soldier. This particular volume, *The Korean War,* is the story of those who served during the Korean War who, as President Clinton said at the dedication of the Korean War Memorial in 1995, "defend freedom for a determined ally halfway around the world—or as the monument says, a place they had never been and a people they had never met."[1]

The term *soldier* here is used to include those men and women who served in the varied services: the Army, Navy, Marines, Air Force, Coast Guard, and Merchant Marines. The primary American force in Korea was the United States Army and is, thus, the focus of this book. Men and women of the other services were deeply involved and their stories too have been included, though not in as much detail. The definition of a soldier in the Korean War has been presented by the *Graybeards,* the Korean War Veterans Association, as those who "fought" in the Korean War, meaning those who served in the Armed Forces between June 25, 1950 and January 1, 1955. This extended date is because those who were in Korea immediately after the Armistice shared much of the hardship and danger. Despite the crisp deadline marked in many narrative histories, the Armistice did not end the fighting or the killing. Korean War service has been extended to those American men and women who were in the armed services anywhere in the world during this period. It is important to remember, of course, that, in 2006, American troops still serve along the Demilitarized Zone in Korea.

Despite the American tendency to bypass it, the Korean War was a watershed in American history. This period marked major changes in the American military and diplomatic strategy post World War II. The United States, and in many respects the world, would never think, or be, the same again. The cold war turned hot for a while and, in that moment, the dangers and frustrations brought the world to the brink of World War III. The fact that the events in Korea did not grow into a global confrontation is one of the many things we must consider when addressing the legacy of this war. For it was in Korea that the United States drew the line and backed up its announcement to the world that communism would no longer be allowed to expand by military effort. Ever since the close of the Second World War, the communist system had been growing, as the necessary compromises among the Allied powers of World War II turned into hostility and fear. Communist military growth had been previously countered with economic and political aid. But, in Korea, for the first time, the United States would commit its armed forces to limiting an expansion, which, many believed, was designed to take over the world.

The conflict in Korea was a war that was fought, somewhat unexpectedly, by the grunt, by the man and woman in the field. As such, it brought an end to the growing myth among the American military that possession of an atomic bomb made conventional warfare unnecessary. The Korea War was a conventional war, and was often fought with the tactics and weapons of World War II. Even as the U.S. assumed that future wars, if there were any, would be decided quickly through the great power available in its nuclear arsenal, it found itself in a war with a small but powerful nation that, among other things, did not provide the kind of target that would be significant in a nuclear effort. Despite the promises of a push-button war, the war in Korea was fought, as wars have always been fought, with the individual in the field.

The desire by some parts of the military to use atomic weapons was not fulfilled; America's nuclear arsenal was not used. The full complement of weapons, therefore, was not available. The war in Korea predicted future confrontations and, unexpectedly, reaffirmed the necessity of maintaining a conventional armed force. It also marked the beginning of the United States' continuous buildup of the military complex that, in the next fifty years, would reflect the consumption of nearly half its annual budget.

Other than the War of 1812, the Korean War was the first that came to a conclusion without a victory—without America's traditional demand for "unconditional surrender." The stalemate it produced was an unaccustomed and uncomfortable situation for the military, just as it was for so many Americans. Yet, evolving strategies of war, and about war, marked the beginning of a long line of such actions that have led us as a nation through Vietnam and beyond. This was a new type of war, a war fought without the assumption of victory. Of particular note, it was a war in which political considerations prevented the military from fighting the kind of war for which it had prepared. It was a powerful lesson: diplomatic considerations in the "cold-war" world made America reluctant to commit all its resources in the fear that an enemy would strike elsewhere.

The changes, coming about as the GI was fighting and dying in a limited war, led to some rather intense controversy. It became common to speak of the Korean War as "a war we can't win, we can't lose, and we can't quit." It quickly became an unpopular war, and left Americans—even until this day—unsure how to consider those who fought it. Besides, it was not characterized by the vigorous protests that have marked our involvement in other conflicts, including America's war in Iraq. The vast majority of those who were called to service in Korea went as called. There was little card burning or draft dodging. This is a brief effort to present the experiences of those who went, to account for the life and times of the American soldiers of the Korean War.

SCOPE OF THIS BOOK

The book contains fourteen chapters, a timeline, a bibliography, and index. The first chapter, called "Overview," provides some context for the outbreak of war and physical and cultural comments about Korea—The Hermit Kingdom—where the war occurred. Korea can be a harsh and hostile environment, and the weather and terrain had a great deal to do with how the war was fought. Chapter 2 provides a brief account of the Korean War as it progressed through a series of phases and campaigns. The phases reflect the changing nature of the war, as the United Nations forces fought first against North Korea, then against Chinese Communists Forces, and finally were caught in a prolonged stalemate. A fourth phase is hinted at and concerns the fighting that went on after the cease-fire was signed. The discussions of the campaigns, usually identified by which side in the conflict was in attack and which in defense, acknowledges the manner in which circumstances encountered altered the course of the war.

The question of raising a military force is discussed in Chapter 3. The U.S. military in 1950 was, to say the least, unprepared for a war such as the one in Korea was to be. The effort to raise a force to carry out the dictates of President Harry S Truman, as well as the United Nations, was far reaching. The First Marine Division, nearly depleted, had to be reconstructed, and the lack of volunteers meant that the other services had to be enforced by reserves, the recall of men who had only recently been mustered out from World War II service, and then draftees.

The extraordinary means used to turn these individuals into a military force is considered in Chapter 4, which deals with basic training, assignments, and eventually transportation into the war zone. Chapter 5 acknowledges the fact that many of the weapons and equipment available to both UN and Communist forces were weapons that had been left over from World War II. Despite this, most of the weapons were fairly good ones. At first they were in short supply, but as the war went on the supplies proved to be adequate.

Chapter 6 takes a look at life at the front and the difficulties of adjusting to life under both garrison and combat environments. It addresses the conditions under which the military lived and worked, how they fought, and what was necessary to keep them well prepared and equipped for the job they had been sent to do. This chapter about life is followed by Chapter 7, which deals with death, and the care of the wounded. The support for the wounded, provided by advances of evacuation methods (the development of the helicopter) and the increased medical procedures (the Mobile Army Surgical Unit, or MASH) gave the wounded GI the best chance ever. This chapter also considers the procedures for dealing with those men and women who paid the ultimate sacrifice.

Chapter 8 shows life behind the line, the garrison as well as the service trains, and investigates some of the more common of the military assignments. Following this is a look into the American soldier's view of those with whom he fought, both in terms of the enemy he faced and the allies with whom he shared the goals of the war. Chapter 9 deals with the questions of attitude.

The conditions of the individual soldiers and the manner in which their actions were reflected in the news media is considered in Chapter 10, as are the questions of morale among the troops, and the myths of service that they had to deal with. It is hard to tell if the censorship imposed by the military really altered the coverage of the Korean War, but what was available, as well as the myths growing up around the war, both contributed to the soldier's morale, or the lack of it.

Chapter 11 takes a look at how the soldier coped with the military, with combat, and how they were taken care of both by the military and by themselves. From the role of the chaplain to the games they played, the soldier's life is considered in terms of activities. Chapter 12 deals with coming home for those who rotated out on leave, those who were wounded, or those who were released as POWs. The transition from soldier was difficult for most of those who returned, and this was particularly true for those who returned after being prisoners of war. The chapter also looks at the home front and the America to which military men and women returned. Some reflections of veterans as well as a brief analysis of these comments are provided in Chapter 13. Taking a look at the responses of individuals who were there, and involved, gives us a picture of the events that are not available in simple narrative. This chapter takes a look at the way that this war is remembered by those who were there. The work concludes with some commentary about the war, the Americans who fought it, and the nation that sent them.

SOURCES

To understand why the Korean War is considered the forgotten war, all you need to do is to visit the local bookstore and see what is available on Korea compared with what is available on World War II and Vietnam. The same is true if you visit the shelves of the local library. The resources are considerably smaller. It is not that there has not been some excellent work done on the Korean War, just that there has not been enough of it. In the preparation of this volume, I have been blessed by the availability of some groundbreaking research efforts, and by some narrative histories that have begun to provide valid interpretations. I am particularly grateful for the insights in Paul Pierpaoli's "Beyond Collective Amnesia: A Korean War Retrospective" (*Military History*, Vol. 14, No. 3 [Spring 2000]: 1–4). Just as certainly this manuscript could not have been completed without the following works: Bruce Cumings, *Korea's Place in the Sun: A Modern History;* Richard Sever and Lewis Milford, *The Wages of War: When Americans Came Home: From Valley Forge to Vietnam;* Ed Ivanhoe, *Darkroom: Eighth Army Special Operations in the Korean War;* Joseph Golden, *Korea: the Untold Story of the War;* S. L. A. Marshall, *The River and the Gauntlet: Defeat of the Eighth Army by the Communist Chinese Forces, November 1950;* James Matray, *Historical Dictionary of the Korean War;* T. R. Fehrenbach, *This Kind of War;* John Bodnar, *Remaking America: Public Memory, Commemoration and Patriotism in the Twentieth Century;* Max Hastings, *The Korean War;* Allan Millet, *Semper Fidelis: The History of the United States Marine Corps;* Clay Blair, *The Forgotten War;* Rod Paschall, *A Study in Command and Control: Special Operations in Korea 1951–1953;* Billy C. Mossman, *Ebb and Flow, November 1950-July 1951: the United States Army in the Korean War;* Walter H. Hermes, *Truce Tent and Fight Front* published in 1966 by the Office of the Chief of Military History; and the recently republished Korean Institute of Military History, *The Korean War,* a three-volume collection.

Research has been conducted at the significant collections housed at the following institutions: The Harry S. Truman Presidential Museum and Library in Independence, Missouri, where most of the political views of the war is available for research; the Eisenhower Presidential Library in Abilene, Kansas, which contains most of the materials dealing with that part of the war directed by President Dwight D. Eisenhower; the Army History Center, Carlisle Barracks, Pennsylvania; the Air Library at Maxwell Air Force Base in Montgomery, Alabama; the Central Plains Region of the National Archives and Records Administration (Kansas City, Missouri); the Library of the University of Missouri at Kansas City, and most helpful the Center for the Study of the Korean War at Graceland University in Independence, Missouri, which maintains a vast collection of materials dealing with the individual soldiers and sailors of this war, including a large number of memoirs and oral histories.

In reading this work, it will be helpful to keep several language related items in mind. First of all the Korean language is written in *Hangul* (meaning great letters) and is very different from Romance languages. Because the sounds of the letters are not the same, many variations of spelling occur ("Pusan"/"Busan") or with diacritical marks ("P'yongyang"/"Pyongyang"). It is also important to keep in mind that the largest share of the maps used during the war had been produced by the Japanese, and thus the names that were in common use were often Japanese rather than Korean. The obvious example is the Chosin Reservoir, which in Korean is *Changjin,* but remembered best by its Japanese name, *Chosin.* There is, as well, some tendency for the language to cause repetitiveness. For example, many know that *ri* means village and *do* means island, but common usage sometimes makes it easier to read if we say Hagaru-ri, or the island of Wolmi-do.

NOTE

1. Korean War Veterans Memorial, Washington, D.C., 27 July 1995.

ACKNOWLEDGMENTS

As I have put this material together, I have been dependent on help from a great many people. First, I have relied on numerous secondary sources for guidance, the most helpful of which have been identified in the notes and bibliography. These works provide an overview that allows the author to put his or her work into perspective. I am also very indebted to the authors of the many monographs that have provided an in-depth investigation on a variety of related topics and are thereby the source of a good deal of factual information and analysis. Third, I owe a debt of gratitude to hundreds of oral histories, memoirs, and personal account that provide information and the "mood" that helps to understand something of what the soldiers felt and thought. To these authors and veterans I offer my sincere thanks. I have also relied on the many stories, insights, suggestions, and criticism of some of the many Korean veterans who come by the Center for the Study of the Korean War to see evidence of their own service.

To this list I would like to add the members of the Missouri Korean War Veterans Association, the Kansas City Chapter of the Disabled American Veterans, and Graceland University for the wide use of the library and archival materials located at their Independence Campus, at the Center for the Study of the Korean War. Particular thanks must be given for the help received by the director of the Center.

Several other individuals must be acknowledged for their help during the preparation of this effort. These must include Tim Reeves and Mark Corriston of the National Archives, Michael Devine of the Truman Library, and Gregg Edwards, director of the Center for the Study of the Korean War. For personal and unusual support I also wish to acknowledge my wife Carolynn;, Paula Jean and Jeff Tennant;, Nancy Eisler of Outreach International;, Lisa Hecht, researcher and graduate student;, Greg Smith, independent scholar and friend;, as well as volunteers and friends Cindy Roberts and Judith Charlton, and Frank Kelley, (Marine, poet, friend). Thanks also to the Third Born Supper Club for listening.

TIMELINE

July 1844	U.S. and Korea sign commercial relations treaty
August 1866	Korean soldiers massacre crew of USS *General Sherman*
June 1870	U.S. punitive kills more than 250 Koreans
May 1882	Korean-American Treaty of Friendship and Commerce signed
November 1905	Japan becomes protector of Korea
1908	U.S. acknowledges Japan's primacy over Korea and Manchuria
1910	Korea annexed by Japan
April 1919	Republic of Korea (ROK) government in exile established in Shanghai
August 15, 1943	U.S. General Order Number One divides Korea at 38th Parallel
December 1, 1943	Cairo Declaration suggests Korean independence "in due time"
August 8, 1945	Soviet Union declares war on Japan and invades Korea
September 2, 1945	Japan surrenders on board the USS *Missouri*
September 8, 1945	U.S. occupation troops arrive in Korea
May 8, 1946	Joint Soviet-American commission fails to reach agreement on Korean reunification
September 17, 1947	Question of Korean independence is referred to the UN
November 14, 1947	UN approves creation of Temporary Commission on Korea (UNTCOK) to supervise national elections in Korea

January 24, 1948	Soviets refuse to permit UNTCOK into North Korea
April 8, 1948	President Truman withdraws most U.S. troops from Korea
August 15, 1948	Republic of Korea (ROK) established—Syngman Rhee claims control of all Korea under its leadership
September 9, 1948	Democratic People's Republic of Korea (DPRK) is established—Kim Il Sung claims control of all Korea
December 31, 1948	Soviets withdraw troops from Korea. Military advisory group remains
April 8, 1949	Soviets veto Republic of Korea admission to UN
May 2, 1949	U.S. Korean Military Advisory Group (KMAG) activated
June 29, 1949	U.S. troops withdrawn from Republic of Korea
August 25, 1949	Soviet government detonates first atomic bomb
January 12, 1950	Secretary of State Dean Acheson proclaims Korea outside America's Far East Security Zone
February 14, 1950	Sino-Soviet Treaty of Friendship and Alliance signed
June 25, 1950	Democratic People's Republic of Korea attacks the ROK with an estimated 135,000 men and 150 tanks
June 26, 1950	U.S. Ambassador John J. Muccio orders dependents evacuated from Korea
June 27, 1950	President Truman authorizes U.S. naval and air support of the Republic of Korea (ROK)—U.S. Fifth Air Force shoots down first enemy plane near Seoul—UN adopts U.S. resolution asking member nations to support ROK
June 28, 1950	United Kingdom forces in Japanese waters join U.S. command
June 28, 1950	Seoul falls—destroyed Han bridge traps Republic of Korea (ROK) Army—507th Anti-Aircraft Battalion downs enemy plane—Truman authorizes blockade of Korean coast—first U.S. casualties when five members of the 507th Anti-Aircraft Battery are wounded—first naval bombardment as USS *Juneau* fires first salvo on east coast
June 29, 1950	Truman agrees with reporter's description of events as a "Police Action"
June 30, 1950	Truman commits U.S. troops to support UN resolution—Republic of Korea (ROK) division crosses Han River—Truman extends Public Law 599 extending the draft
July 1, 1950	U.S. Task Force Smith, first contingent, arrives in Korea
July 2, 1950	USS *Juneau* destroys attacking Democratic People's Republic of Korea torpedo boats near Chumunjin, in only naval battle of the war—Truman rejects offer of Nationalist Chinese troops

July 3, 1950	First UN carrier strike as planes from USS *Valley Forge* hit DPRK airfields
July 6–8, 1950	34th Infantry Regiment (24th Division) delays North Korea at Osan
July 7, 1950	General Douglas MacArthur gets command of all UN troops—United Nation Command created
July 12, 1950	Eighth U.S. Army given ground command in Korea
July 13, 1950	General Walton "Johnny" Walker takes command of Eighth Army in Korea—U.S. and Republic of Korea (ROK) form defensive line along Kum River
July 13–16, 1950	Battle of the Kum River, 24th Infantry Division delays DPRK
July 18, 1950	8th Cavalry Regiment arrives at Pohang
July 19, 1950	Truman authorizes Secretary of Defense to mobilize reserves
July 20–21, 1950	5th and 8th Cavalry Regiments defeated at Yongdong
July 24, 1950	Fifth U.S. Air Force relocates in Korea
July 26, 1950	Eighth Army withdraws to defensive positions near Pusan
July 29, 1950	General Walker is reported to have issued a "stand or die" order
July 31, 1950	General MacArthur visits Taiwan to discuss island defense
August 2, 1950	First Provisional Marine Brigade lands at Pusan
August 3–4, 1950	First aeromedical evacuation of UN troops by Marine VMO-6 (Marine Fighter Squadron) helicopters
August 10, 1950	First air raid on Rashin—Tenth Corps activated and ordered to Korea—Truman authorizes call-up of National Guard unit
August 17, 1950	Massacred American prisoners found on Hill 303
August 18, 1950	First tank-to-tank conflict of the war
August 25, 1950	General William Dean taken prisoner
August 29, 1950	United Kingdom's 27th Brigade lands at Pusan
September 15, 1950	Tenth Corps lands at Inchon harbor
September 18, 1950	Eighth Army breaks out from Pusan Perimeter
September 19, 1950	Battle of Naktong Bulge
September 25, 1950	Joint Chiefs of Staff (JCS) authorize MacArthur to cross 38th Parallel
September 29, 1950	MacArthur returns Seoul to President Rhee
October 1, 1950	Republic of Korea (ROK) troops cross 38th Parallel—first Greek and Netherlands troops arrive
October 7, 1950	U.S. troops cross 38th Parallel

October 9, 1950	Troops of 1st Cavalry Division cross 38th Parallel
October 12, 1950	Chinese Communist Forces (CCF) begin crossing Yalu River into Korea
October 15, 1950	President Truman and General MacArthur meet at Wake Island
October 18, 1950	Republic of Korea (ROK) troops occupy Hungnam and Hamhung
October 19, 1950	Pyongyang, capital of North Korea, is occupied
October 20, 1950	187th Airborne jumps at Sukchon
October 26, 1950	1st Marine Division makes administrative landing at Wonsan
October 27, 1950	Eighth Army is halted by Chinese
November 1, 1950	First Chinese MiG jet appears near the Yalu
November 8, 1950	First all-jet combat when F-80 shoots down (Soviet) MiG-15
November 12, 1950	U.S. 3rd Infantry Division arrives in Korea
November 16, 1950	President Truman declares a state of emergency
November 25, 1950	Chinese release 50 UN prisoners in public relations move
November 26, 1950	French forces arrive in Korea
November 28, 1950	President Truman hints at use of atomic bomb
December 11, 1950	First Marine and 7th Infantry Divisions in fighting retreat from Chosin
December 16, 1950	Greek Battalion arrives in Korea
December 20, 1950	Military imposes press censorship on all allied journalists
December 23, 1950	General Walker is killed in jeep accident—Chinese leader Chou En-lai rejects cease-fire proposal
December 24, 1950	Evacuations completed at Hungnam
December 25, 1950	Chinese cross 38th Parallel
December 26, 1950	General Matthew B. Ridgway takes command of Eighth Army
January 4, 1951	Seoul is abandoned
January 7–14, 1951	Ridgway stabilizes UN line near the 38th Parallel
January 25, 1951	Operation Thunderbolt moves out as UN offensive
February 1, 1951	UN votes to end conflict by peaceful means
February 10, 1951	United Nations Command retakes Inchon and Kimpo
February 16, 1951	Siege of Wonsan Harbor begins
March 18, 1951	Seoul retaken
March 23, 1951	187th Airborne drops near Munsan-ni

March 24, 1951	General MacArthur's "pronunciamento" demands full surrender of Chinese Communist troops
April 1–22, 1951	Operations Rugged and Dauntless drive north of Kansas Line
April 7, 1951	President Truman fires General MacArthur
April 15, 1951	General James Van Fleet takes command of Eighth Army
April 22, 1951	U.S. begins rotation system based on time in Korea
April 28, 1951	Joint Chiefs of Staff authorize bombing bases in Manchuria if Chinese Communist Forces planes threaten U.S. forces on the ground
May 16–22, 1951	May massacre
May 20, 1951	American George Kennan meets with Soviet leader Jacob Malik to discuss cease-fire
June 10–16, 1951	Battle of the Punchbowl
June 13, 1951	General Van Fleet is ordered to stop offensive action
June 23, 1951	Ambassador Jacob Malik proposes truce talks during radio broadcast
July 2, 1951	Communists agree to cease-fire discussions at Kaesong
July 10, 1951	Cease-fire discussions begin at Kaesong
June 12, 1951	UN takes and holds Iron Triangle area
July 28, 1951	Commonwealth Division formed from smaller units
August 1-September 18, 1951	Battle of Bloody Ridge
September 13, 1951	Battle of Heartbreak Ridge begins
September 21, 1951	Operation Summit, first helicopter deployment of a combat unit, is executed
October 7, 1951	Negotiators agree to move cease-fire talks to Panmunjom
November 12, 1951	Operation Ratkiller begins against enemy guerrillas in South Korea
November 27, 1951	Peace talks resume at Panmunjom—Cease-fire line agreed on
December 5, 1951	45th Infantry Division replaces 1st Cavalry at front
December 18, 1951	U.S. and Communists exchange POW lists
January 2, 1952	UN Prisoner of War repatriation exchange proposed
January 8, 1952	Chinese reject prisoner voluntary repatriation
February 18, 1952	Riot at the Koje-do Prisoner of War camp
April 8, 1952	Truman seizes steel mills to end strike
May 7–11, 1952	General Francis T. Dodd taken prisoner at Koje-do POW camp

May 12, 1952	General Mark Clark succeeds General Ridgway
May 26, 1952	President Syngman Rhee declares martial law in Pusan
July 11, 1952	Operation Homecoming releases civilian internees
October 6–15, 1952	Battle of White Horse
October 8, 1952	Chinese reject final POW compromise
October 24, 1952	General Eisenhower says he will go to Korea if elected president
October 26, 1952	Battle of the Hook
November 4, 1952	Eisenhower elected president
January 20, 1953	Eisenhower replaces Truman as commander-in-chief—John Foster Dulles becomes Secretary of State
February 2, 1953	Eisenhower's speech unleashes Nationalist China
February 10, 1953	General Maxwell Taylor replaces General Van Fleet as Eighth Army commander
February 22, 1953	China accuses U.S. with germ warfare
March 5, 1953	Joseph Stalin dies
March 23–24, 1953	Battles of Old Baldy and Pork Chop
March 28, 1953	Democratic People's Republic of Korea and CCF agree to prisoner-of-war exchange
March 30, 1953	Cease-fire talks resume at Panmunjom
April 11, 1953	Operation Little Switch (exchange of sick and wounded) agreed
May 22, 1953	Plans for Operation Everready (overthrow of President Rhee) approved
June 4, 1953	Communists accept major portions of UN peace proposal
June 11–16, 1953	Chinese Communist Forces launch major attack against Republic of Korea (ROK) troops
June 18, 1953	Syngman Rhee releases 27,000 North Korean POWs—cease-fire talks break off
July, 1953	Naval Task Force 77 equipped with nuclear weapons
July 13–20, 1953	Marines overrun Outposts Berlin and East Berlin
July 20, 1953	UN establishes new Main Line of Resistance (MLR) on south bank of Kumsong River
July 24–25, 1953	CCF launch attack on the Hook, UN holds
July 27, 1953	Cease-fire signed, effective 2200 hours

July 28, 1953	First meeting of the Military Armistice Commission, meetings have continued for fifty years, and continue in 2006
September 4, 1953	Repatriation of prisoners begins at Freedom Village
September 5, 1953	Operation Big Switch (release of POWs) begins
September 26, 1954	Geneva Conference on Korean reunification
January 1, 1955	Closing date for identifying Korean War Veterans
December 1985	Korean War Veterans Association organized
July 27, 1995	Korean War Veterans Memorial dedicated in Washington, D.C.
December 1999	Defense Act of 1999, signed by President Clinton, changes official reference from Korean Conflict to Korean War

1 OVERVIEW

It is my contention that the Korean War so dramatically changed the course of the Cold War–not to mention the history of its chief protagonists–that to view it as anything less than one of the great historical catalysts of the last half-century is to misunderstand the entire evolution of the cold war.

—Paul G. Pierpaoli, Jr., *Military History*, 2000

Time magazine, in naming the "U.S. Fighting Man" as the 1951 Man-of-the-Year, described him in the following way: "He was the most comfort-loving creature who had ever walked the earth–and he much preferred riding to walking. As well as comfort, he loved and expected order; he yearned, like other men, for a predictable world, and the fantastic fog and gamble of war struck him as a terrifying affront. Yet he was inevitably cast for his role as fighting-man in the middle of the 20th Century."[1]

At this point, the war had been going badly for the United Nations Command and many opinions about the war had already been formed. (The Korean War was the first and, in many respects, the only war fought under the UN flag.) Since that time, the American fighting man has been judged, sometimes unfairly and unkindly, against some undefined standard. Defined by *Time* as "destiny draftee," the man of the year was to be the American soldier, chosen so in preference to the many diplomats involved in the political time-bomb that was Korea, or one of the scientists or industrialists, who might well have qualified.

Some have called the American soldier tough and callous as well as soft and cowardly. He was called resourceful and poorly trained; he was portrayed as a disciplined man and as a rebel. He was, as *Time* pointed out, a peculiar product of a peculiar country: "a man more comfortable with victory than defeat, to advancing rather than retreating, to individualism rather than to team work, he is, in the main, a thinking, deciding, man."[2]

TIME

THE WEEKLY NEWSMAGAZINE

MAN OF THE YEAR
Name: American. Occupation: Fighting-man.

"G.I. Joe, Man of the Year." January 1, 1951. *Time* magazine cover, 1951. Artist: Ernest Hamlin Baker. (© *Time Life Pictures/Time Magazine, Copyright Time Inc./Time Life Pictures/Getty Images*)

War, we are often told, is the ultimate political act. No intelligent person wants war and many devoted persons work against the outbreak of war. Peace has always been the ultimate goal of the military. But sometimes, there seems to be no other way to maintain the peace and security we seek as a nation. When the nation selects war as an extension of its political agenda, peace-loving men and women leave their homes and the normality of their lives to go and fight a war for their country. In a very real sense, they give up control of their personal destinies so that the rest of the nation can continue to enjoy and pursue their own destiny. In the services, they commit themselves to a team that lives and fights under the harsh conditions of a war.

Today, more than fifty years after the conflict, the experience of being a soldier during the Korean War is generally unknown. A good many persons tend to see the war and the soldier's experience as simply a continuation of World War II. Many Korean veterans consider that their role has been generally misunderstood and primarily forgotten, their struggle lost between the passionate and patriotic period of World War II and the anger and disillusionment of Vietnam. This is both true and false but, nevertheless, the distinction between Korean service and other military involvement is worth noting.

Those who serve during a war, and survive, share in common a bond that is hard to describe. It is perhaps only explained by the experience they have shared. This bond is stronger when those involved have faced combat. What they share is not just their role in the conflict. They are also members of a single community, which, for lack of a more descriptive term, we call "the military." In this community, they share common experiences of training, of discipline, of mutual effort, of sacrifice, of food and drink, of transportation, of entertainment, and the emotional attributes of homesickness and community, as well as fear and boredom.

The men and women who fought the Korean War were first of all soldiers and, as soldiers, formed a community unlike any other. Despite the increasing number of narrative accounts of this war, the historiography of the war remains flawed, for there is still very little available about the day-to-day experience of those who fought. Even those who have written of their experiences in the war have tended to do so in the sweeping terms of their combat memories, rather than in an effort to help others understand the essence of their lives as members of the American military. Today, these men and women, thousands of them, still walk quietly through history, not saying much, but in the main with a common memory and inner pride.

When the time arrives, the United States has always been able to call on its young men and women, and they have answered the call to arms, to fight, and sometimes to die, in defense of national goals. When it becomes necessary to fight, the military is called into action. It is so organized that it can be expanded fairly quickly. It is composed of a wide variety of persons including those who belong to the standing force, which we call the regular army, and those who enter the war for the period of the conflict—draftees or "hostilities only." These men and women come for a variety of reasons: for some it is their profession, many come out of a sense of duty and because they have been called. Some respond because they believe in the goals of the conflict, some are simply caught up in the pressures of the events. But, in the main, they fight because they believe in the nation and see participation as a part of their duty as a citizen of the United States.

While we still have much to learn about the Korean War, the war itself has a great deal to teach us. Today, the world continues to live under the cloud of a divided Korea, the questions that brought the war to a head in 1950 have still not been answered. It was the first major clash between the forces of the cold war. The war in Korea was fought on the land, and the sea, and in the air, and covered most of the peninsula. It was America's most intense war. It lasted a little more than three years and ended with an agreement—not a settlement—that remains unfulfilled even in 2006.

While Korea has a long and illustrious history, it has little national history, other than that influenced by the Japanese annexation in 1910. A brief effort at rebellion in 1919 was put down and Japan took control of her people and her resources. Korea became a major resource in Japan's Greater East Asian Co-Prosperity Sphere, and it was in Korea—hidden among the east coast mountainous regions north of Hungnam—that the research was conducted, as Japan struggled to be the first nation to build an atomic bomb.

Historians disagree when the cold war started, but most would agree it became "formalized" with the acceptance of National Security Document 68 and the Korean War.

Events during 1949 called on President Truman to order a new study of Soviet intentions. The result of the study was Document 68, prepared by the Policy Planning Staff of the U.S. State Department, which called on the United States to contain communism with military force if necessary. The document identified the USSR as the enemy and implied that every part of the world was a place where communists might test America's commitment to containment. The politicians called it "symmetrical containment." It appeared on President Truman's desk in March 1950, but it was the Korean War that moved it into the forefront. From 1950 forward, the arms race, military intervention, and massive defense spending became a permanent part of the life of the American.

America's involvement in the war in Korea can be traced to roots deep in both American and Korean history. Since the earliest days of her history, Korea has been a gateway, the natural battleground for nations interested in maintaining control in the Far East. During these centuries, Japan, China, and the Soviet Union all sought control of Korea. While the Japanese were successful in establishing control in 1910, the Soviet Union never lost interest. Seven days prior to the Japanese surrender in 1945, the Soviet Union entered the war against Japan and later, with Allied approval, accepted the surrender of Japanese forces in Korea north of the 38th Parallel.

Most historians recognize that the Korean War was first of all a civil war stoked by the desire among nearly all Koreans to unite their nation. It is also generally believed that in the early stages, neither the United States nor the Soviet Union considered the peninsula as being vital to their security concerns. The play of events suggests that of all the outside nations, the Chinese were far more concerned with whom and what was in Korea.

There is no doubt that the war was an act of aggression by the North, the Democratic People's Republic of Korea (DPRK), and that it was supported by the Soviet Union. Work by both Kathryn Weathersby and Mun Su Park show that the leader of DPRK, Kim Il Sung, was the one who originated the plans for invading South Korea (also called the Republic of Korea), but that he did not receive the necessary Soviet support until February 1950. It is increasingly obvious that when Mao Tse-tung's (Zedong) effort at some sort of peace settlement failed, he decided to put China's economic problems on hold and go to the aid of the Koreans. In September 1950, Joseph Stalin had promised to provide a protective Soviet air umbrella for the Chinese attack, but, on October 10, went back on his promise and told Mao that no Soviet aircraft would be available for several months. *Uncertain Partners* says that Stalin changed his mind because he believed Mao was trying to force them into a war with the United States. He also believed, according to Goncharov, that the American presence close to the Yalu River, would make Mao more dependent on the Soviet Union in the future. When, some months later, Stalin did send significant aircraft to Korea, they did not provide the air cover that Mao had anticipated, but rather protected the Chinese border from UN air attacks.[3]

But there is no evidence that the war in Korea was planned by the Soviets in an attempt to drive the democracies from the defense of western Europe. Certainly the communists viewed the South Korean government as being puppets to the saw the South Koreans as puppets of the United States. The North Koreans were fighting for the unity of their "cruelly amputated nation," and they had the advantage of knowing that if they could win their nation would be reunited.

When the Soviets sent air power, it included about 5,000 pilots and the necessary ground and security force to maintain them. It is obvious that neither the U.S. nor the Soviet Union wanted the intervention to be known, for neither wanted a full-fledged war. The USSR secretary restricted the use of Soviet aircraft to defensive operations.

The Soviet used North Korean and Chinese markings and ordered pilots to avoid capture at all costs. Stalin's orders were that the planes could be used only in defensive operations within the vicinity of the border. The Soviet pilots were not allowed to attack ground forces, nor airfields, nor to fly farther into North Korea than the Changchun River, north of Pyongyang, the region the UN pilots called MiG Alley. While it was believed that Soviet pilots often spoke Russian while in combat, most Americans could not tell the difference between Russian and either Chinese or Korean. Some intelligence sources suggested these pilots came from communist territory, like Poland and Romania. One war correspondent reported, flying with a bomber command, that he recognized the language, but was told by the military to kill the story.

The Soviet Union also sent anti-aircraft defense teams into Korea, and they were able, with suffocated electronic equipment, to shoot down many UN aircraft. They were successful enough that concern for safety forced the U.S. Air Force to change its pattern from daylight to night-time bombing by the end of 1951.

There is little doubt that the United States was caught by surprise. Both military and political analysts held to the theory that a satellite nation would not move without the authority of the Soviet Union, and that such an act would set off World War III. Confident that the Soviets were not yet ready to make such a move, they believed that no invasion would take place.[4] They were wrong.

SOME BACKGROUND FOR KOREAN WAR STUDY

In using this book, it will be helpful for the reader to keep several things in mind about the context of world events leading up to, and at the time of, the Korean War.

First of all, the United States had other military concerns on its plate during this time. Despite the conflict going on in Asia, as commander-in-chief, President Truman did not feel that he could withdraw troops and resources from Europe for the support of the war in Korea. In the context of the larger American policy, Europe was considered far more significant than Korea. Concern over the Soviet intentions in Europe dictated that the Department of Defense needed as many resources available in that command. In 1948, for example, as a result of the Berlin Blockade, the U.S. had transferred nearly a half of the Far East Air Forces' medium bombers (B-29) and large segments of its supporting units to Europe. This was done despite the strong protests of the Far East Commander, General Douglas MacArthur.[5]

Second, neither side in this struggle brought the full complement of their military might into the conflict. The U.S. was occupied in other places and did not mobilize to the full extent it might have done had it been totally committed to the war in Korea. Nor did the U.S. make use of atomic weapons in the struggle. At the same time, the Communists did not commit a large portion of their air force and certainly held back from attempting to control the air. Nor did the Chinese bring into play the full force of their ground strength. The Soviet failure to bring its vast navy into play allowed U.S. convoys to be moved across the more than 5,000 miles of open ocean almost without restriction. UN ships were also able to approach the coasts of Korea unmolested by either enemy planes or submarines. Both sides, as Stanley Sandler has so well pointed out, "held off committing their full military assets for precisely the same reason: fear of igniting a major war, perhaps even the Third World War.[6]

Third, the war in Korea came very close to being a world war. More than thirty-five nations took part in the war to one degree or the other. The Republic of Korea, the

Democratic Peoples Republic of Korea, the United States, and the People's Republic of China bore the brunt of the war. There were many other nations involved: some primarily as token assignments to support the United Nations and some, such as the Soviet Union, that were involved in fairly large numbers. On the United Nations side, other than the United States, Great Britain (supported by members of the Commonwealth) provided the largest contingent of support.

HISTORIOGRAPHY OF THE WAR

Despite its identification as a forgotten war, the last fifty years have seen a considerable amount of scholarly work designed to bring some understanding to the origins of the war, the process by which it was fought, and the legacy it produced. Like most historical inquiry, it has fallen into three fairly identifiable parts. The first, sometimes called the orthodox period, sees the war in the larger context of the cold war. The second phase is called revisionist, and it is designed to see the war more from the domestic perspective than from international ones. The third wave, encouraged by an increasing amount of material recently made available from the Soviet Union, attempts to reinterpret the war using this new information, taking on the seemingly limited efforts of the first two accounts. Nevertheless, despite the significant ways in which the Korean War has been studied, and the changes in those efforts, there is a great deal about the war that remains unknown.

The availability of new archival data since 1990 brings many of the early assumptions about the Korean War into serious question. This material challenges both the traditional view of the war and what is called the revisionist's view. The early historical response—the traditional view—accepts that the North Korean invasion was somehow a part of a larger Communist plan, and that it convinced President Truman that the communists were willing to use military power to expand their influence. It holds the United States pretty much blameless for the war.

During the 1970s and 1980s, a new interpretation—that of the revisionists—began to appear. This view openly blames Truman and the United States' policies on Korea for the behavior and attitudes that led North Korea, and later the People's Republic of China, to attack South Korea. This view is inclined to see the war in Korea as an extension of the Korean Civil War that began shortly after the miscalculated division of the peninsula.

Now, with new evidence coming to light, another phase of historical inquiry has begun. This view is more inclined to look at the influence of the Chinese and the Russians while, at the same time, identifying—but not so clearly blaming—President Truman's policies. The issues at stake suggest that the relationship that existed between Moscow and Beijing, following Mao's successful civil war in China in 1949, was anxious, at the very least. The new evidence tells us that Joseph Stalin did not in fact order the North Korean attack, but rather it was Kim Il Sung who persuaded the Soviet leader to support the attack promoted by Kim. Open for consideration, as well, is just why China was willing to intervene in support of the North Koreans and, perhaps more important, why was Mao interested in supporting the conquest of the entire Korean peninsula. It seems evident that Mao considered the war an opportunity to challenge the United States, and in doing so, to establish the new Chinese state as a world power.

Another interesting factor in changing some of the more traditional and revisionist history is that while the Soviet Union secretly sent nearly 70,000 Soviet military personnel to aid the North Korean cause, it was never an issue. New data suggest that both President Truman and Eisenhower were aware that the Soviet troops were in Korea, but for reasons still being identified, they chose to keep the situation secret. Nor did Stalin acknowledge their presence. Surely both knew that if the word got out, that Americans, at least, would pressure for a larger and expanded conflict.

Looking back, there are obvious reasons why both sides did not want to acknowledge the involvement of Soviet troops. In the first place, the secrecy was to the UN's advantage because the Soviets went to considerable effort to hide the fact that they were there, thus avoiding UN action or inquiry. This played into the UN's hands. Soviet planes were not allowed to either attack UN ground troops, or to fly further into North Korea than the Changchun River that lay north of Pyongyang. This region was eventually identified as MiG Alley. This restriction served the UN well.[7]

KOREA, WHERE IS IT?

It would be safe to say that the majority of those who served in Korea did not know where they had been sent. Few Americans in 1950 could have located Korea on a map. Nor, usually, did the serving GIs know where in Korea they had ended up. This occurred for a variety of reasons, but the most obvious one is that no one thought to tell them. But it is also true that they were in a place where few of the surroundings made identification possible. Not only were maps of local areas extremely scarce, but the few maps available were of Japanese vintage and almost consistently at variance with the terrain. Grid systems were confusing, villages misnamed and misplaced, roads either not listed or plotted inaccurately. Lack of contour lines left the conformation and extent of ridges entirely to the imagination of the map-reader. These were a constant source of frustration and often led to troops being completely lost.

An excellent example of the inconsistency of the maps occurred when the planning was underway for the invasion at Inchon. Japanese and American maps showed different tide levels, a matter of some importance when the plan was to invade from the sea on Landing Ship, Tank (LSTs). Frequently, cartographers used elevation for names of hills. Heights on the Korean map are given in meters, and many of these hills derived their name from their elevation. This figure in meters is arrived at by using the conversion factor of 3.28. The practice of naming hills and valleys as well as lines and outposts ended April 28 1953, after which the entire front, from coast to coast, was known as the main line of resistance. At the same time, the Eighth U.S. Army in Korea became simply the Eighth Army.

Soldiers' Knowledge of Korea

As suggested, few of those who were sent to Korea had ever heard it mentioned. Fewer still knew anything about it. Those in the military stream knew a little about the area, but they too had very little knowledge of the land they had been called to defend. The first thing most American soldiers identified with Korea was the smell. For the American nostril, the human manure with which Koreans fertilized their fields filled the air with a terrible smell. And it could be smelled far out to sea, greeting the incoming soldier with a dreadful beginning to their stay.

Dangling like an appendix from the mainland of Asia, the nation of Korea was not an area about which much of the world had heard. Little in its history, or in that of the United States, encouraged any real knowledge of this small and traditionally isolated country. There were few Koreans living in the United States prior to 1950, and few examples of Korean culture were available. In the midst of America's own rampant emergence in the world, what was going on in the obscure nation of Korea made little difference. The fact that the history of the two nations had mingled since the 1870s had not made it into most history books, and the implication of these early contacts was totally misunderstood.

In many respects, Korea resembles an island. Officially, the Korean Peninsula drops about 1,000 kilometers southward from the Asian land mass. Its northern border is identified along the Amnokgang (Yalu) River on the west and the Dumangang (Tumen) River on the east. Sixteen miles along the Dumangang, the border separates Korea from the historical Soviet Union. The rest serves as the border with the Chinese satellite of Manchuria. Korea is surrounded on three sides by the Korean Bay to the west, the Yellow Sea to the south, and on the east the East (Japanese) Sea.

The nation is about 380 miles wide, but this varies considerably because of deep inlets and narrowing in the south. Longitudinally, the nation lies along a path shared by the Philippines and Australia. It shares the meridian 135 degrees east with Japan. Geographically, it lies adjacent to China, Russia, Manchuria, and very close to Japan, all of which have, over the centuries, had the most cultural influence on the Korean people.

In terms of size, it has about the same square kilometers (222,154) as Great Britain (224,100). Of this area, about 55 percent (121,300) lies in North Korea, and about 45 percent (93,000) in the South. Between these two nations lies the area that makes up the Demilitarized Zone, a no-man's-land four kilometers wide (2.4 miles), which runs about 241 kilometers (151 miles) from the east coast to the west. The coastline is 5,400 miles long. There are approximately 3,000 islands that traditionally belong to Korea. While the majority of the islands are in the South Sea, a few islands are found in the East Sea. The largest island called Jujudo lies off the southwest corner of the mainland. Most of the islands are rocky and uninhabited and generally have a population of fewer than 100 people.

Mountain ranges serve as natural boundaries between regions that, especially in its early history, tended to isolate the people and prevent much interaction. Therefore, most of the area—now defined as provinces—developed differences in both language and custom. The regional distinctions, which are generally the same as those developed during the Joseon Dynasty (1312–1910), divided the Korean peninsula into three distinct areas. The regions were also subdivided into provinces. In many cases, these regions also served as administrative channels. Prior to 1945, the term "north" was used to mean the area of Pyongan and Hamgyong Provinces. The term now refers to any area north of the Demilitarized Zone.

Seventy percent of Korea is composed of mountains and uplands. The primary ranges are the Taebeaek, Sobaek, and Chiri Massif. The tallest mountain, the volcanic cone, Mount Halla, is 1,950 meters and is located on Cheyu Island. The highest point on the mainland is Mount Pact. The longest rivers, and those that gave the UN the most trouble, were the Naktong River (521 kilometers), the Han River that flows through Seoul (514 kilometers), and the Kum River (401 kilometers). Korean rivers are usually unnavigable, filled with rapids and waterfalls. About 20 percent of the land is arable and rice is the primary crop. The wet paddies where rice is grown takes up about 10 percent of the arable land. At one time, the Peninsula was highly wooded, but now (and in 1950) most of the remaining forested areas were in the north. Some oak, alder, pine, spruce, and fir trees remain in the south, generally in the west-central area.

Some geographical characteristics played a significant role in the Korean War. Perhaps most significant was the Chosin (Changjin) Reservoir located about 56 miles north of Hamhung and extending more than 40 miles northward. The Iron Triangle was formed by the villages of Chorwon, Kumhwa, and Pyongyang, and a relatively flat area surrounded by mountains. Also important was the area called the Punchbowl, a volcanic crater about five miles in diameter and twenty miles from the Hwachon Reservoir, with a hill rim about 2,000 feet high. The Naktong Bulge, which played a significant role as it changed hands, was a semicircular area created by a westward turn of the Naktong River

A Quick History of Korea

If we accept archaeological finding, the first settlements appeared in the land that is now Korea, about 700,000 years ago. The beginnings of a nation are traced to the mythical figure Dan-gun, who was the founder of the Go-Joseon kingdom about 2333 BCE. In the period between 57 BCE and 676 CE, three kingdoms were identified called Goguryeo (Koguryo), Baekje, (Paekche), and Silla (Shilla). The Korean people were under the Sillian kingdom that reigned until about 935, when the nation fell from within and was annexed by Goryeo. There was a brief period of government under Dae Joyeong, but the Goryeo Dynasty was far stronger and ruled from 918 to 1392. The Joseon Dynasty was formed about 1392 and would last, in one form or the other, until 1910. In 1876, Korea was forced into a series of alliances with Japan and finally, with the approval of the Western nations, was annexed by Japan. The Korean people lived under Japanese rule until the end of World War II. The surrender, in 1945, divided Korea into two segments—North and South—and in 1950 caused a vicious civil war that quickly became a conflict between East and West. Both nations now live under their respective government in accordance with the cease-fire signed in 1953.

The modern Korean is believed to be the descendant of Mongol tribes that migrated, during the Neolithic Age (5000–1000 BCE), into the Korean peninsula from Central Asia. Later migrations occurred during the Bronze Age (100–300 BCE). By the beginning of the Christian era, the Koreans were a primarily homogenous people. Today, most of the cities and large towns are very crowded, and personal space is at a premium. The "personal bubble" held by the Korean people is much smaller than that of people in the West and Koreans tend to stand close, even touching, when speaking or walking together.

Climate

Korea has a surprisingly diverse climate that runs through four seasons. Spring, with its rainfall, tends to run from late March to May; the summer season, which is also the monsoon season, begins in late June with the heaviest rains in July. Autumn begins toward the end of September and falls into November when the air is dryer but the wind blows from the north. The winter is cold with snow and ice.

Summers are dominated by monsoons and are best defined as hot and humid. The temperature often reaches 110 degrees (F) or higher, with humidity that hovers at 90 percent. On average, 60 percent of all precipitation in Korea falls between June and September. Typhoons hit the coastline at an average of one or two a summer. The difficulty in climbing the steep hills that made up much of the battleground was made nearly impossible by the heat and was a major challenge for the young soldiers.

While the summers could be hot and the humidity high, it was the cold that most American military men and women remember. There is no way to describe the sort of cold that was experienced by the GIs who were in Korea during 1950–1951, and it was not much better in other years. Now, even fifty years later, men try and explain what it was like and fail. The cold was a major enemy, and it came as a shock to those who had to face it. This is true even of those people who lived in cold climates. Though Korea is in the same general parallel as the state of Indiana, it has extremes of heat and cold. The United Nations troops got as far north as the 40th Parallel, which also runs through Denver and Philadelphia, but the winters, especially in North Korea, were made more desperate by the bitter winds blowing off the Manchurian plains turning everything into a solid, making moving parts immovable and human blood freeze. The average snow-fall is thirty-seven days during the winter. It was not as cold in the south, but January in Seoul usually meant 22 degrees F. Annual rainfall varies from year to year but usu-ally averages 100 centimeters, two-thirds of it between June and September. During the winter months, this was translated into heavy snow and blowing winds. Admiral Arleigh Burke remembers in his oral history: "the winds are terrific, they come down from Siberia, the snow comes down horizontally and it's frozen, it not like snowflakes. It's ice."[8]

Cold weather was a far greater threat to the soldiers than they at first understood. The extreme cold decreased the soldier's ability to think and weakened the will to accomplish anything not directed toward getting warm. It dulled the body and weak-ened the desire to survive. As the ground froze, a whole series of new problems arose. Ordinary trenching tools became inadequate for digging once the land froze three inches deep. Picks and shovels were better for the task, but they were far too heavy to be carried by the troops. One infantry unit met the problem by issuing two-pound blocks of TNT to each soldier for the purpose of breaking through the frozen top layer of earth.

NOTES

1. "American Fighting Man: Destiny's Draftee," *Time* (January 1, 1951).

2. "American Fighting Man: Destiny's Draftee," *Time* (January 1, 1951).

3. Sergei Goncharov, John W. Lewis, and Xue Litai, *Uncertain Partners: Stalin, Mao and the Korean War* (Stanford CA: University Press, 1993), 188–189.

4. P. K. Rose "Perceptions and Reality: Two Strategic Intelligence Mistakes in Korea," *International Social Science Review* (Fall-Winter, 2001).

5. Stanley Sandler, *The Korean War: No Victors, No Vanquished* (Lexington, KY.: University Press of Kentucky,1999), 39.

6. Stanley Sandler, *The Korean War: No Victor, No Vanquished* (Lexington, KY.: University Press of Kentucky, 1999), 5.

7. Lester H. Brune, "Recent Scholarship and Findings about the Korean War," *American Studies International* 36 (October 1998): 4–13.

8. Stephen Howarth, *To Shining Sea: A History of the United States Navy* (New York: Random House, 1991) 489.

2 PHASES AND CAMPAIGNS

But the deeds of those who fought, the men who died and those who lived, beget their own posterity—the human drama of life and death in the stinking valleys and denuded hills of a peninsula where wars have raged since man first raised fist to man.

—Hanson Baldwin, *New York Times,*
as quoted by Richard Kolb, VFW, 1991 reporter

War is often seen as one continuous action, but this generally not the case. An individual soldier might well pass through several campaigns or phases that look very much the same to him. But in stepping back to look at the war in total, it becomes obvious that the nature of the war changes even as it is being fought. These changes are reflective of many factors: the political environment, military strategy, weather, equipment availability, morale, supplies, and the stamina of those doing the fighting, both in terms of their background and in terms of their longevity. Wars are also fought in terms of campaigns with separately established goals and conditions. There is an ebb and flow to combat, movements of aggression and defense, advances and retreats, which reflect both the military strategy of the leadership and the conditions and locations of the armies. In Korea, there are three generally recognized phases as well as one not so-well recognized. To further define the fighting, there were, depending on the service, somewhere between five and ten campaigns. Here, for the sake of clarity, the war is broken into ten campaigns.

THE AMERICAN VIEW OF KOREA

Whereas the United States and Korea had been involved in a small war in the latter part of the nineteenth century, the first modern contact between the United States and Korea took place in September 1945. It was then that the first members of the American Occupation Forces (Operation Black List Forty) landed at Inchon, to be met by Japanese dignitaries in formal dress. This marked the beginning of the occupation of postwar Korea. The American forces were greeted warmly by the Koreans, who were enjoying a sense of freedom unfelt by them since the 1901 occupation by the Japanese Empire. Under relentless pressure from the Japanese military, the Korean emperor had signed away all the rights of Korean sovereignty on August 22, 1910. The United States and Great Britain had given their blessing to this action in return for Japan's support of the U.S. and British expansion in the Philippines and in India. Now, with the end of World War II, the Korean people anticipated their freedom and independence as seemingly promised in the 1943 Cairo Declaration issued by the leaders of the Grand Alliance.

As World War II began to wind down, however, American and British concern about the internal character of the Korean nation was challenged by an increasing fear of what the Soviet Union was planning for the Far East. It was true that a Soviet occupation of Korea might produce a significant alteration in the strategic balance in the Far East. On the other hand, the Japanese in Korea were still strong, and there was some advantage to leaving that problem to the Soviet Union, which, late in the game, had promised to enter the war against Japan. The scene changed again on August 10, just two days after the destruction of Nagasaki, when the State-War-Navy Coordinating Committee decided that America should be involved in the occupation of at least a part of Korea. The proposed, and fairly arbitrary, dividing line was the 38th Parallel. Much to the relief of many, the Soviet Union accepted the arrangement. The Soviets had troops in what is now North Korea a month before the United States was able to get its troops into the south. But even at this point, American leaders felt that Korea was of little interest either politically or militarily.

Lieutenant General John R. Hodge, a fighting general who was given command of the American occupation forces, was told to create a government that supported U.S. policy. But just what that policy was had not been determined, or, at least, it had not been made clear to General Hodge. Setting up his headquarters in the Banda Hotel in Seoul, he began an occupation made even more difficult by the lack of English speakers among the populace and Korean speakers among the military. Unfortunately, the Americans tended to relate better with the Japanese, sharing with them the camaraderie of military service. They were appreciative of Japanese knowledge and administrative skills, which they did not find among the Koreans for whom they had little understanding or respect. As it turned out, the American military found it much easier to deal with the correct and reasonable Japanese than with the vast array of divergent opinions and political groups they discovered among the Korean people. By the time administrative pressure forced the Americans to disavow this dependence, and brought about the release and shipment home of nearly 70,000 Japanese civilian administrators as well as nearly 600,000 Japanese soldiers, the damage had already been done. In the eyes of many Koreans, the Americans were as bad as the Japanese.

The political situation in Korea was also unstable. The democratic (conservative) party, headed by exiled Korean leader Syngman Rhee, had only a fraction of the political support enjoyed by the more aggressive Korean People's Republic (KPR), but was the choice of the occupation administration. A determined, egotistic man, who was hated by many of his countrymen, Syngman Rhee nevertheless had the advantage of being an uncompromising foe of communism. His backing by the American military was at odds with the views of the American Department of State, and yet Rhee, probably with the support of the military, was returned to Korea, despite the fact that the State Department had refused him a passport. The political difficulties were enhanced as Hodge grew increasingly determined to rid the KPR of its power.

Between 1945 and 1947, it became clear that Korea was becoming a pawn in the struggle between the United States and the Soviet Union. Attempts to create a unified government for Korea had failed. In September 1947, the United States, arguing that the mutual talks with the Soviets about unification had not been productive, sent the Korean question to the United Nations (UN). The Soviet Union objected, but the UN took up the challenge and accepted resolutions that would provide UN-supervised elections in Korea. This was to be followed by the withdrawal of American and Soviet forces. The Soviet Union and North Korea made it quite evident that whatever the UN decided about Korea would pertain only to that area south of the 38th Parallel. The UN Temporary Commission on Korea supported the idea of elections, nevertheless. Despite the North's refusal to take part, an election was held, and 7.8 million South Koreans went to the polls to select a government supportive of Syngman Rhee. He was inaugurated president on July 24, 1948.

Rhee immediately went to work setting up a powerful, dictatorial, government that used the military, the courts, and the jails to control political opposition. He was anxious to keep the American military in South Korea as a buffer, but the Americans had agreed with the Soviets to a mutual pullout of occupation troops. When the Soviets peacefully withdrew their forces, the Americans soon followed suit. In the north, it left the strong, charismatic Kim Il Sung in command of the Democratic Peoples Republic of Korea (DPRK), which had come into existence in September 1948. The American occupation of Korea was over, and the troops, with the exception of a small 500-man group that made up the Korean Military Advisory Group (KMAG), left.

Most Americans were glad to be gone. Korea was of small importance and by January 1950, the area had dropped to such low priority in American policy that on January 5, 1950, President Truman declared that the United States would not intervene in the clash between the Chinese on Taiwan (Formosa) and those on mainland China. Seven days later, Secretary of State Dean Acheson was able to tell the world, in an address to the American Press Club, that Korea was now outside the American sphere of interests. Although the United States and the Republic of Korea (ROK or South Korea) had signed a mutual security and military assistance pact on January 26, 1950, only a 1,000 dollars worth of signal wire had reached Korea by the outbreak of war. Looking back, it is easy to be shocked at the Secretary of State's comments. But he said nothing that was outside the thinking of American policymakers. Korea did not appear to have any potential value either politically or militarily.

THE INVASION OF SOUTH KOREA

There is little doubt that the war in Korea was set off by an invasion of the forces of the DPRK. North Korean troops crossed the 38th Parallel in force in an effort to unite the nation under the communist leadership of Kim Il Sung. They had Soviet permission and the promise of some support. They also had somewhat vague promises of help from China and, if nothing more, the release of those Korean soldiers who had been fighting alongside during the Chinese Communist in their Civil War.

Many Soviet-watchers, including President Harry Truman, were afraid that the invasion was the first stage of World War III. The attack was seen as a diversion orchestrated by the Soviet Union to be followed up by aggressive action in Europe. Perhaps

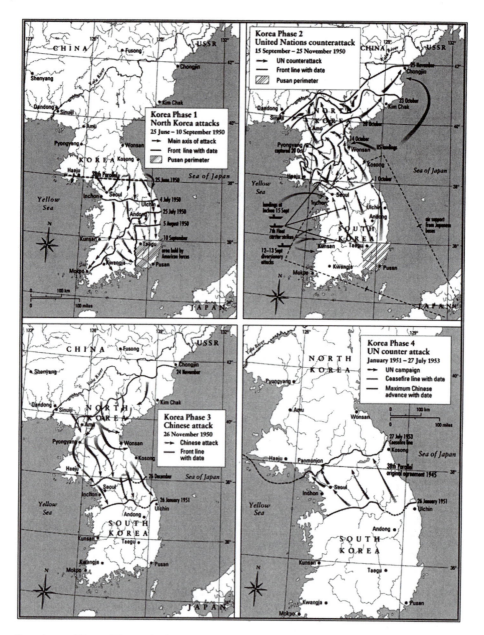

Four phases of Korean War attacks, 1950–1953.

this helps explain what appears to be President Truman's seemingly abrupt decision to support the South Korean people in this fight. To many, the decision did not appear to be a part of any carefully considered Korean policy. Rather, it appears to have been the result of the thinking behind National Security Council Document #68, which called for limits on the military expansion of communism. These discussions behind America's decision to go to war, while fascinating, are well outside the scope of this study, so will not be pursued here.

President Truman was at his "Summer White House" in Independence, Missouri, when he received the news of the invasion. The decision to take responsive action, made on the day of the invasion, was worked out in five days of meetings at Blair House in Washington, D.C. (The White House was being remodeled.) There, President Truman and his advisors tried to respond to what appeared all too clearly to be an act of aggression by the Soviet Union. During these five days in June, in a series of decisions made by America's leading political and military men, the American government committed itself to the defense of South Korea and sought to bring the United Nations into the struggle.

The decision to enter combat was made under the shadow of a moral crusade, keeping with Reinhold Niebuhr's thesis in the *Irony of American History*, so widely believed: an evil action undertaken for the sake of the good was legitimate. It was what *Newsweek* magazine would call an act of knight-errantly, but Truman would later express the idea that he made the decision for the sake of the United Nations. Some historians have reported that only 7 percent of the American people agreed with the president's argument for entering Korea, but in the early stages far more than that were supportive.[1]

Jacob Malik, the Soviet delegate to the United Nations Security Council, had walked out of the sessions on January 13, 1950 to protest the UN's failure to seat Red China. The Soviets were still absent on June 25, when the UN passed a resolution condemning the North Korean attack. Without the Soviet delegate to challenge the effort, a resolution calling for the withdrawal of North Korean troops was passed 9-0. The attack was seen as a challenge not only to America, which many still considered a protector of the South Korean regime, but to the United Nations, which was struggling to play a role more significant than the League of Nations had done in the past.

During the first day of the meetings at Blair House, Truman determined to evacuate Americans in Korea and authorized whatever military force was necessary to protect them. The Seventh Fleet was sent to the Taiwan Straits (then called Straits of Formosa) to prevent either the Nationalist or Chinese Communist from using the war in Korea to take any action in their ongoing struggle, and authorized General Douglas MacArthur to spare stored ammunition and equipment to the South Korean government.

In the long run, it was probably the decision to quarantine Taiwan (then Formosa) that had the greatest long-term effects on the war and its outcome, for Premier Mao of Communist China interpreted the move as evidence that the United States had taken a stand on the side of the Chinese Nationalist government of Chiang Kai-shek. The American people appeared, at this point, to be supportive of Truman's decision to take a stand. An hour after Truman's announcement of support, Congress passed a bill that extended the draft. It was passed by 314 votes to 0.

At the president's request, Major General John Church did the preliminary analysis of what was happening in Korea. He and his staff of some 15 officers went to Korea and were met by Ambassador John Muccio at Suwon. They were looking for a realistic determination of the situation. Shortly after this, General Douglas MacArthur arrived for his own survey. MacArthur saw the enemy advancing, the South Korean military in retreat, and the need to commit an American army to the defense of the fledgling nation. After five days of meetings and seven meetings of the UN Security Council, America's involvement in Korea was set.

The American cause was greatly strengthened when the British government immediately made available her Far East Fleet: there were only eight ships, but it was a representation that made up in internationalizing the conflict what it lacked in firepower. Soon other nations, called on by the United Nations, came to support the cause. Twenty-one nations contributed in some form or other, seventeen sending contingencies of troops.

When the United Nations asked President Truman to name a commander for the gathering force, General Douglas MacArthur was called on. While there were some administrative concerns about selecting General MacArthur for the role, there was really no way that he could be ignored. A military hero, a highly capable administrator, the highest-ranking officer in the American military, and one of the best-informed men on the Asian mind, he was considered a natural. So, as the nation committed itself, the call went out for an army to be raised.

THE COMMUNIST VIEW OF KOREA

An uneasy truce had existed in Korea for some time. A series of South Korean raids along the border caused great concern for Soviet Premier Joseph Stalin, as well as for North Korean leader Kim Il Sung. The Soviet leader, not seeing much hope for unification, had refused to sign a separate cooperation treaty with the North. Most of Stalin's concern, and eventual cooperation, was apparently affected by a series of events during 1948–1949, including the Chinese Communist victory over the Chinese Nationalists and the establishment of the People's Republic of China. The Soviet leader's position was strengthened as well by acquisition of the atomic bomb.

Believing the time was ripe for a forced unification, Kim Il Sung, the leader of the DPRK, had requested Joseph Stalin's support for an invasion of Korea as early as March 1949. At that time, he had written suggesting that "We believe that the situation makes it necessary and possible to liberate the whole country through military means."[2] Stalin, however, did not agree and pointed out the weakness of the North Korean military machine. He also expressed concern that the United States might enter into the war. During the fall of 1949, North Korean leaders tried again reaffirming their belief that under the circumstances, unification of the nation was not possible under any other means. Kim Il Sung insisted that the Korean people on both sides of the parallel sought the unification of their nation and could not understand why such an opportunity was being missed. He also insisted that his forces were superior to those in the ROK. Since the U.S. had withdrawn from Korea, the 38th Parallel as a dividing line was meaningless. He also felt it was no longer feasible to assume that South Korea might attack, and thus justify a North Korean invasion. The Soviets were not convinced, however, and again raised the possibility that any unwarranted action might bring the Americans into the war.

However, by January 1950, Stalin was beginning to see it Kim's way. During April 1950, the North Korean leader spent considerable time in Moscow. The talks apparently included Mao Zedong, the Chinese premier, but he was not asked to join in the war, but only to support its North Korean neighbors. There seems to have been some concern on the part of the Soviets that Mao would tie any help in Korea to expectations of Soviet assistance in a military venture to rejoin Taiwan to the Chinese Communist regime. The prime motivation that was consistently expressed by Kim, and endorsed by Stalin, was the unification of Korea. Stalin's reasons for agreeing to the invasion are less clear, but there is certainly evidence that he believed Washington's interest in Korea had lessened.[3]

There is still disagreement as to what was arranged between Stalin and Mao to secure the eventual Chinese intervention. Stalin apparently promised to provide air cover to any Chinese advance, but when it came time for the attack, no air cover was provided. This supposed betrayal was a major factor in the later breakdown of Sino-Soviet relations. As it turned out, of course, Stalin did deploy air units, but primarily for the defense of Chinese industrial areas along the east coast.

Kim Il Sung apparently believed that he could conquer South Korea quickly. He had estimated it would take five days and that Koreans in the south would rise up to support his effort at unification. He believed that the existence of large numbers of communist cells in the south gave him a significant advantage.

PHASES OF THE KOREAN WAR

In terms of how it affected the life of the GI, the war in Korea was fought in three (possibly four) rather broad phases. These are not distinct, and the dates provided to identify them are arbitrary, perhaps more helpful to the historian who would write about it, than the young men and women who were involved. The phases of the war reflect the manner in which it was fought and, in this case, could well be titled retreat, advance, stalemate, for these are their primary characteristics.

The First Phase of the War

The first of these phases (June 25, 1950 to September 15, 1950) reflects the war that started with the invasion of South Korea. It began with ROK's efforts, supported by the KMAG, to halt the rapid advance of North Korean troops. It led to the involvement of the United States, and then the United Nations, and was characterized by hard-fought battles and general retreat. For nearly three months, the defensive lines moved consistently south, as American and ROK troops were pushed farther into the small pocket of resistance that was later identified as the Pusan Perimeter. The retreat concluded with the quick turnaround made possible by the invasion through Inchon Harbor and the breakout of Eighth Army from the Pusan Perimeter. Following on the heels of this victory, the Eighth Army on the west and the semi-independent X Corps on the east moved into North Korean territory with their eyes on a complete takeover of the north. In the initial stage, the United States was fighting: first, to delay the North Korean aggression, and second, to drive the North Korean Army from the territory of ROK.

This phase of the war was primarily fought in the warmer months in Korea. The environmental enemies were the seemingly endless hills to be climbed, the heavy rain, and the mud that turned trails into bogs. It began with the American and, eventually, the early United Nations', forces being greatly outnumbered and, in some significant respects, out-equipped and supplied.

Moving with no small degree of arrogance after their successful landing at Inchon, neither President Truman nor the UN paid much attention to warnings coming from China, by way of India, that they should not come any closer to the Yalu. The area near the Yalu River, which divided the Korean nation from that of Manchuria was a highly sensitive area. It was not only too close to China, but it housed highly important industries and hydroelectric plants. Recently declassified documents show, however, that the Chinese intervention was being planned long before the decision was made to head north across the 38th Parallel. The warnings appear now to have been a means to justify a course already selected.

The Second Phase of the War

The second phase (December 1950 to November 1951) is marked by the entry of the volunteers of the Chinese People's Liberation Army, who crossed the Yalu in support of the government of North Korea. Moving to the 38th Parallel following the X Corps invasion at Inchon, and the recapture of Seoul, Truman, with UN approval, ordered UN forces north of the 38th Parallel. The new goal was to destroy the North Korean army and end its threat to the ROK. The hope was the reunification of the nation. It went beyond the original goal of the war, which was to roll back the enemy forces and restore to South Korea its sovereignty.

This phase of the war continued on the west with the Eighth Army moving north and the X Corps, on the east coast, moving into the area of the Chosin Reservoir. It was here, at Chosin, that the Chinese hit the 1st Marine Division and the 7th Infantry Division, initiating a long retreat, a regrouping, and an eventual steady withdrawal. On the west, the Eighth Army moved back, evacuating soldiers as it went, until it regrouped south of Seoul. The Allies faced a far stronger and seasoned army. It was, as General MacArthur would remark, the beginning of an "entirely new war."[4]

After the Chinese attack was slowed, then stopped, it became a different war. It was a different war as it entered a stalemate, with both sides digging in. Identified by an awful winter in which men actually froze in their tracks, this was a period of hardship that was to be dominated by the armistice negotiations at Panmunjom.

The Third Phase of the War

The third phase is often called a stalemate, or sometimes the Hill War, and was, as the names imply, basically a defensive war fought between the hills and ravines of an area hardly wider than the future Demilitarized Zone (DMZ). It began with the United Nations command's decision to end the aggressive war and maintain a battle line reasonably close to that of the 38th Parallel. Each of these periods had their distinct character, and each required something different of those who were doing the fighting. This phase was marked by the static battle line, the aggressive patrols and probes, the failure to seek major land gains, and the willingness to hold on while negotiations continued.

The shift from mobile warfare to a more static one allowed for fairly permanent defensive positions to be built. This, in turn, got the men and the weapons out of the elements and allowed for better care of both. Lulls in the fighting provided time for routine cleaning and maintenance, which solved many of the problems that arose in automatic weapons that had not been adequately cleaned. This phase continued as armistice negotiations were going on. The military action was primarily associated with the political necessity and the fighting, generally conducted by small units and patrols, and was more interested in position than territory or casualties. It continued, fought on one hill after another, until the cease-fire was signed and the troops, at least most of them, could end the fighting.

The Fourth Phase of the War

There was a fourth period, one which is not often discussed, but which was no less significant to those involved: this was the postwar involvement. This reflects a period of the war that needs considerably more study. While the armistice was signed on July 27, 1953, the danger—and in many respects the combat routine—went on for several additional months after the armistice was signed. There was still considerable danger, as it was necessary for American troops to aid in the prisoner exchanges. As well, there were

Unidentified GI at construction site. Punchbowl, Korea, 1953. (*Used by permission of the Center for the Study of the Korean War, Graceland University*)

men on the line who, for reasons best known to the military, moved into the DMZ for occasional patrols and reconnaissance.

Technical Sergeant Michael Dorsey recalls:

After Christmas of that year [1953] [Sam] Fire received orders up to the Demilitarized Zone where he worked on a surveying crew. His crew took on the task of heading up past the front lines to try and determine the exact locations of enemy strongholds so they could be accurately targeted. Fire said there were countless times that fear was almost overwhelming from the constant sniper fire and ever-present danger of land mines.[5]

There was little recognition of this phase, after both sides had signed a cease-fire. However, this last period, extended until 1955, was significant enough to be used by the American government to identify soldiers eligible to be called Korean War veterans.

CAMPAIGNS

While the phases provided a quick overview of the war, the fighting took place in a series of campaigns. The Republic of Korea (ROK), the UN, and, within the UN command, the Marines, Army, Navy, and Air Force, identify a somewhat different campaign structure.

UN Defensive: June 25 to September 14, 1950

The first campaign began with the invasion of South Korea and the introduction of American forces. The first American unit was Detachment X and consisted of thirty-five men from the 507th Anti-Aircraft Automatic Weapons Battalion who defended the evacuation of American dependents. They were followed by Task Force Smith, the first American infantry unit to be involved. The task force consisted of 406 men in an infantry battalion and 134 men in an artillery battery, which arrived in Korea on July 1, 1950. Elements of the 24th and 25th Infantry Divisions continued to arrive, but the limited forces were unable to stop the North Korean march toward the south.

Brigadier General William L. Roberts, who was en route to the United States when the war began, placed great faith in the ROK, suggesting they had the best army outside the United States. But the poorly guarded frontier was an easy egg to crack, and the reserves, sometimes ten miles or so from the line, were moved back in the face of the violent North Korean tide. On June 25, Yak-9P fighters of the North Korean Air Force came over Kimpo Airfield near Seoul to discover the field busy with Americans evacuating. The North Korean planes shot up the control tower and destroyed some C-54s sitting on the ground. Nearby, a flight of Yaks destroyed seven ROK aircraft at the Seoul International Airport.

On June 28, Seoul fell, and the North Koreans took up points along the Han River. By July 4, they had reached a line along Suwon-Wonju-Samchok. The retreat was resisted along the way, but it appeared that little could be done. Most American troops, the largest number coming from occupation duty in Japan, were neither as well-trained nor equipped as would be expected and they, along with the ROK Army, were forced to trade ground for time.

On July 20, 757 untrained recruits of the 29th Infantry Regiment were ambushed at Hodong and 313 killed. More than 100 were captured. The North Koreans crossed the Kum River and captured Taejon. The U.S. and South Korean forces were driven, by means of hundreds of small battles at Korean villages and crossroads, toward the southeastern port of Pusan. Efforts to take a stand occurred at the Battle of Kum River, the Battle of Taejon, and the Battle of the Notch. As July came to an end, there were desperate battles along the 200-mile UN front and, as August began, UN troops had withdrawn behind the Naktong River. Lieutenant General Walton Walker, Eighth Army commander, determined at this point that trading space for time was over. He ordered a stand along the 140-mile perimeter around the port of Pusan. Here, on August 4, 1950, the Pusan Perimeter was established.

The eventual defensive line was established in a half circle around the port of Pusan, anchored in the hills north of the city and along the Naktong River to the west. The sea, and potential evacuation, lay to the south and east. The North Koeran forces were slowed, but continued to crack the line. Between August 31 and September 11, the North Korean troops made important gains against the entire Pusan beachhead. As the defense of Pusan waged on, however, the Eighth Army was getting stronger. The location and collection of equipment and supplies had produced much of what was needed which, after a 5000-mile journey, were arriving at Pusan. The port city provided excellent facilities and, as each day passed, more and more supplies were landed. There was an increase in troop strength heralded by the arrival of the 1st Provisional Marine Brigade and four battalions of medium tanks. At the same time, the supply lines for the DPRK were increasing in length, and it was now facing continued attacks from American land- and sea-based planes.

While inside the Pusan Perimeter, in August 1950, the remains of the ROK Army were reorganized and rebuilt with as much speed as possible. The shattered 2nd, 5th, and 7th ROK Infantry Divisions were dissolved and reincorporated into the ROK 1st, 3rd, 6th, 8th, and Capital Infantry Division. During the first part of September, the men of the ROK I and II Corps managed to hold the right sector along its northern edge and, when ready, participated in the breakout from Pusan.

The battle for Pusan was perhaps the most deadly, taking an estimated 3,603 casualties. Breaking out led to the Second Battle of the Naktong Bulge, which slowed the momentum of the North Koran advance and promoted the defense of Pusan between August and September 16, 1950. It was a desperate battle but, as the days went on, the American forces were able to grow in strength and supplies brought in through the port, whereas the supply lines of the North Korean forces grew longer and less efficient.

The combat during this period was difficult, to say the least. Those Americans selected to take the war to the North Koreans were not prepared, materially or psychologically, for what they were to face. Troops who were heading into battle for the first time were told such things as "the North Korean were poorly equipped, poorly led, and marched till they dropped." It was a common perception, and their forces were often identified as a "peasant army." It took only a few days to determine just how wrong this was. The North Korean army was well equipped, well trained, and well led.

When members of the 27th Infantry Regiment (Task Force Smith) were ordered to Korea, they were instructed to pack their footlockers so they could be retrieved on arrival. The war, it was assumed, would be short. Similar instructions were given to other U.S. commands. C. Lyle Rishell, a platoon leader of the 24th Infantry "thought that they were going into combat for a few months and would certainly be home for Christmas and that Korea would be an extension of our training in Japan."[6]

None of the divisions that were deployed to Korea from Japan during July 1950 did so with new equipment. The men left with what they had. And what they had was in poor shape. Many of their supplies were old or inappropriate for what they were being sent to do. Basic ammunition supplies were limited. During the first battle of the war, Baker Company, 27th Infantry Regiment, was issued cartridges that were in twenty round cardboard boxes. The men had to remove the cartridges and load them into eight round M1 clips. Not only was this time consuming, but the clips had to be saved to be used again. Machine gun ammo was often issued in web belts that were left over from World War II. In some cases, the cartridges were corroded to the belt. In this case, individual rounds had to be forced out and inserted into modern metal-link belts. Some of the unit vehicles were not even running and had to be towed aboard the ships for the trip to Korea. Cannibalization was often needed to get some of them in operation. Equipment was not the only problem. Many of the men heading toward Korea in 1950 did so in under-strength units. In terms of personnel, eleven of the twelve regiments sent at first had only two of their three authorized battalions, and the artillery battalion had only two of its firing batteries. Each had only about 14 percent of the authorized tanks.

With them, were sent C rations, the basic combat ration of the day, that had been left over from World War II. Taken out of storage, these rations were designed for three meals for one man for one day: sugar, coffee, cocoa, a can of crackers, small cans of fruit, and cans of food for the main meals.

While the men involved may not have known it, they were being sent to Korea to deliver a message. Some believed that the appearance of American troops at the front would be enough of a warning to halt the North Korean advance. Others were well aware that what they were doing was more realistically an effort to slow the enemy in order to gain time to bring in more substantial numbers of men and equipment. Task Force Smith took the brunt and paid the price. PFC Kenneth Shadrick, with Task Force Smith, made the first payment, becoming the first U.S. soldier killed in Korea when he was struck in the chest by machine-gun fire.

The nature of the combat took on a pattern. American troops would be brought up a road by trucks and offloaded in order to set up a defensive block designed to slow the North Korean advance. The North Korean People's Army would bring its troops up close to the roadblock and then send elements through the hills in order to take up positions to the rear of the American troops. Then they would attack the line and, having successfully blocked off any chance for retreat, were able to destroy the infantry involved, destroy the transportation, and be free to move on. In most cases, the Americans and their ROK allies would stand and fight, but sometimes they would move into the hills in the hope of escaping. The scenes were chaotic with refugees everywhere; the attacking North Koreans, it seemed, could not be stopped.

It was early in the war, at a place called Hill 303 near Waegwan, while defending the Pusan Perimeter that soldiers of the 5th Cavalry regiment counterattacked only to discover the bodies of twenty-six American mortar men who had been found and executed by North Korean soldiers. Among those shot was Private Frederick M. Ryan who though wounded five times managed to survive.

Some relief came, however, in the form of the British 27th Brigade sent from Hong Kong, which arrived on August 29, 1950. By September 1, the strength of UN forces in the Pusan Perimeter was an estimated 180,000. Credit must be given to Lieutenant General Walton Walker for a magnificent defensive effort. During the fight, he shuttled his troops from weak spot to weak spot, staying a little ahead of the North Koreans. At some points, the outcome was in question, but he held his ground.

UN Offensive: September 15 to November 21, 1950

The specially organized X Corps, made up of the 1st Marine and the 7th Infantry Division, broke out of Pusan and invaded at Inchon on September 15 (Operation Chromite) in an end-around exercise, much like the successful efforts General MacArthur had planned in World War II. The troops at Inchon moved in quickly and took Kimpo Airfield, and then reached the outskirts of Seoul on the night of the 18th. They had been joined by the 7th Infantry Division and the remainder of the Marine regiments. The 187th Regimental Combat Team (RCT) was flown into Kimpo Airfield to strengthen UN defenses. On the 26th, MacArthur deemed Seoul liberated (a little early) and by September 29, the city was returned to the South Korean president. By early October, the North Korean forces were moving back across the 38th Parallel.

On the day following the invasion, the Eighth Army began its breakout from Pusan. At that time, the UN had about 230,000 combat troops. The 7th Cavalry Regiment had to fight its way across the Yesong River, and the 8th and 5th Cavalry got into a terrible fight with elements of two North Korean infantry divisions as they moved north of Kaesong in a battle known as Kumchon Pocket. Three days later, the 1st Cavalry and

2nd, 24th, and 25th Infantry Divisions began their advance, moving quickly so that on the 26th they joined up with elements of Corps X. After retaking Seoul, the two forces advanced across the 38th and began to move toward the Yalu River.

Although large numbers of North Koreans escaped through the mountains, more than 100,000 prisoners were captured. General Walker's Republic of Korea (ROK) I Corps crossed the 38th Parallel on October 1 and advanced up the east coast, capturing Wonsan on October 10. By mid-October, the UN forces had penetrated North Korean territory to about twenty miles.

In an effort to cut off a few of the retreating North Korean officials, and hopefully to retake some prisoners of war being moved with them, the 187th Airborne was dropped thirty miles north of Pyongyang, with half of the unit hitting near Sukchon and the other half near Sunchon. The troops, once they arrived, were quickly engaged in stiff combat. The next day, they moved toward Pyongyang.

After the success at Inchon and Seoul, the Eighth Army moved northward along the western half of the peninsula, and Corps X, still operating independently, was transferred to the east coast—the Marines to Wonsan and the 7th Infantry Division to Iwon—where they advanced north. Men of the Eighth Army reached the northernmost point with the capture of the North Korean village of Chonggondo, just a few miles from the Yalu River.

Under orders, General Almond's Corps X began to withdraw from combat and prepare for an amphibious landing on the east. The Marines made an administrative landing at Wonsan on October 26, despite being held up for several days by the heavily mined harbor. The 7th Infantry Division, having made the trek, landed unopposed at Iwon about eighty miles to the north. On the east, after landing in Wonsan, which the ROK had previously captured, Corps X headed toward Hamhung in the north and then turned northwest toward the Chosin Reservoir. Units of the 1st Marine Division advanced up the west side of the reservoir, while the 7th Infantry Division moved up the west. On October 21, near a railroad tunnel north of Sunchon, the Americans found a mass grave of an estimated seventy-three prisoners who had been taken off the train and shot while they waited for the evening meal. Three days later, the ROK 6th Division discovered another grave with twenty-eight executed prisoners.

While the UN forces moved north, the Chinese Communist People's Liberation Army (called volunteers) were massing in preparation for a move south across the Yalu.

Corps X moved out in an effort to capture the industrial, communication, and power production of the North. The Republic of Korea (ROK) I Corps moved along the coast reaching Chongjin more than 100 miles north of Iwon. The Marines moved fifty miles north of Hamhung then turned inland toward the reservoir at Changjin (Chosin) nearly fifty miles to the northwest. The 7th Infantry moved north toward the Pagan Reservoir with its eye on the Yalu River. There was some evidence that Chinese troops were involved in combat as early as October 15, and stout resistance in a few locations beginning on October 25. But after a few interventions, the Chinese troops seemed to disappear. There was some belief among the military leaders that these men represented a few volunteers and presented no threat. On the other hand, both Lieutenant General Walton Walker and Lieutenant General Oliver Smith were concerned with Almond's order to keep moving north.

Chinese Intervention: November 22, 1950 to January 15, 1951

When men of the 7th Infantry Division leading the Eighth Army reached the town of Hyesanjin near the Yalu, the rest of Eighth Army began moving forward from

Chongchon. They were hard hit on November 27, when the UNC positions began to crumble. The same was true on the other side of the country where Corps X had been advancing. When, during the end of November, 260,000 Chinese appeared without much warning, the surprised Americans and Republic of Korea (ROK) Army found that the tide of battle was turning.

On the west, the primary assault was against the ROK II Corps, which collapsed in the face of the massive force of fire. General Walker raced his reserve composed of the 1st Cavalry, the British 27th Commonwealth, the Turkish Brigade, and the 29th Independent Infantry Brigades, but they were unable to stop the advance. As they tried, Walker withdrew steadily south, so that by December 5 he had fallen back from Pyongyang and by the middle of December formed a perimeter north and east of Seoul.

Corps X began its attack to the north on November 27 and had made some slight advances when a second Chinese force that was moving down both sides of the Changjin (Chosin) Reservoir hit both the 1st Marines and the 7th Infantry Divisions. The ROK I Corps and the U.S. 17th Regiment were in danger of being cut off and they were ordered back. The 1st Marines and 7th Infantry retreated carefully "advancing in another direction," and were forced to fight their way until they approached reached Hungnam, where a defensive perimeter was established. Air units were in support and cargo planes were dropping needed supplies. On December 9, the two forces met in the mountain somewhat south of Koto and joined in their redeployment toward Hungnam and evacuation. headed toward Hungnam to be evacuated.

The evacuation at Hungnam was one of the great military rescues. North Korean guerillas in American uniforms—apparently posing as KATUSAs—attacked the rear guard areas around Hungnam as shells from the Naval Task Force whistled overhead and American planes bombarded the advancing Chinese. On December 19, it was necessary to abandon Yonpo, the air base near Hamhung. As the evacuation progressed and most of men and refugees were withdrawn, Navy frogmen were called in to begin the destruction of areas not needed in the withdrawal.

The situation at Hungnam was serious. From shore to shore the area was bracketed by mountains and there was no easily identifiable terrain feature where the Americans could try and keep the Chinese back, so the military relied on firepower. About a mile from the main harbor, the USS *Missouri* began its fire mission, sending 16-inch shells over the defenders' heads. The fire was continuous, beginning at one point and then moving on to another, as a ring of fire was laid around the retreating Americans. The USS *St. Paul* and the USS *Minneapolis,* cruisers, sent rockets against the same targets. Overhead land-based and sea-based planes bombed the area and strafed the Chinese troops they could see. The last of the men were finally taken off in the early morning hours of Christmas Eve. As these men embarked, the engineers planted mines and blew the harbor from one end to the other destroying everything they were not able to take with them. "There was nothing but clouds of dust left," reported Lieutenant Colonel Margaret Brosmer.[7]

British historian Max Hastings makes an informative comment about this period of massive retreat:

> The simple truth remains that the very speed of the retreat saved many units from annihilation and left the Eighth Army with forces that could be rebuilt to fight another day. . . . American mobility was not entirely useless. It enabled many thousands of men, who would not otherwise have done so, to outrun their pursuers and escape to fight another day.[8]

On the west, the Eighth Army began the longest retreat in United States military history, as troops began to move out. General Walker started his withdrawal from the Sukchon-Sunchon-Songchon line on December 2, 1950. As he moved, he destroyed and left behind whatever equipment and supplies that he could not take with him. At the Battle of Kunu-ri, Chinese forces nearly destroyed the 2nd Infantry Division. By December 15, the UN command had managed to slow the enemy enough to establish a defensive line along the Imjin River south of the 38th Parallel.

As men from the service units worked to clear the supply depots, General Walker sent his forces in a semicircle about twenty miles north of Pyongyang, creating a temporary line on December 3, which he reached without major resistance. Walker planned another retreat, moving his line to about fifteen miles south of Pyongyang to establish a defensive line. Another fifty-mile withdrawal was planned and by 4th or 5th December, he had set his units in the Yesong Valley in terrain that would provide better defense. As Walker saw it, the badly bloodied Eighth Army was not prepared to create a static defense line, and, therefore, he considered a series of delaying actions as the only course. He established a series of delaying lines behind him, with the intention to move south from one to the next, avoiding any flanking or enveloping actions, moving back until his forces could be re-established.

Although Chinnampo was under fire by December 5, the port continued in operation, almost without harassment, and troops were loaded aboard Landing Ship, Tanks (LSTs) LSTs from the Japanese merchant marines, as well as from U.S. Navy troop and cargo ships. The troops were taken to either Inchon or Pusan. What supplies had been preserved were landed at Inchon, while personnel, including the wounded, were taken to Pusan. Walker deployed troops, by December 6, across the peninsula where he planned a fighting, rather than a static, defense. Despite the argument of the Joint Chiefs of Staff that MacArthur consolidate the Eighth Army and Corps X in order to prevent the North Korean force moving between them, this was not done.

However, on the 7th of December, General MacArthur directed another withdrawal and the assignment of Corps X to Walker. By December 20, the force was withdrawing to Line B, with plans available for further withdrawal to Line C. At the same time, General Walker brought in ROK I Corps as reinforcement, but still the line was shallow and contained serious gaps. Preparations for withdrawal south of Seoul continued despite the promise to hold Seoul as long as possible. As late as the 23rd, General Walker had not had any significant contact with the Communist forces.

The evacuation on the east and the retreat on the west left the communists once more in control of North Korea. On December 30, General MacArthur warned the Joint Chiefs of Staff that the Chinese Communist Forces could drive the UN forces out of Korea if they so desired. The Joint Chiefs ordered him to defend his position and if necessary to retire back to the former Pusan Perimeter Line.

In late December, Lieutenant General Matthew B. Ridgway replaced Lieutenant General Walker as Commander, Eighth Army, Korea. Walker had been killed in an automobile accident. Ridgway established a defensive line near the 38th Parallel. The North Koreans launched a massive attack on January 1, and with seven Chinese armies and two North Korean corps pushed deep in the UN lines, driving them back toward the capital on the west and toward Wonju at the center of the line. When Seoul fell on January 4, Inchon was evacuated. As pressure from the offense increased, Ridgway moved south to a line near the 37th parallel. On New Year's day, 1951, a massive Chinese force advanced on the UN lines and drove the defending forces another fifty miles south, but was finally slowed by the hard-fighting defenders. The defense was aided by the fact that the expanded lines were making it increasingly difficult for the Chinese to keep up with the demand for supplies.

At home, there was some evidence of panic thinking as *Life* magazine, one of the few recorders of the war, published an editorial that called events in Korea a disaster and warned that World War III was coming ever nearer. "Out leaders are frightened, befuddled, and caught in a great and inexcusable failure to marshal the strength of America."[9]

First UN Counteroffensive: January 16 to April 21, 1951

Following the death of General Walker and the arrival of Lieutenant General Ridgway, the UN forces begin a series of operations designed to return to the 38th Parallel. Operation Wolfhound, named after its primary force, the 27th Infantry Regiment, moved forward as a reconnaissance in force until it met the Chinese near Suwon. This was followed by Operation Thunderbolt on January 27, as a general offensive by Corps I, IX, and X (returned to Eighth Army). The generally successful Operation Thunderbolt was followed by Operation Roundup. Elements of the U.S. 25th Division secured Inchon and Kimpo airfield, portions of Corps X captured Hoengsong. Strong North Korean resistance continued until February 9 and then, rather abruptly, gave way in the face of UN efforts to move their lines northward toward Hongchon. The UN Forces met with a stiffened response, as a powerful Chinese counterattack penetrated their lines and attempted to set up roadblocks to harass any attempt to retreat. Communist forces nearly annihilated the ROK 8th Infantry Division, but the drive was stopped when they reached the position held by the 2nd Infantry Division. Using artillery, air, and armor, the UN forces were able to hold Chipyong-ni and break the North Korean advance. Other communist probes directed against sectors held by the 1st Cavalry, the 7th, and elements of the 2nd Infantry Division were met with fierce resistance, as gaps were closed and the communist drive halted.

Evidence suggests that on February 18, the communists were withdrawing along the front, and General Ridgway ordered Corps IX to move forward. Operation Killer was launched on February 21 by the 1st Cavalry, the 2nd, 7th, and 24th Infantry Divisions, and the 1st Marine Division to drive the communists north of the Han River. Only moderately successful, it did, however, improve the UN lines and set up the situation for Operation Ripper, which followed in March. Ripper, which involved all of the divisions of Eighth Army including airborne troops of the 187th Regiment Combat Team and the 2nd and 4th Ranger companies (in a related operation called Tomahawk), finally drove the communist forces north of the 38th Parallel. In Operation Rugged, during April 1951, the Eighth Army advanced to what would become the Kansas-Wyoming Line, north of the 38th Parallel. Utah Line, an extension of the main defensive line, was achieved by the 3rd, 24th, and 25th Infantry in Operation Dauntless. With Seoul back in UN hands, the Eighth Army set about improving their defensive line along the Kansas Line.

One of the more vicious battles to take place during the Korean War occurred near Osan, South Korea. Wolfhound's (27th Infantry) Easy Company had regrouped after being driven back during February. The vanguard for their unit, having discovered that the communists were dug in at Hill 180, moved up and under a hail of grenades and gunfire took the hill in hand-to-hand combat, wounding sixty-one and killing forty-one. For action during this battle, Captain Lewis Millett was later awarded the Medal of Honor.

Retaking the area near Hoengsong, men of the 7th Marines uncovered evidence of the earlier rout, where they found hundreds of GI's bodies that remained where they had fallen, frozen into positions. The men were astonished by the evidence of the estimated

Village after being liberated, Korea, 1951. (*Used by permission of the Center for the Study of the Korean War, Graceland University*)

204 dead men of the 15th Field Artillery (2nd Division) who were caught there by Chinese forces, and dubbed the area "Massacre Valley."

By March 1, the entire Eighth Army line was relatively stable as the North Koreans had withdrawn during the bad weather. On March 11, Corps IX reached the first phase line, and three days later patrols moved into Seoul, after which the capital changed hands for the fourth time since June 1950. On March 23, the 187th Airborne Regimental Combat Team was dropped at Munsan-ni about twenty miles forward from Seoul in an effort to trap the Communist forces, but failed because of the latter's rapid retreat. On April 9, the U.S. Corps I and IX and the ROK I Corps reached Line Kansas.

On April 11, President Harry Truman released General Douglas MacArthur, listing as his reasons, differences between them concerning national policy and military strategy. The old soldier went home with some presidential aspiration, but all too quickly "faded away."

On April 14, just before the Chinese Spring Offensive, Lieutenant General James A. Van Fleet succeeded Lieutenant General Ridgway as commander of the Eighth Army, Korea. General Ridgway replaced General MacArthur. On the 16th, the Hwachon Dam was taken and on the east coast ROK Forces captured Taepo-ri while others crossed the Imjin River. By April 19, all the units of the U.S. Corps I and IX were in positions along Line Utah.

Chinese Spring Offensive: April 22 to May 19, 1951

In late April, the Chinese launched a movement toward Seoul and Kapyong. Despite a strong defense along the Kansas Line, the Chinese, after cutting up the South Korean 6th Division, managed to break through at Kapyong. As a result, the UN forces were required to move south about thirty-five miles where they dug in and established No Name Line; here the line held. Seeking to prevent another attack against them,

General Van Fleet ordered the Eighth Army forward, and by the end of May it had progressed to an area just short of Line Kansas. During eight days of combat between April 22 and 30, 1951, there occurred one of the greatest single battles of the war: a victory by the Eighth Army when it repulsed the Chinese offensive and inflicted more than 70,000 casualties.

A devastating battle occurred during this period at Gloucester (Gloster) Hill, also called Hill 235. After the withdrawal from North Korea, the Eighth Army began a series of attacks in an effort to take Line Kansas that lay just north of the 38th Parallel. These operations, Thunderbolt, Killer, and Rugged, began to push the North Koreans, who countered by attacks in April in an attempt to double-envelop Corps I and IX. In the withdrawal of the Corps, the Gloucester Battalion was isolated and repeated efforts to relieve them were unsuccessful. The battalion was cut off and overrun. Responding to a Chinese attack on April 22–23, 1951, the British soldiers fought until their ammunition was gone, and then only four officers and 36 enlisted men made it back to UN lines. Casualties: 1,100.

On May 16, the Chinese tried again and sent twenty-one Chinese divisions and nine North Korean divisions against the UN lines. The line cracked at several points, bringing about limited retreats, but the majority of the line managed to hang on. Along the Soyang River, the Chinese casualties were so large it was referred to as the May Massacre. The line held for the most part, however, and by the 20th, American and UN divisions were forming up for a counterattack. On the 17th, the North Koreans moved down the Pukhan River toward the Han River and against Corps IX. While they enjoyed some early successes, they were contained after three days. By the 20th, the UN line had stopped them, the second time in two months. On the 18th, Van Fleet opened a series of local attacks and by the 31st, South Korea was primarily cleared of North Koreans.

UN Counteroffensive: May 20 to November 12, 1951

At this point, the Joint Chiefs of Staff determined that the Eighth Army was not to move beyond the general vicinity of the Kansas Line. Acting on these orders, General Van Fleet directed his reserve forces to strengthen Line Kansas in an effort to make it as impregnable as possible. As spring arrived, UN divisions were ordered to carry out a series of operations designed to retake positions lost in the Chinese Offensive or to close gaps in the line. In Operation Detonate, the Americans moved forward to retake the Kansas Line. In Operation Piledriver, troops succeeded in driving the communists out of the Iron Triangle and reformed the Wyoming Line. Operation Commando succeeded in establishing the Jamestown Line, and Operations Nomad and Polar took up positions at what would be called the Missouri Line.

On June 23, 1951, the character of the war changed once again. Jacob Malik, Deputy Foreign Minister of the U.S.S.R. recorded a broadcast that implied that the Chinese and North Koreans were willing to discuss an armistice. When Chinese radio backed this up, Truman authorized Lieutenant General Ridgway to make the arrangements. At the first meeting of the potential armistice negotiators, it was agreed that military action would continue unrestricted while the talks went on. The war thus took on the character of a small-unit exercise. Battles were now fought over hilltops, including the Battle of Tessin and the Battle of Bloody Ridge, which dislodged the Chinese, forcing them to nearby Heartbreak Ridge. Bloody Ridge was a piece of high ground formed by three hills—773, 940, and 983—and was a part of the area known as the Punchbowl. The armistice talks broke off again on August 22, and Van Fleet launched a series of limited attacks to improve the Eighth Army's defensive position. The objectives, seven terrain features about six miles above Line Kansas, were secured by October.

Second Korean Winter–Spring: November 13, 1951 to June 19, 1952

This begins the period of the war known as the "battle of the outposts" or, sometimes, simply, the hill wars. During this period, there was a relative lull that settled over the battlefield, as Ridgway ordered a halt to offensive operations. On November 21, he ordered the Eighth Army to cease offensive operations and begin an active defense of the front.

As the second Korean winter hit, the opposing forces had established lines from one coast to the other, very much in the same pattern as that used in the static fighting of World War I. In Operation Clam-up, an effort was made to bring the communists out to fight, but the Chinese did not take the bait. Though the grand maneuvers had ceased, however, the fighting did not. In fact, more than half of the 140,000 casualties of the Korean War were killed or wounded during this phase. Raids by small units, heavy air strikes, and artillery bombardments were the order of the day. Most of the action took place at the company level, occasionally at battalion level, but rarely of units larger than that. There were also raids against small-unit locations. Operation Counter, a series of raids, was launched by the 45th Infantry Division to establish patrol bases around Old Baldy, and a series of Chinese small-unit attacks occurred against UN outposts on Snook Hill, Pork Chop Hill, and Old Baldy.

The decision had been made to continue efforts to achieve a negotiated settlement and, in consideration of this decision, most of the aggressive action was limited. While this change in the ultimate goal altered the size and the scope of action, it also changed the role of the individual soldier. From the standpoint of the men involved, these relatively small battles for hills and outposts were fights as bloody and intense as any being fought. Life on the line, while no less dangerous, became more static, and semipermanent fortifications took on new significance. Bunkers and trench lines, outposts and listening stations became the order of the day.

As 1951 came to a close, most of the fighting now occurred during routine patrols, raids, and the bitter struggles of small units' objectives. Attacks were permitted only to strengthen the line or to establish the high ground.

Korean Summer–Fall: June 20 to December 20, 1952

As the war dragged on into the third year of combat, the stalemate continued. Efforts to achieve some success led to small attacks by both the UN and communist forces. The weather took a hand and torrential rains prevented much activity through the latter part of July and most of August.

When reporting that there was little activity during this period, it needs to be remembered that what this meant primarily was that there were no large-scale attacks by either side. Assaults on isolated positions, sieges of specific posts, and heavy artillery bombardments continued. There were repeated attacks on Old Baldy, Bunker Hill, Outpost Bruce, and a Chinese assault on Outpost Kelly. The Chinese, apparently believing that they could erode the UN desire to fight by daily harassments, resorted to trench warfare and avoided the big offensive. During June, the communists' guns were firing nearly 6,800 shells a day at UN positions. The UN response was sometimes five to ten times that amount. There was rarely a day when communist and UN troops did not tangle somewhere along the front line. It was not until October, however, that each side would launch a significant operation designed to improve their defensive positions.

One of these efforts was the Battle of White Horse Hill that followed a Chinese attack against several hills, White Horse perhaps being the most important. Forces of the Chinese 38th Field Army attacked, and what followed was a seesaw battle where the hill changed hands many times. After several days and high casualties, the Chinese withdrew. At the same time, the Chinese launched a second diversionary attack against Arrowhead Hill that, at the time, was occupied by the French Battalion. The French were able to hold on.

In Operation Showdown, the UN set out to capture four major hills—Triangle Hill, Pike's Peak, Jane Russell Hill, and Sandy Hill. All of these were northeast of Kimhwa in the area known as the Iron Triangle. Soldiers of the 31st Infantry regiment (7th Division) moved out toward their goal, but were met by the elite Chinese 15th Field Army entrenched on Triangle Hill. On the 15th, the Americans captured Triangle Hill and moved on to take Jane Russell the next day. After the UN briefly held Pike's Peak, the Chinese counterattacked and took it back. Later, after the Republic of Korea (ROK) 2nd Division had moved up, the Chinese attacked again, driving the ROK first off Triangle Hill and then Jane Russell.

Third Korean Winter: December 21, 1952 to March 20, 1953

During January and February, the fighting was again limited to a few patrol clashes and small-unit activities. North Korean forces increased their attacks during March, striking at outposts held by the 2nd and the 7th Infantry Division and against the 1st Marine Regiment. But as the winter returned, soldiers on both sides of the line were hoping for the cease-fire to be reached. The stalemate still existed at the conference table, and both sides had constructed seemingly impregnable defensive lines. Combat consisted of artillery duels, small (platoon and squad sized) ambushes, and skirmishes between patrols. During this time, the Eighth Army defended its terrain and its outpost positions. On occasion, they were required to let the North Koreans have an outpost when the cost of its defense outweighed its potential value.

During the early months of 1953, though the Eighth Army sent out an estimated 5,000 patrols, only a few—about 200—actually made contact with the North Koreans. Starting in February, the Chinese directed their limited efforts to break the UNC lines, particularly moving against ROK troops. During February and March, the Eighth Army carried out a series of raids, which, supported by artillery and air power, hit Chinese and North Korean positions, killing large numbers and weakening their emplacements.

When Lieutenant General Maxwell D. Taylor took command of the Eighth Army in February 1953, talks at Panmunjom had come to a halt once again. In mid-March the Chinese again hit the line, primarily at the Corps I sector, attacking at both Old Baldy and Pork Chop Hill. Both hills changed hands on two occasions until General Taylor, determining that Old Baldy was not worth the costs, called off raids against it. On one occasion, a patrol of thirty-four men from the U.S. 7th Infantry Division was ambushed and decimated. Other ambushes were addressed against the men of the 2nd Infantry Division. The operation called Smack, a combined-arms attack against communist-held Spud Hill was unsuccessful.

In some indication of the fierce nature of this period—which was called a stalemate—approximately 13,000 Marines were killed, wounded, or captured during the period from March 1952 to July 1953.

Korean Spring–Summer: March 21 to July 27, 1953

Again, waiting for some sort of cease-fire to end the killing, military operations were limited to small actions. Unfortunately, the casualties were not small. Battles, such as they were, were fought between companies and directed toward the high ground. The Chinese continued to attack hilltops to make clear their resolve, and the UN fought to maintain the line in case of a cease-fire. The last Chinese offensive was directed toward the Kumsong River Salient, and U.S. fought their final battles near the Boulder City section of the Berlin Complex. As spring approached, North Korea began a series of attacks against the outpost line established by the Eighth Army. Both mortar and infantry attacks increased along the line.

During this period, the UN forces were not permitted to advance into any new territory, but they were ordered to hold the Main Line of Resistance (MLR) at all costs. Most of the fighting took place near outposts, most of them from one thousand to five thousand yards ahead of the MLR. The outpost held the closest high ground and was designed to cover the area through which an enemy force might try to move against the MLR.

There was also heavy fighting at Old Baldy, the Nevada Cities outposts of Carson, Reno, and Vegas held by the 5th Marines, as well as Outpost Harry. The most telling, perhaps, were the on-and-off battles of Pork Chop Hill. In a series of attacks, one side and then the other took control of the hill. Even as the armistice talks were reaching their conclusion at Panmunjom, the hill had become a test of the moral determination of both sides. As the talks reached an end, the Chinese divisions were trying to dislodge the UN forces. General Maxwell Taylor decided the cost was too high to pay for the worthless hill, and the Chinese took control of Hill 234. After the armistice, the hill was located along

Command post, executive bunker, Korea, 1953. (*Used by permission of the Center for the Study of the Korean War, Graceland University*)

the DMZ and partly in North Korea. During three days in April, UN artillery rounds on Pork Chop numbered more than 77,000, with the Chinese firing approximately that many.

The weather during this period was awful, with seemingly unending downpours and massive mud. Constantly flaring gunfights crackled all along the front. Every night, in darkness as black as the inside of a cave, the Chinese would fight and slog their way through slippery and restricting ankle-deep mud. All along the line, there were eruptions of gunfire that lit up the night as Marine and Chinese patrols, suddenly exposed, stumbled on to one another.

On the night of June10, three Chinese divisions struck the ROK II Corps near Kumsong. The attacks were moderately successful, forcing these units to withdraw, but both sides lost heavily during the conflict. On July 7, 1953, the Chinese infantry advanced in waves through their own artillery barrage toward the forward slopes of Berlin and East Berlin. The defenders were hopelessly outnumbered, and the Chinese took East Berlin. The battle continued on the next day and night. Again, on July 13, the Chinese hit with three divisions against the flank of the ROK III Corps and with a division against the U.S. Corps IX, forcing a withdrawal of about eight miles to positions just below the Kumsong River. By the 20th, UN Forces had retaken the high ground along the river and established a new line of resistance. By the 18th of the month, the attacks had subsided, and by the end of the month patrol action was once again the primary activity along the line. On the 18th, the terms of the armistice were all but complete, but it all heated up again as South Korean President Syngman Rhee ordered the release of 27,000 anticommunist North Korean prisoners of war.

The last open combat of the war was fought by the 1st and 7th Marine Regiments on Hills 111 and 119 along with units of the 3rd Infantry Division who occupied Sniper Ridge.

CEASE-FIRE

The road to the cease-fire was a long and costly one. Several attempts had been made earlier and the Chinese Communists Forces had rejected every effort. But in June of 1951, the Soviet delegate to the UN suggested some discussion of the possibility of a cease-fire. The U.S. wanted to curtail, if not totally stop, the war and its drain on men and materials. On July 8, a meeting was held at the old Korean capitol at Kaesong. The Chinese, who came to the table as a world power, were in no mood for an immediate agreement and even the discussions on the agenda took two weeks. It was clear that the Communists wanted to tie several political items—the question of the Nationalists on Taiwan for example—but finally agreed to a primarily military agenda. For months both sides argued, presented their proposals, rejected items and, when everything else failed, adjourned the meetings, sometimes for months. In October 1951, the site of the negotiations moved to Panmunjom, where they remained during the rest of the negotiations.

Whether it was the death of Joseph Stalin on March 5, 1953, or the suggestion that America was considering the use of the atomic bomb, the two sides began discussions again during the first of April and, in those discussions, agreed on an exchange of sick and wounded prisoners of war. Finally, the discussions took on a note of expectancy, and item after item was worked out so that by early July it looked like a cease-fire could be concluded. President Rhee put a wrench in the gears, however, with the premature release of North Korean POWs that he believed wanted to stay in the South. The Communist reaction was swift, and military, but did not really delay the discussions.

Finally, on July 27,1953, the delegates met and signed eighteen copies of the agreement—the fighting was to stop twelve hours later, but everyone was aware that it was a cease-fire, not a peace treaty.

It is important to note that while it was Communist "feet-dragging" that is primarily blamed for the lack of progress at the negotiations, the major roadblock was presented by the United Nations, and basically by the United States. While one must accept the existence of humanitarian motives, and that certainly was the interpretation accepted by most Americans, there were other perhaps more politically motivated reasons behind the demands. Among other things, of course, the demand for the repatriation of those who wanted to stay behind was in violation of the Geneva Convention that requires the "return of all prisoners." James I. Matray suggests that an armistice could have been signed a whole lot earlier had the United States not taken the hard stand that it did on prisoner repatriation.[10] This is not a judgment about the decision, but rather a realization that the negotiations had arrived at a reasonable agreement prior to the call for total POW repatriations.

OPERATIONS

The Korean War, like most military efforts, involved a significant number of focused events called operations. These operations were usually designed to accomplish a specific goal within a specified time frame. There were more than a hundred of these operations during the Korean War. Most of them were short-lived and were conducted on a small scale. At the beginning, General MacArthur maintained the World War II practice of naming these from a pre-established code list. But he moved beyond the tradition in Korea by announcing the names to the press while they were still in operation. Lieutenant General Ridgway, realizing the need to motivate his army, adopted a set of highly aggressive operational names for his counter-offensive that ran from February to April 1951. Among his names were Thunderbolt, Roundup, Killer, Ripper, Courageous, Audacious, and Dauntless. These may well have helped the fighting spirit, but the home front, apparently ashamed to talk about what they were not ashamed to send their soldiers to do, thought the names were unpleasant and poor public relations. Ridgway would later comment that he could not see why the nation should not be made aware that war involved killing.

THE SERVICES

Army

The armed forces consist of men and women who take the fight to the enemy when it is deemed necessary by the political leaders of the nation. Many find their way to the front line. Some spend their entire service doing one of the thousands of jobs necessary to keep the fighting men on the front. Of those jobs in the army, all of them are required, all of them are essential, and no role that is played is done so in vain. While it is perfectly natural for many to focus their attention on those in the front line, that man or woman is but the point of a long spear that runs all the way from the recruiting sergeant to the artillery forward observer. With very few exceptions (when civilians are employed for a specific task), the vast majority of jobs in the military are filled by a member of the Armed Forces.

The U.S. Army carried the brunt of the UN mission in Korea. Under staffed, widely dispersed, and lacking in modern equipment, the Army responded immediately, landing the first combat troops with a few days of the initial attack. As the situation worsened, President Truman authorized General MacArthur to use all troops available to him. At the time, this consisted of the Eighth U.S. Army (EUSA) with the 1st Cavalry and the 7th, 24th, and 25th Infantry Divisions. Available, but farther away, were the 29th Regimental Combat Team on Okinawa and the 5th Regimental Combat Team in Hawaii.

Quickly formed as the United Nations Command, with General Douglas MacArthur as Commander-in-Chief, United Nations Command (CICUNC), the Eighth Army moved to Korea under the command of Lieutenant General Walton H. Walker. During the initial months, the Army engaged in a fighting retreat as they withdrew, line by line, in the face of a massive North Korean attack. Eventually, they set up a defense around the port city of Pusan. Holding at Pusan while gaining reinforcements and supplies, the Army—slowly being joined by the Marines and fighting men from assisting UN members—prepared for an attack through Inchon. As Corps X moved inland, the Eighth Army broke out, moved north rapidly and, in October, crossed over the 38th Parallel into North Korea.

Crossing the parallel, the Eighth Army moved north along the west coast and (in the designation of Corps X) along the east. The Chinese intervention forced the Army into a massive retreat, along both coasts, that continued until December 1950. The assignment of Lieutenant General Matthew B. Ridgway renewed morale and, under his direction, the counter-campaigns began. Through a series of operations—Thunderbolt, Killer, Ripper, Rugged—the Army forced its way back until, in November 1951, it began to assume more defensive positions closely related to the 38th Parallel, in coordination with the armistice talks.

As the war grew more static, the pressure increased. Except for brief encounters, the battlefield was a place of patrols, small skirmishes, artillery duels, mortar battles, and ambush raids. During the final phase of the war, the Chinese Communist Forces made several offensive attempts but were held back.

Certainly without discounting the role of the other services and the particular skills attached to those units, the American soldiers carried the war. Greatly outnumbering the other services, more directly involved in the daily trench, outpost, and hill attacks, and living through every imaginable weather catastrophe, they were there every day, in every event—from delivering the mail to firing the rockets—during every phase of the war. Army personnel received 78 Medals of Honor.

Navy

At first, President Truman hoped that naval and air power would be enough to stop the North Korean advance. This was not to be the case, however, and the navy quickly became part of the team. Besides, this was not a traditional war, and the navy did not fight it in a traditional way. There were no battles with the enemy on the high seas, nor were they called on to protect desperate convoys trying to keep the supply lines open. Rather, the navy's role was to seize and control the waters around Korea, keeping both coasts open. And to use their massive power against enemy supplies and communication lines, provide carrier-born air support, and stand guard against any attempt by the communist forces to move in from the sea.

The first step was taken by the U.S. 7th Fleet, which was sent into the Taiwan Straits in order to prevent any movement, either way, between Red China and the Nationalists in Taiwan. Then, by the June 29, 1950, Task Force 77—made up of Australian, Canadian, New Zealand, and United States ships—began the bombardment of communist targets, an activity that would last during the entire war. By July 3, planes from the carrier the USS *Valley Forge* were attacking North Korean airfields.

The focus of naval combat operations was to seek and maintain control of the seas. It is difficult to imagine how different the outcome of the war might have been if the UN forces had to deal with a communist presence on the high seas. During the Korean War, the merchant and troop ships crossed the nearly 5,000 miles of sea in convoys but, unlike in World War II, they did not have to fight their way to their destination. The freedom available was because the navy had moved quickly against the small but annoying North Korean fleet, and control of the sea became a reality. Other than the brief period at Wonsan, when the Marine landing was delayed by sea mines, the UN had fairly free access to both coasts. By September, whatever coastal navy the North Koreans could bring to bear had been destroyed, and the navy achieved supremacy of the sea. Neither the Chinese Communist nor the Soviet Union committed naval forces.

The navy was present in great abundance during the Inchon landing and swept the harbors of mines to make movement in-and-out possible, supported the landing at Wonsan, and then, later, moved into Hungnam to provide bombardment and to aid in the evacuation of the retreating troops. At Wonsan, the U.S. Navy conducted the longest naval blockade in U.S. history, preventing the communists from using the port and, it has been calculated, diverting 80,000 troops from serving on the front line. The navy provided air–ground troop support, acting as artillery for advancing units.

A major service performed during the war was carried out by those few men of the vastly understaffed Minesweeper force. Sea-mines were a major hazard, deposited by the North Koreans and—it was believed—floated down from Soviet bases to the north. Though mines had appeared elsewhere, the first major confrontation was at Wonsan harbor, where the U.S. Marines were delayed for several days because their ships were not able to get close enough to shore. To fight these mines, the navy pulled into service several wooden and metal minesweepers. They were aided by efforts to destroy the mines by naval gunfire, or even to explode them using planes. Lieutenant Commander Harold Elston, aboard a destroyer in the Korean Theater of Operations, recalled this event when a sea-mine struck back at a plane. He was watching a U.S. Navy flying boat (USN PBY try and explode mines by gunfire, when it was suddenly successful and the "entire line exploded all at the same time. The plane was making a turn at the moment, crossing the line of mines. A wall of water was sent skyward as all of the mines fired simultaneously."[11]

Naval support at Chosin was extremely important. The operation began on December 10, when Task Force 90 embarked to support the withdrawal from the reservoir area. Fleet carriers USS *Philippine Sea* (CV-47), USS *Valley Forge* (CV-45), USS *Princeton* (CV-37) and USS *Leyte Gulf* (CV-32), along with three escort carriers, provided support for the ground troops, carrying out in excess of 1,700 sorties during the primary week of withdrawal. As the evacuation began, the battleship USS *Missouri* and the cruisers USS *St. Paul* (CA-73) and USS *Rochester* and twenty destroyers and rocket ships provided bombardment, slowing the advancing communist forces. By Christmas eve, when the evacuation was over, the naval explosive teams destroyed the facilities at Hungnam. During the evacuation, the navy had withdrawn more than 200,000 military and civilian personnel.

The navy manned the ships that provided most of the transportation, cargo movement, blockade, interdiction, and mine clearance. In addition, navy corpsmen provided the medical aid personnel for the Marine units. The U.S. Navy Amphibious Construction Battalions were attached to Task Forces. During the war, they undertook hundreds of construction tasks under very difficult situations.

While life aboard a ship was both boring and exciting, it was better than life on the front line. There was every chance that living conditions on board ship would be cramped, and that life itself would be monotonous—particularly when looking at nothing but water for more than a year—but it was certainly better duty that dodging death every day on the front line. On the larger ships, there might be as many as 3,200 billeted on a ship, sleeping twenty-seven to a compartment, five beds high, all together in a space that was not much larger than the living room of a modern home. But at least naval personnel did not spend days in knee-deep mud avoiding bullets. More than 265,000 navy personnel served during the Korean War. Four hundred and seventy-five were killed in action, another 4,043 died of disease or injury, and 1,576 were wounded in action.

While primarily unheralded, the U.S. Navy submarine service was also very active during the Korean War. They were some of the first boats to appear on the scene in Korea. During the war, they screened naval surface forces, surveyed Soviet and Korean minefields, performed photo reconnaissance, surveyed landing sites, kept an eye on Soviet shipping, were significantly involved in the neutralization of maritime forces in the Taiwan Straits and patrolled the Sea of Okhotsk. All in all, thirty-one submarines saw service during the war. One of the primary activities in which the submarines were engaged was in the transport and support of clandestine activities. One sub, the USS *Perch* (SSP 313), had been refitted to carry about sixty troops and transported a skip inside a bulbous projection fitted to its deck. The "Pregnant Perch" was responsible for several raids along the coasts.

Admiral Burke was to remind Americans later: "Another simple point, that is just so obvious that people have forgotten it. We had absolute control of the sea around there. It was never contested in Korea. If our control of the sea had been contested just a little bit . . . Korea would have been lost forever."[12]

Air Force

The Air Force had only recently become independent from the Army—no longer the Army Air Corps but now the United States Air Force—and in this organizational form had never fought a war. The Air Force had been dominated by the delivery of nuclear weapons, and it had few plans for fighting a conventional war. The air war began in Korea when two North Korean planes first attacked Seoul, and General MacArthur called on American naval and air forces to respond. Almost immediately, the Far East Air Force established air superiority over the battlefield. The United States Air Force supplied 85 percent of the land-based combat aircraft. Through the war, the Air Force conducted more than 730,000 sorties.

The air war began almost immediately, as President Truman authorized the use of air power to defend the evacuation of American dependents from Korea to Japan. The Far East Air Force, commanded by Lieutenant General George E. Stratemeyer, initially served to provide air cover for the evacuation of American nationals. At the time, it was composed of the Third Air Force in the Philippines, the Fifth Air Force in Japan, and the Twentieth Air Force in Guam. Only 657 planes were combat ready and, to compensate,

Project Holdoff was set in motion to recondition mothballed aircraft and return them to service. Some new planes, the F-86, F-94, C-119, and C-124, were also deployed.

One of its primary missions was to gain air superiority over the North Korean Air Force. Within a month, it had established this superiority. When China entered the war, however, the situation changed, and control of the skies became more difficult. Though the Soviets were less aggressively involved in the ground war, they did pose a challenge to U.S. air control. The Soviet-built MiG-15 was 100 miles faster and could climb better than the American F-86A.

The battle for air superiority against the MiG was more glamorous, and the pilots involved in such skirmishes received the greatest recognition and press coverage from the UN side. In reality, most pilots were engaged in the less glamorous but equally lethal work of bombing and strafing ground targets. Anti-aircraft artillery and ground fire took the greatest toll of UN pilots over the battlefield. Close-support aircraft and the night-flying B-26 and B-29 bomber pilots flew more missions and died in greater numbers than did the high-flying Sabre pilots.

As the war progressed, the air war was directed toward ground support and interdiction. During the summer of 1952, the air war intensified with raids against troop concentrations, supply centers, factories, and power plants. The largest raid of the war was carried out on the 29th of August against Pyongyang, the North Korean capital. Beginning on August 15, 1952, the Far East Air Force launched the interdiction campaign, Operation Strangle, against railroad trucks, bridges, and highway traffic. Carrier-based planes blasted railroad tracks, bridges, and boxcars.

In addition to the primary mission of maintaining control of the air, the Air Force tasks were sixfold. A major assignment was close air support, carried out mostly over the front lines, and was conducted by F-51s, F-80s, and F-84s. The Air Force not only protected the fighting men from harassment by Chinese planes, but also fired on their ground forces. In many cases, these attacks were controlled by T-6 aircraft, called Mosquitoes, which observed and maintained radio direction.

The Air Force was also responsible for air interdiction, which was primarily carried out by the Fifth Air Force. High-flying B-26s and B-29s flew numerous missions against trains and rail lines, destroying more than 900 locomotives and cutting up tens of thousands of rail lines. The planes destroyed or interrupted supply columns, destroyed depots, weakened industrial areas, and downed bridges. Strategic bombing was highly significant and carried out at great risk. Flying most of the time at night, UN bombers, usually B-29s, flew hundreds of missions over North Korea to wipe out the nation's industrial complex, destroy hydroelectric plants and irrigation dams. The Air Force was also involved in conducting reconnaissance and photo-reconnaissance flights.

Certainly of high priority, especially to those on the ground, was the Air Force's delivery of critical supplies when and where they were needed. The Combat Cargo Command (later the 315th Air Division) undertook constant supply flights, combined, on their return, with medical evacuation. The use of aeromedical evacuation, using primarily H-5 and H-19 helicopters, was initially designed to work in emergency cases only, but soon built up to such an extent that they were considered normal flights. The air arm was also responsible for search-and-rescue missions both behind enemy lines and over the water. Using a variety of planes—SA-16 flying boats, L-5 liaison planes, and H-5 and H-19 helicopters—they rescued more than 250 persons.

Marines

The Marine Corps was in fairly desperate condition when the war broke out in 1950. During the years following the end of World War II, the Corps had been downgraded to the point that when General MacArthur called for the 1st Marine Division, it existed in name only. Disagreements between the services, and the mistaken belief that the day of the amphibious landing was over, had allowed the Corps to release a major portion of its men into the reserves.

Gathering its resources, the 1st Provisional Marine Brigade was quickly activated based on the 5th Marine Regiment and was supported by Marine Aircraft Group 33. By July 12, the group was aboard ship heading for Korea. Coming ashore on August 2, the Brigade, attached to General Walker's Eighth Army, first engaged the North Koreans at Chindong-ni in the defense of Pusan. As the Pusan Perimeter held, and with the rest of the division (minus the 7th Regiment) becoming available, General MacArthur attached the division to Corps X, joined it with the 7th Infantry Division, and launched an attack against Inchon and eventually the capital at Seoul. Following the success at Inchon, the division was moved to the west coast where it landed without opposition administratively, at Wonsan. The Marines were to advance into northeast Korea. Caught near Chosin by the Chinese, they engaged in a prolonged fighting retreat and were evacuated at Hungnam. It was in this battle, in November 1950, that Colonel Lewis B. "Chesty" Puller made the remark attributed to him, "We've been looking for the enemy for several days now, we've finally found them. We're surrounded. That simplifies our problem of getting to these people and killing them."[13]

During 1951, the Marines participated as the United Nations regrouped and counterattacked, taking their objectives at the Punchbowl. They deployed there in defensive positions until March when they were reassigned to the far western end of the Eighth Army line. In 1952, they were involved in the defense of Bunker Hill, the Battle of the Hook, and in defense of a segment of the MLR. During 1953, they came in defense of outposts Reno, Vegas, and Carson, while waiting out the armistice negotiations. The last days of the war found them in defense of outpost Reno, Berlin, and East Berlin, and they were in support of the 24th Infantry Division (Army) as the war ended. Forty-two Marines were awarded the Medal of Honor.

Segments of the Marine Air (VMF) flew in raids against North Korean installations, in harassing their positions, and in support of ground troops. The Marine Helicopter Transport Squadron was involved in early experiments with the movement of troops and supplies, as well as providing medical evacuation.

Coast Guard

After major service during World War II, it was decided that in future wars the Coast Guard should be limited to an expansion of its peacetime roles: that is, ports security, maritime inspections, search and rescue, and ocean patrols. In addition, Coast Guard units, personnel, ships, and aircraft were to be utilized in their traditional service rather than indiscriminately integrating them into navy assignments. This was the thinking as the war broke out and was implemented during the period.

Interestingly, it was well before the Korean War began that the American Coast Guard made one of its major contributions. On August 23, 1946, a small unit of the Guard, under command of Captain Frank McCabe, was sent to Korea to organize and train the South Korean Coast Guard. Using former Japanese warships and basing their program on the U.S. Coast Guard Academy, they established an officer training school for the maritime services. When the Republic of Korea decided it needed a Navy more than a coast guard, many of the Guard members were sent home, but a significant number of retired and reserve officers stayed on to help train the navy.

During the war, the U.S. Coast Guard was involved in manning Ocean Stations. These cutters provided weather observations, checkpoints for military and commercial maritime and air traffic, relay stations for aircraft on transoceanic flights, and served as search-and-rescue platforms. Several aircraft ditched near the cutters (mostly Navy destroyers that had been taken from mothballs and re-commissioned). At the beginning of the war, there were two stations, and three additional ones were established in the North Pacific. The ships remained at these stations generally steaming around in endless circles for three or four weeks at a time. As well they established a chain of detachments on islands to aid in the search-and-rescue missions.

Duty in the Coast Guard was hard and monotonous. Day after day of being slammed around by rough cold sea swells that could rise as high as fifty feet, with the winds sometimes hitting gale force, was exaggerated by trying to stay on station within an ocean grid the size of a postage stamp. Fortunately, the routine kept them quite busy: radar and radio were manned around the clock; twice a day, six-feet helium-filled balloons were launched to measure air temperature, pressure, and humidity; the temperature of the water was checked every four hours; and passing aircrafts and ships were contacted by radio to provide radar and radio fixes. For recreation, the Coast Guard had movies, pistol matches, skeet shooting, volleyball games, and fishing.

Twenty-four cutters serviced on the stations that fell within the perimeters of the Korean War and their crews earned the Korean Service Medals. A number of Pacific air search-and-rescue detachments were commissioned on Wake and Midway Islands. The Guard often refers to itself as the "unknown service of the unknown war."

Merchant Marines

The term merchant marine generally refers to those ships used for commerce that, in times of war, complement the navy. In the United States, the term is used to identify the U.S. Merchant Marine that serves as an auxiliary to the U.S. Navy. On March 13, 1951, the Secretary of Commerce established the National Shipping Authority (NSA) to provide ships to meet the needs of the military. During times of war, the NSA could requisition privately owned merchant ships and make them available. About 700 ships were activated for service in the Far East. This included 130 laid-up Victory ships that were taken out of mothballs and made available. At the same time, the marine services had also identified 600 ships to take coal to Europe and grain to India.

During the Korean War, only about five percent of the men and materials needed in Korea was sent by air. The rest was transported on commercial vessels. It had been estimated that seven tons of equipment was required for every soldier or marine bound for Korea and that one ton was needed every month after that. A bridge of ships, much as was done in World War II, spanned the Pacific Ocean during the years of combat in Korea.

The ships were involved not only in the routine transportation of materials. When the American troops went ashore at Inchon, they did so in twenty-six chartered American and thirty-four Japanese-manned merchant ships. During the evacuation at Hungnam, one merchant ship, SS *Meredith Victory*, built to take on 14 passengers, carried more than 14,000

Korean civilians from the battle area to Pusan. They filled the holds, between deck spaces, main and boat decks, clung on the rigging, and to cargo nets let over the side. Captain Leonard P. LaRue and his crew were appropriately honored sixteen years later by Congress.

Men serving on the ships of the Merchant Marines were authorized to receive the Korean Service Medal and the United Nations Service Medal.

Secretary of the Navy Charles S. Thomas was quoted in the October 1954 *MSTS* magazine:

> In every war, the Merchant Marines has played a vital though sometimes an unpublicized role. The war in Korea is the most recent example. Every fighting man sent to Korea was accompanied by 5 tons of supplies and it took 64 pounds of supplies and equipment every day to keep him there. Five million passengers, 22 million tons of petroleum products, and 54 million tons of dry cargo were transported to, from, and within the Korean theater to support that war. Of these totals, more than 80 percent of the dry cargo was carried by merchant shipping.[14]

CONCLUSION

To say that the United States was unprepared to accomplish what President Truman and the United Nations agreed to accomplish is an understatement. The intelligence provided prior to the war was inadequate. The CIA, only a couple of years old and deeply distrusted by the military, was still basically unable to perform the duties for which it had been created. The focus of the United States was on Europe, and the military-planned war games were played against a Soviet invasion of the NATO countries. The military, spread thin over several continents, was primarily concerned with occupation, more focused toward getting the utilities working again than training and maneuvers. At home, the services were at odds with each other and the government, some fighting for their existence. The policy for security was based on the concept of strategic air strikes, and many who should have know better assumed that the nation could bomb its way to any victory.

When the Truman administration committed U.S. forces to the fight in late June 1950, there were few available to counteract the well-planned and executed attack by the DPRK. The military arm of the ROK, despite the role of the KMAG, was ill-prepared, ill-equipped, and relatively small and disbursed. The violence of the initial attack forced the ROK and eventually the United States. into a defensive war that demanded that men and women, once again, give their lives in return for time to prepare.

When the call went out, it was necessary to draw men and women who had served in World War II, to recall individuals from reserve units to fill vacancies. Marines from all over the world were called back to help in the reformation of the 1st Marine Division. Men from the occupation forces in Japan and on Okinawa were pulled out of their units to fill out hastily called and under-strength units. The draft was extended, calling men into service who had been just too young to serve in the Second World War.

What was produced was, at first, a diverse mixture of men formed quickly into battle groups—many trained on the job and sent to Korea unaware of what they were getting involved in—to bring stability to the lines facing the advancing North Korean forces. The military rose to the occasion, but it was a task that would take the best America could provide.

NOTES

1. Richard Kolb, "The First Moral Crusade," *VFW* (June, 1998): 20–21.

2. Evgueni Evgueni, "The Origins of the Korean War: An Interpretation from the Soviet Archives," Conference paper, "The Korean War, an Assessment of the historical Record" Georgetown University, (24–25 July, 1995): 2.

3. Bajanov: 4.

4. Alonzo Hamby, *A Man of the People: The Life of Harry S. Truman* (New York: Oxford University Press, 1995), 552.

5. 50th Anniversary Committee, National Salute to Korean Veterans, Department of Defense (July 9, 2003).

6. W. Uzal, "War on a Shoestring," *Military History* 17 (July, 2000): 7.

7. Sandy Strait, "What was it Like in the Korean War?" (New York: Royal Fireworks Press, 1999), 15.

8. Max Hastings, *The Korean War* (Garden City, NY: Doubleday and Company, Inc. 1987), 173.

9. "Life on the Newsfronts of the World," *Life* 34 (January 19, 1953): 46.

10. James Matray, "Revisiting Korea: Exposing Myths of the Forgotten War, Part 2." *Prologue Magazine* 34 (Summer, 2002): 2.

11. Mines: www.minewar.

12. Stephen Howarth, *To Shining Sea: A History of the United States Navy* (New York: Random House, 1991), 490.

13. Burke Davis, *Marine! The Life of Lt. General Lewis B. (Chesty) Puller, USMC (Ret.)* (Boston: Little Brown, 1962), 280–281.

14. Charles S. Thomas as quoted in *MSTS* (October, 1954): 5.

3   PREPARING TO FIGHT

Koreans are not yet capable of exercising and maintaining independent government and . . . they should be placed under a forty-year tutelage.

—Franklin Roosevelt to Joseph Stalin, 1943

The United States eventually furnished 50.3 percent of the United Nations ground forces, 85.9 percent of the naval forces, and 92.4 percent of the air forces that fought in the Korean War. The second largest contributor was the Republic of Korea, which provided 40.1 percent of the ground troops, 7.4 percent of the naval forces, and 5.6 per cent of the air forces. Other United Nations contributors provided the equivalent of two additional divisions. At the beginning of the hostilities, the United States did not have the necessary men at arms to meet the commitment that President Truman had made. After years of demobilization and cutbacks, there were simply not enough men in the armed services for such an endeavor. Mobilization was necessary and had to be accomplished fairly quickly. Once started, there were, eventually, 6.8 million men who served on active duty during the Korean War; 1.8 million during the period of hostilities. A very significant statistic is that an estimated twenty percent of the servicemen who served in the Korean War had also served in the armed forces during World War II.

MOBILIZATION

When the war broke out in Korea, the existing mobilization plans were based on the expectations of an all-out war. There were no plans to fight a limited war, which would require military men for combat assignments, and at the same time allow military forces to be maintained in numerous other spots all over the world. The limited mobilization, as it was later called, was designed not only to meet the needs of putting an army into the Korean peninsula, but also to meet the expanded needs to confront current and potential communist threats all over the world. Several basic administrative decisions were made early. First of all, the mobilization for Korea was to be considered as partial and would be implemented in a manner that would not ignore the needs of the military in other parts of the world. A second was that while materials mobilization should have some priority, and that there would necessarily be a significant increase in industrial production, it was not to be a total effort. This was not to be an all-out preparation like that which occurred during World War II. The Korean mobilization was to cause the least possible effect on the domestic economy. There would be both guns and butter.

The authorized strength of the U.S. Army, on June 10, 1950, was 610,000, but in fact it consisted of only 593,167. This figure was determined by Congress. Among those on active duty, 348,904 were in the continental United States (generally called the Zone of Interior, ZI). There were 111,430 in the Far East, mostly on occupational duty, 88,956 in Europe, and the rest scattered in the Caribbean and Alaska. The Army, at the time, consisted of ten active divisions, four training divisions, and the necessary supporting troops. Most of the units were badly under-strength and those in the Far East—the units most quickly affected—were each short one battalion and many support elements. At this point, particularly in areas of occupation, a significant amount of the military support service had been turned over to civilians.

From the beginning, it was acknowledged that the services would need to draw from the organized reserves. In June 1950, the organized reserves consisted of 217,435 officers and 291,182 enlisted men designed to serve as the core of the units. Of this number, 68,785 officers and 117,756 enlisted men were available, but were widely disbursed in 10,629 units located all over the United States, for their paid participation in drills. The National Guard strength at 324,761 was nearly 25,000 under-strength. The National Guard had a strength on paper of twenty-seven organized divisions and numerous supporting units but, in actual fact, they had only about 46 percent of what was considered to be required equipment. The main strength of the reserves was to be found in the large numbers of its members who had seen action in World War II.

Recognizing the seriousness of the military situation in Korea, General Douglas MacArthur had asked for additional units. But he also badly needed replacement personnel to upgrade his existing units to Table of Organization and Equipment (TO & E) strength. It was also becoming necessary to fill in for increasing battle losses. The only immediate source was from the organized or general reserve. By the end of July 1950, so many individuals had been drawn for service that it had only one complete unit available—the 82nd Airborne with about 90,000 men from vastly disorganized units.

To meet the growing need for troops, a "creeping mobilization" was initiated. First President Truman raised the authorized size of the Army from 630,000 to 680,000. The authorized strength was again raised on July 14 to 740,500, and then on the 19th to 834,000. Congress followed suit on August 3, 1950 and finally removed existing limitations on the size of the armed forces, leaving it up to the Secretary of Defense. On August 10, the ceiling was raised to 1,081,000; on November 22 to 1,263,000; and finally on April 17, 1951 to 1,552,000.

As the war went on, more and more troops were required. Part of the demand was caused by a tremendous turnover in Army personnel during the last two years of the war—caused by a liberal rotation system and increasing casualties. In many cases, the armed services were losing ground. During the fiscal year of 1952, 500,000 men entered the Army but that number only provided an increase of 65,000. The next year 742,300 men were inducted into the armed forces, but the overall strength of the Army fell 62,600. The increasing influx of selectees was changing the nature of the armed forces as well. In June 1951, the breakdown of the Army had been 45 percent regular army, 40 percent selectees, and 15 percent reserve and National Guard. In June 1953, these figures had changed dramatically to regular army 41 percent, selectees 57.5 percent, and 1.5 percent reserve and national guard. This was a different army.

FILLING THE SERVICE

Draft (Selective Service)

In the United States, conscription was called the Selective Service. It was established in 1863 to provide troops for the Civil War. Never popular, but determined to be necessary, it was reintroduced in World War I with the Selective Service Act of 1917. This act required all men in the twenty-one to thirty age group to register for the draft. It was later changed to eighteen to forty-five. By the end of World War I, about 2,800,000 young men had been inducted. The first peacetime draft was initiated in the Selective Training Act of 1940 that authorized conscription, but provided that no more than 900,000 men were to be in training at one time and limited the term of service to twelve months. The period of service was extended in 1941 to eighteen months. After entering the war, yet another act was passed that required all men from eighteen to sixty-five to register, and designated men from eighteen to forty-five as being eligible for military service. The time of service was extended to six months after the end of hostilities. During the war, more than ten million persons were inducted. In 1948, another act required all men from eighteen to twenty-six to register; those between nineteen and twenty-six were liable for twenty-one months of service, to be followed by five years of duty in the reserves.

When the Korean War broke out, the 1948 law was still in effect. It was replaced by the 1951 Universal Military Training and Service Act with the length of service extended to twenty-four months and the minimum age for induction made eighteen and-a-half. The Reserve Forces Act passed in 1955 required six years of duty, a combination of active duty and reserve status.

When news of the war hit the streets of America, young men, unlike during World War I or II, did not rush to the recruiting station. The great patriotic appeal provided by Pearl Harbor was not available for the recruiting officers who faced the massive task of filling the services. As Selective Service Director Lewis B. Hershey put it, "Everyone wants out; no one wants in."[1] Thus, in response, the United States Congress, on July 9, 1950, extended the existing Selective Service Act for another year. The first call for the draft was issued in July for induction in September. It also aided the depleted reserves by imposing a six-year reserve obligation on those who had completed their active duty service. During the period June 1950–July 1951, there were 550,397 inductees brought into the armed service.

Understandably, many used all possible means to avoid the draft. The largest percentage of the methods was totally legal. The draft dodgers, as they were called, numbered less than 10,000 during the war years. The largest loophole was for students. President Truman had issued an executive order deferring students who scored at least seventy on an intelligence test. The following year, 65 percent of the 400,000 students tested met this qualification and were deferred. This created what the radio commentator Edward R. Murrow considered a bias of the elite. Whether intended or not, the result was that the bulk of the combat forces in Korea were drawn from the lower-to-middle working classes, with limited education.

Army

During the war, the Army in Korea consisted of the Eighth Army composed of four corps—I, IX, X, and the XVI (which remained in Japan), eight divisions—1st Cavalry, 2nd, 3rd, 7th, 24th, 40th, and 45th Infantry Divisions, the First Marine Division, and three Regimental Combat Teams—5th, 29th, and the 187th Airborne. Arriving, and remaining at this composite, was to prove very difficult. The need was met by a variety of responses, many of them short-term. The first move was to extend the existing term of enlistment of those already in service for an additional twelve months. The second was to promote volunteer enlistment in the regular army. During the period June 1950–July 1951, more than 176,000 volunteers joined but this was not enough. To meet the needs, the Army turned toward involuntary mobilization, accomplished first by calling Reservists and National Guardsmen into active duty both as individuals and units. These men served as trainers and filled the ranks in Korea and elsewhere.

To add to the pool of manpower, individuals and units of the organized reserves were called into active service, authorized by Congress on June 30, 1950, for a term of twenty-one months. Within a few weeks, the president had called up 25,000 men. More than 10,000 of these were junior officers and noncommissioned officers with combat experience. By the end of the year, another 135,000 had been called. A call for volunteers from the reserves on July 22, 1950 produced so few that the Army resorted to an involuntary recall of both officers and enlisted men. It was decided to take men on Volunteer and Inactive Reserve and not disturb total units that were functioning on a pay-for-drill basis. This was done to preserve the integrity of units in case they might be needed elsewhere. As a result of this decision, most who were called were World War II veterans. During the period June 1950–July 1951, 172,496 members of the Inactive and Volunteer Reserves, 34,225 from the organized reserves, as well as 95,000 National Guardsmen were ordered into federal service.

The second stage was to absorb volunteers and selectees and their training organizations into units. By June 1951, eighteen divisions and supporting units were formed, eight of which were in Korea, two in Europe, and the rest in training in the United States. After this date, there was little net increase in the Army strength. Most of the increases through mobilization were necessary because of the release of reservists, the increasing casualty rate, and to replace men who had earned rotation.

Navy

The Navy had gone through a very hard time, with intra-service difficulties and the "revolt of the admirals." The revolt occurred in the late 1940s, and is relevant here because it epitomized the problems the United States faced in its efforts to establish a postwar military identity. During discussions about the unification of the armed forces, the generals of the newly formed Air Force proposed that strategic bombing (primarily nuclear), supported by a fleet of long-range bombers, was all that was needed to defend America. The Navy disagreed, considering the aircraft carrier a necessary and proven weapon. The cancellation of the proposed carrier USS *United States,* as well as efforts to transfer the Marine Corps' aviation units to the Air Force, plus some talk that the Navy and Marines should be abolished, led to a revolt among the admirals. While still being argued, the outbreak of the Korean War brought the first test of unified command; it would provide the evidence necessary to support the altered but continuing role of the Navy and Marine amphibious forces. The role of the Air Force in Korea, vital but limited due to the nature of the available targets, tended to prove once again the great truth of war; that in the final analysis, it is the man and the woman on the ground who complete the victory.

The naval presence in Korea was a fleet consisting of three Task Forces—77th, 90th, and 95th. The naval force was made up of ninety destroyers, sixteen aircrafts carriers, eight cruisers, and four battleships. In June 1950, the Naval Air Reserve consisted of about 1,700 aircraft, mostly planes of World War II vintage, but there were a few units that had the early jets. These aircraft were scattered at air stations from Miami to Spokane and maintained by thousands of reservists, most of whom were World War II veterans.

Even before the call went out, more than 3,400 naval reservists asked to return to active duty. Nevertheless, when the call was issued, it fell on a good many men who had only recently returned to normal after service in World War II. This was to be another disruption in their lives. One unit from Olathe, Kansas, nicknamed themselves the "Bitter Birds" in reference to their discontent at being recalled.

Patrol aircraft were the first elements of the reserves to see service in Korea but reservists also flew attack craft in considerable numbers. Of the twenty-four squadron deployments by fleet carriers during the war, nearly one third had at least one reserve squadron on the flight deck. The first carrier-based squadrons deployed in spring 1951 and the *Naval Aviation News* reported in 1951 that every third plane that flew over Korea was in the hands of a reservist. Of the 153 officers in Carrier Air Group 101 on the USS *Boxer,* 133 of them were reservists, while 73 percent of the enlisted men were reservists. The job of these reservist pilots was beautifully portrayed in James Michener's novel *The Bridges at Toko-ri.*

Marines

The Marine Corps was expanded from a force of 75,000 regulars in 1950 to 261,000 men and women in 1953. Most of this expansion came from the reserves. A complete mobilization of the organized ground reserves was accomplished between July 20 and September 11, 1950, within the first fifty-three days. Seventeen percent of the Marines that participated in the Inchon landing were reservists and, by the end of the first year of the war, reservists made up 50 percent of the Corps. At the conclusion of the war, the Marine Corps was at its highest peacetime strength in history.

Also immediately effected were the Air Reserves. A forward unit of the First Marine Air Wing arrived in Tokyo on July 19,1950, with the remainder arriving by jeep carrier on August 1. The wing was sent into combat on August 5. It maintained its own ground-control intercept and tactical air control squadrons. The Marines were first to fly in support of the 1st Provisional Marine Brigade in the Pusan Perimeter, and they were with the 1st Marine Division at the Inchon landing. Until the Inchon invasion, the Marine Air Wing was using its 72 F4Us to carry out about 45 sorties a day. These units also offered excellent close support, flying off jeep carriers close to the coasts.

Between August 1950 and July 27, 1953, units of the 1st Marine Aircraft Wing flew more than 118,000 sorties, of which more than 39,500 were close air-support missions.

During this same period, Marine helicopter squadrons evacuated almost 10,000 personnel, contributing greatly to the low casualty/death ratio.

Forty-eight percent of the 1st Marine Aircraft Wing combat sorties flown during the Korean War were flown by Marine reservists who had served during World War II. New York Yankee star second baseman Jerry Coleman and Red Sox batter Ted Williams were called back to fly Marine combat missions.

Ultimately, forty-two Marines were awarded the Congressional Medal of Honor, twenty-seven posthumously. Twenty-two Marines received Navy Crosses, and more than 1,500 Silver Stars were presented. Reservists received 13 Medals of Honor, 50 Navy Crosses, and more than 400 Silver Stars.

Air Force

Shortly after the end of World War II, the U.S. Army Air Corps became the United States Air Force. The war in Korea was its first. At the time, the Air Force in Korea consisted of the 5th, the 20th located on Okinawa, and the 13th located in the Philippines, plus the 314th Logistical Force and the 315th Combat Cargo Command.

The reservists played a very significant role in the Korean War. The deficiencies they showed were the result of neglect following their demobilization after World War II. To their credit, however, they made a significant contribution. When the Air Corps became the Air Force, the flying units of the then National Guard were identified as the Air National Guard. The air national guard was activated the same day the Air Force became a separate service.

National Guard

Authorized by Congress on June 30, 1950, units of the Army National Guard were ordered into federal service. The terms of service were to be twenty-one months. Selected units of the National Guard were recalled beginning September 1950, with four divisions and supporting units identified. In January 1951, two more were ordered in. During the period June 1950–July 1951, more than 130,000 National Guardsmen were called up and, by the summer of 1951, a significant number of nondivisional engineers and artillery units were sent to Korea.

The first guard units to arrive in Korea in January 1951 were transportation outfits, who were immediately dispatched at Pusan area to carry supplies and personnel. The following month field artillery units began to arrive, as did engineer and quartermaster units. The first to arrive in Korea were the 40th from California and the 45th from Oklahoma. Also, as a part of the Korean War package, the 28th of Pennsylvania and the 43st of Connecticut, Rhode Island, and Vermont were sent to Europe.

Much of the time, National Guardsmen were levied. That is the Army practice of identifying guardsmen with combat experience and pulling them out to be sent as replacements to units in Korea. While it met the urgent demand for replacements, the process harmed some of the units by weakening them. Because there was no tracking system to separate guardsmen from other casualties, there is no accurate account of the number of National Guardsmen killed or wounded in combat.

Essential to meeting the needs of the armed service was the Air National Guard. During the period between World War II and the Korean War, Air Force planners did not place much faith in the reservists. They hoped, instead, to build and maintain the largest standing force they could. The concern, primarily, was the belief that reservists could not be as well trained and thus would be unable to deal with the complex weapons of a modern war without considerable retraining. It is true that many were not as well trained as those on active duty, but, on the other hand, many individuals were veterans of World War II with considerable experience. Despite the Air Force concerns, the Air Guard was maintained partly as a collateral against plans for a smaller active duty force.

As hostilities began, the Air Force Air National Guard was called into action. This included 45,000 airmen, which amounted to the mobilization of about 80 percent of the force. The difficulty was that much of their equipment was obsolete and they were not well prepared for combat. Despite the difficulties, the Air National Guard flew 39,530 combat sorties and destroyed 39 enemy planes. One hundred and one of its members were killed during the conflict. Twenty-two wings and sixty-six tactical squadrons were called up during the war. Four of these were sent to Europe. Seventeen wings remained in the U.S. and two wings fought in Korea. Four of the thirty-six jet aces were air guard pilots. These units were equipped with F-84E Thunderjets assigned to the primary mission of guarding B-26 and B-29 bombers. During the Korean War, as in other conflicts, the most significant service by the members of the guards was as individuals, with four individuals identified as aces.

> Sometimes, a statistical look can provide some understanding of the make up of the armed services in Korea. According to the United States census of 1990, of the 4.9 million Korean Veterans who served in Korea, 4.5 million (92 percent) of them were Caucasian. Of the total number, 339,400 (7 percent) were African American. Less than one percent (30,400) were American Indian, and 133,500 (3 percent) were Hispanics.

The Volunteer Services

Both the Coast Guard and the Merchant Marines filled their ranks by volunteers. Those coming up for the draft often saw the Coast Guard as a good alternative to one of the ground forces and the need for men, never very large, was rather easily filled. The Merchant Marines were, in the main, civilians doing the job they usually did, but under more hazardous conditions. The services in which women were called to duty is discussed in the section dealing with various women's corps.

INTEGRATION

It was during the Korean War that the armed services, earlier ordered to integrate its units, actually began the process. For most of its history, the armed services separated black and white soldiers, usually assigning blacks to duties involving physical labor and placing any black combat unit under the command of white officers. In 1948, President Truman issued Executive Order 9901, which mandated an end to racial discrimination and segregation in the Armed Forces. Some military leaders were reluctant to implement the president's order, believing the military was not the place for a "social experiment" And yet, the intent of the order began to be carried out immediately. Six years later, the Department of Defense announced that segregation had been eliminated in all the armed forces.

American history provides us with all the illustrations we need to show that segregated combat units have succeeded in battle. During the Civil War, black regiments performed well against both the Confederacy and on the frontier against the Native American Indian. The black regiments of the 93rd Division in World War I and the segregated units that fought in World War II, including the Battle of the Bulge, were highly successful. The failure, real or imagined, of the segregated black 24th Infantry in Korea was more the product of the treatment of blacks prior to the integration than it was to any questions of their individual or collective bravery. The record of the 24th Regimental Combat Team is unique and expressive. Despite both prejudice and seemingly irrational assumptions being made about it, the unit went on to perform at a high level of competence and courage. Even accepting the discontent among some concerning the behavior of black groups, the achievements of black units at Yechon and the Han River crossings provide adequate evidence of the courage and determination of the black soldier.

The Army had been experimenting with integration since the late 1940s, but it was not really until July 1950, as a part of the Army Organization Act, that Congress repealed the statutory requirement of the service's four all-black regiments. Faced with serious replacement shortages and aware that the Selective Service was sending a surplus of black replacements, the situation began to change. By early 1951, nearly 10 percent of the blacks in the theater were serving in integrated units. The change continued, basically because it worked and the Army could report that the "the performance of integrated troops was praiseworthy with no reports of racial friction." By March 1951, the Army's nine training divisions were integrated. By April 1951, blacks in Korea served in combat positions at about the same ratio, 41 percent, as whites.

On May 14, 1951, General Matthew B. Ridgway, Eighth Army Commander, formally requested authority to abolish segregation in the Eighth Army. By the end of July, the Army announced the integration of its Far East Command. The 77th Engineer Combat Company was the last unit to lose its asterisk, the Army's way of identifying a black unit. The integration, once determined, came about fairly quickly.

Despite some minor changes, the Navy's Steward's Branch was still 65 percent black. By early February 1951, however, the Navy ended the separate recruitment of stewards and, by 1961, blacks were in the minority in this branch for the first time.

In the Marines, there was a sudden and dramatic rise in the number of blacks. Prior to the war, there were about 1,525 blacks in the Marines, more than half of them serving as stewards. Within a couple of years, there were nearly 17,000 blacks with less than 500 remaining as stewards. The assignment of large numbers of black Marines began in September in what is probably the clearest instance of a service that abandoned a social policy because of the demands of combat. Eventually, some black officers began to find themselves serving as Infantry platoon commanders beginning with company Baker of the 7th Regiment. By 1952, blacks constituted more than 5 percent of the enlistment into the Marines. When the Marines were ordered back into division status, it was necessary to include black service units and they were assigned to the Far East as needed. The combat efficiency of these troops did a great deal to dissipate the racial tensions. Soon, those already in service were joined by thousands supplied through the nondiscriminatory process of the selective service system, which resulted in a 100 percent jump in the number of black Marines during the first year of the war. The figure would be multiplied six times before the end of the war.

The Air Force, with its short history, had moved more quickly and in September of 1952 it had only one segregated unit in operation. Soon after, blacks were serving in 3,466 integrated units. In 1946, New Jersey began to integrate its National Guard.

Several of the southern states, however, had no blacks in the guard units. In those units in which women were the primary personnel, there was also a noticeable integration. There were several African-American nurses assigned to the Korean Theater as well as to Japan and Hawaii. The same was true of African-American members of the Women's Army Corps (WAC) who served on military bases in Japan.

Finally, on October 30, 1954, a year following the cease-fire, the Secretary of Defense announced that the last racially segregated unit in the armed forces of the Unites States had been abolished.

WOMEN IN THE WAR

Army leaders viewed women as a means of releasing male soldiers for combat duty. As the heavy fighting called for more combat soldiers, commanders in the Far East Command and other overseas installations requested women to work in Far East Command Headquarters and regional Japanese commands and station hospitals. In these locations, women performed a wide range of jobs, though they were prohibited from combat-related assignments. They served primarily in personnel and administration, communication, intelligence, medical, supply, and food service units. The shortage of male personnel in overseas commands provided the opportunity for women to serve in supervisory responsibilities as well, and to undertake some military occupational specialities that had traditionally been reserved for men.

Whatever the character of the military action in Korea, there were women on duty from the start. Of those who served, about one-third were health professionals. By law, the Women's Army Corps (WAC), Women Accepted for Volunteer Emergency Service WAVES, and Women in the Air Force WAF could only enlist women up to a number representing 2 percent of the total military strength in each service. Even then, by 1951, women service members made up only about 1 percent. By 1951, 26,000 female soldiers were serving in the Far East Command.

Despite considerable effort to recruit women, the previously unpopular response to women in the military hampered recruitment. In 1948, Congress had passed the Women's Armed Forces Integration Action, giving women increased prospects for careers in the military. However, the effort to recruit women met with limited success and was discontinued in 1952. Although many women served during the Korean War, in light of the increase in the size of the Armed Forces, the percentage of women declined. Among those who served, there was a great variety.

Army Nurses

The Army Nurse Corps (NC) had a strength of about 3,450 women when war broke out in 1950. A year later, the size of the service had grown to 5,397. Most of these women were veterans of World War II who had joined the reserves following the war. A total of about 570 nurses served in Korea. Captain Viola B. McConnell, working with KMAG, was the only military nurse in Korea when the war began. She would later receive the Bronze Star for her service during the evacuation of American dependents from Korea. On July 5,1950, fifty-seven nurses arrived at Pusan, Korea and began setting up aid stations and hospitals. Two days later, twelve nurses moved forward to Taejon with a Mobile Army Surgical Hospital unit. By August, more than 100 Army nurses were in Korea and on duty in support of UN troops on the line.

At Inchon, landing with the troops, nurses took over the operation of an improvised civilian hospital at Inchon, living and working in the same conditions as the troops they served, wearing fatigues, combat boots, and steel pots, as well as eating the same food, sharing the same facilities, and accepting much of the same danger. The nurses accompanied the troops at the Inchon landing, the advance to the Yalu, the retreat, and during the long sieges of the static war.

Nurses from the United States, as well as from Belgium, Denmark, France, Greece, Italy, the Netherlands, Norway, Sweden, Thailand, and Turkey, as well as some Japanese nurses, cared for members of the Republic of Korea (ROK) Army as well as patients in prisoner-of-war hospitals. Fortunately, there were no nurses killed due to enemy action despite the fact that many were in highly dangerous positions. Major Genevieve Smith, however, was killed in the crash of a C-47 while en route to her assignment as chief nurse in Korea.

Navy Nurses

To meet the increasing demands for personnel to staff the medical facilities in Japan and aboard hospital ships, the Navy recalled Reserve World War II veterans, reduced staff at hospitals in the United States, and commissioned some civilian nurses. About 35 percent of all casualties went through a hospital ship, as the boats moved from location to location following the action.

Two nurses, Commander Estelle Kalnoske Lange and Lieutenant Ruth Cohen, received the bronze star for their work on hospital ships. One aviation accident claimed the lives of eleven nurses while en route to hospitals in Japan.

Air Force Nurses

Flight nurses performed all their medical duties while sharing the hardships of regular flight crews. They administered to thousands of young wounded men as they participated in the machineries of casualty evacuation. At the high point, on December 5, 1950, they assisted in the evacuation of about 4,500 wounded men following the Chinese intervention. In recognition of this service, the 801st Medical Evacuation Squadron received the Presidential Unit Citation. It was dangerous work and two Air Forces nurses, First Lieutenants Virginia May McClure and Margaret Fae Perry, were killed in aircraft accidents.

UN Nurses

The medical team was expanded by the participation of a number of nurses from UN members allied with the United States. Often coming individually, the women were both military and civilian participants who represented their nation's support of the UN causes in Korea. Qualified nurses from Belgium, Denmark, France, Greece, Italy, The Netherlands, Norway, Thailand, and Turkey as well as some nurses from Japan, served in the military hospitals in Japan.

Women's Army Corps

To supplement the numbers in the Women' Army Corps (WAC) when war broke out, the Army called up reserves and suspended the separation-on-marriage rule. Nearly

1,600 members of the Organized Reserve Corps volunteered for active duty. Fewer than 200 were involuntarily recalled. The Women's Army Corps, WACs worked in the Far East Command Headquarters and other regional commands. A WAC unit in Okinawa, staffed by medical and administrative personnel was opened in 1951. Seven WACs served in Korea during 1952 and 1953: two stenographers, four interpreters, and one an aide-de-camp. Women became senior Non-Commissioned Officers NCOs serving in motor pools, mess halls, and post offices.

By the time the Korean War broke out, the WAC strength had more than doubled to 7,259. In June 1951, the number reached 11,932 but as the negotiations began the number dropped to 8,924. About a dozen WAC served in Seoul and Pusan. Though few were stationed in Korea, they did fill significant positions in Japan. By 1953, 1,764 WACs were serving in the Far East.

Women Marines

The number of women Marines peaked at 2,787. At the outbreak of the war, Women Marines, who were in reserves, were placed on active status and the unit developed as trained professionals who had a minimum requirement of active duty. The Marine Corps determined that women were capable of fulfilling forty-three military occupational specialities and women served in most of these: personnel and administration, intelligence, logistics, mapping and surveying, fire control, instrument repair, electronics, motors, public information, and communication. Most, however, served in the more traditional roles as clerical and administrative staff. For female Marine officers, only nine professional fields were considered appropriate.

Women in the Coast Guard

Following the end of World War II, the SPARs (Semper Peratus, Always Ready) were demobilized and reserve units closed. The Women's Armed Services Act of 1948 integrated women into the Army, Navy, Marine Corps, and the Air Force, but no mention was made of the Coast Guard. With the need for replacements, former SPAR enlisted personnel and officers to the rank of lieutenant only were invited back. The Coast Guard made no effort to mobilize. Approximately 200 former SPARs volunteered and served during the war. In the main, they served at the Coast Guard Headquarters in Washington, D.C. After the Korean War, most SPARs were released so that, in 1956, only nine enlisted men and twelve female officers were on active duty with the Coast Guard. The *Coast Guard Magazine* reported that the "chances of seeing a SPAR on active duty today have a slight edge over the possibilities of your running into Greta Garbo at the corner drugstore."[2]

AVOIDING SERVICE

There were few organized anti-draft activities during the Korean War. There were some, but the times and conditions were not such as to encourage this sort of political action. The percentage of those individuals who avoided service by one means or the other was not much different from the percentage in World War II. Reasons for this ranged from a lack of interest by the majority of Americans to the liberal nature of the deferment system.

Deferments

One way to deal with the possibility of being drafted into the infantry and sent to Korea was to volunteer for some other service. Ferhrenbach, in *This Kind of War,* says that young men entered in this priority: Coast Guard, which could pick and choose the best; then Navy and Air Force, where skills were more at a premium; and combat dangers – in this particular war – where the skills required were less. The Marine Corps, which had written some of its most glorious history at Changjin and which kept its standards high, had difficulty recruiting up to authorized strength."[3]

Due to the conditions set by the Universal Military Training and Service Act of 1951, just about any normal young man could avoid the draft by going to college. The eligibility was based on class standing and their scores on college qualification tests. While individual draft boards had the right to make the decision on who might be given such a deferment, students were almost universally deferred.

Conscientious Objection

Almost from the beginning, the United States has recognized that some men called into service objected to killing on religious or moral grounds. In 1948, a congressional misconception provided a legal hole that exempted Conscientious Objectors (COs) from all service. When the war broke out, however, public outrage over the CO exemption caused Congress to cancel the exemption and replace it with a two-year required alternative service. During the Korean War, a fair share of men who objected to being put in a position to take a human life, applied for Conscientious Conscious Objection status. But the number involved during the Korean War was at about the same scale as those who applied during World War II.

The military classification I-W was inaugurated in 1951. The programs provided a broad variety of opportunities for those who claimed religious and philosophical objections to serve in the armed forces. A number of farmers were given duty at a dairy or experimental farm duty. The Brethren Service arranged relief and welfare work and the Mennonites created PAX service, which employed COs around the world in construction, agricultural development, and relief work. The majority of those in the I-W program filled low-level jobs in health facilities. By the end of the war, in 1953, more than 1,200 institutions and agencies had been approved for I-W members. Of the nearly 10,000 men who were in the program, only about twenty-five left their jobs without prior authorization.

By June 1951, less than 0.1 percent of those classified in the selective service, some 8,609 men, had been granted classification as COs. The major fault of the I-W program was that it focused on staying out of military service rather than dealing with conscription. The Vietnam War would bring this issue to the fore in 1969.

Desertions

While there were desertions during the Korean War, it was about half of the occurrence during World War II. The primary reason given was that a man was about to be sent overseas. However, of the 46,000 men listed as deserters, more than 35,000 of them returned to duty. About 20,000 men were reported absent without leave (AWOL) each month, but there were a variety of reasons for this, most of them administrative rather than criminal. It is estimated that the number of men who were deserters or AWOL at any one time would add up to the size of about two divisions.[4] All in all, they represented a very small percentage of the men who were called and inducted into the armed service and had little adverse outcomes on the war.[5]

INDUSTRIAL MOBILIZATION

While the average GI did not think too much about it—probably only considering the problem when he was out of what he needed—the difficulties of supply were as massive as the personnel problem. The logistics is not a significant part of our story of the American soldier, but it deserves some brief mention. As World War II ended, a good deal of the military production stopped and factories retooled for civilian production. When the situation in Korea heated up, there was some effort to direct manufacturing to the production of what was needed. Because of the average of eighteen months to two years industrial time needed for retooling, much of the early part of the Korean War was fought largely from World War II surplus, either revitalized in Japan or withdrawn from reserves.

The Department of Defense production program developed during the early part of the war consisted of a five-point objective. They had to provide the facilities and installations to accommodate the expansion of the armed forces, as hundreds of thousands of men and women were brought into the system. They had to provide the support necessary and the equipment required for an armed force estimated at three-and-a half million service men and women. They had to replace the supplies and materials that were being sent to the Far East and to meet whatever other requirements might be necessary for armed forces in other parts of the world, and to build up a reserve of materials that were difficult and time-consuming to produce. In order to do this, it was necessary to tool up and enlarge the industrial facilities to meet the higher levels of production in the future.

In order to meet these needs, the Defense Production Act of September 8, 1950 gave the president authority to establish priorities and direct the allocation of materials as they were needed for the armed forces. Shortly after this, on December 16, 1950, a National Emergency was declared. As a part of this, the Office of Defense Mobilization was established with broad powers.

Following the outbreak of war, there was a reactivation of many plants. The difficulty of programming requirements and scheduling production combined with delays in tooling up to produce critical shortages of certain types of materials during some stages of the war. The enormous demand for artillery ammunition after the front had been stabilized produced a tremendous drain on available ammunition in the U.S. In 1952, the reserves for contingencies outside Korea fell to a dangerously low level, while the 8th Army commander complained that sufficient ammo was not available for the type of operation he was conducting.

Even after the beginning of the Korean War, many believed that stockpiled materials would be enough. Still others believed the war would be a short one. Both of these beliefs played a part in slowing down industrial mobilization. The other side of the problem was the difficulty of distribution. After the Chinese entered the war, Congress, in January of 1951, made its first large ammunition appropriation. At the line, the conditions of the battlefield led many to believe that there was an ammunition shortage. This was probably not true. The biggest problem was distribution, though Korea was an artillery war and the increased use put a lot of pressure on reserved stocks. During the winter and spring of 1951, the army had to reduce the rate of daily fire in order to maintain their reserves.

The armed services, long desperate for funds, suddenly found themselves benefiting from congressional support as the First Supplemental Appropriation Act, September 27, 1950, allocated $3,166,403,000 for support of Korean operations. Within a few months, the Second Supplemental Appropriation, January 6, 1951, provided $9,161,799,000 for the armed forces. The Fourth Supplemental, May 31, 1951, provided an additional $2,847,570,000.[6]

CONCLUSION

The United States armed forces in the 1950s was based on the cadre system, wherein the services maintain the core of trained men and leaders in the expectation that if war breaks out, the ranks will be filled by volunteers and conscription. But at the time of the Korean War, even the cadre was small and widely scattered. When it became necessary to fill the ranks, the call went out for those who had previous service. As they reported, and assumed their positions, the U.S. began the job of training vast numbers of young men and women to fill the vacancies and expand the services.

At this time in American history, there were few volunteers for this role, many having already served and not anxious to return, and other who were eligible but not interested in the military. Some did not agree with the war in Korea but, in the main, those who were called reported and performed as Americans have always done.

Each of the services was to be involved. The Army, as always, carried the bulk of the commitment, but the Marines were engaged as well in the daily fight for land. The Navy, in blockades and bombardment provided control of the seas, as the Air Force, newly created and untried, took control of the skies and held it. The Coast Guard, not legally available for combat duty because no war had been declared, nevertheless took on the role for which they were so qualified, providing sea stations for rescue efforts, weather forecasting, and picket duty. The Merchant Marines, the mainstay of the transportation system, provided men, equipment, and supplies to an area nearly five thousand miles away.

NOTES

1. Richard Kolb, "Korea's Invisible Veterans Return to an Ambivalent America," *VFW* (November 1997): 1.

2. Coast Guard: www.uscg.mil/hg/g-cp/history

3. T. R. Fehrenbach, *This Kind of War*, (Washington, D.C.: Brassey's, 1963), 422.

4. "Life on the Newsfronts of the World," *Life* 34 (January 19, 1953): 33.

5. R. W. Coakley, P. J. Scheips, E. J. Wright, with G. Horne, "Antiwar Sentiment in the Korean War, 1950–1953," in Stanley Sandler (ed.), *The Korean War: An Encyclopedia* (New York: Garland Publishing, Inc.1955): 25.

6. Robert W. Coakley, "Highlights of Mobilization, Korean War," Office of the Chief of Military History, Department of the Army (March 10, 1959): 3.

4 LEARNING TO BE A SOLDIER

Politics, as a practice, whatever its professions, has always been the systemic organization of hatred.

—Henry Adams

It was not long after the war broke out that a good many young men began to receive invitations from their "friends and neighbors" to report for a physical and induction. For many, this early call is only remembered sketchily but, in retrospect, it does not appear that most men felt very strongly about it one way or the other. Few actually wanted to go into the service, but it was not a reality for a good portion of those called. It is not that they were particularly courageous or even unusually patriotic, but many just did not take it too seriously. What concerned most was getting through the next few days in the unexpected and unfamiliar environment. At that point, few gave thought to the war itself. "It was something that had to be done. I milked all the attention I could get from the fact I had to go, but to be real honest, it was just something to be done. I really didn't connect being in the army with going to war," said David Wilson, thinking back fifty years.[1]

Emergence into the military stream of life is accomplished with crafted efficiency, though it might appear to the draftee or recruit that it is arbitrary. On the appointed day, newcomers reported to an induction area where, in a large room with hundreds of other young men, they were given a cursory physical examination and the oath of military service. There was not a lot of time wasted and, after about six hours, the new inductees were ready to move out. The first day was a shock. A typical experience is recorded by David Oglethorpe, who was inducted in Kansas City, Missouri:

> The train load of us arrived at Camp Crowder, Missouri, in the middle of the night. The night was very dark and cold. Met at the train by buses we were taken into camp by a

crisp looking drill instructor (DI) marched us to our barracks, several blocks away. When we arrived, the place looked like a circus—as there was a GI Party going on and we were immediately drafted into the job. I ended up scrubbing the wooden floor with a tooth brush.

After about two hours of sleep the whole barracks was awakened by the whistle of the man I later identified as the Drill Sergeant. Given twenty minutes to wash and shave we were then marched off to the mess hall where we waited half an hour or so for cream gravy on soggy toast. Then we spent the day in an effort to try and make us look like soldiers. Moving into large buildings that looked like warehouses we gave up our civilian clothes, our hair was cut, and were measured (a sight measurement taken by the man passing out the clothes) for uniforms – fatigues, a dress uniform, boots, a helmet liner and a M-1 rifle. When we completed the rounds, we managed to all look alike. Then it was a period of drilling as angry NCO tried to teach us the basic of moving around. This was followed by a supper of shredded beef of some kind, and another GI party.[2]

In April 1949, a 14-week Basic Military Program was adopted. This new program was designed to provide progressive individual training in basic military subjects common to all soldiers. But during the Korean War, the Regimental Training Command was unable to handle the demands of rapid mobilization. More than half of the nonprior service personnel, who were trained during this period, were trained in an operational TO & E unit. As a result, in October 1953, the replacement training cycle was modified to reduce the number of persons in the pipeline at any one time. All recruits would receive eight weeks of basic combat in a common branch Army Training Program. This was followed by eight or more weeks of advanced individual training. Shortly after the war, the use of division designations to identify training centers was discontinued and the designation United States Army Training Center was adopted. But as far as the inductee was concerned, most training outfits were the same.

Every military man or woman begins their career in the Armed Forces by undergoing basic training. As the name implies, it is a period in which the individual is introduced to military life and taught the basics of their new (usually) temporary profession. During basic training, Americans do not lose their civil liberties, but they certainly have them curtailed. It can be safely said that for most recruits these are difficult days, and there are times when individuals think they will not make it, and some thought is given to opting out. Some do, of course, but are usually caught very quickly. The vast majority just buckles down determined to get through it, and they do.

There were two primary purposes behind basic training. First, to teach the soldier about primary infantry weapons, to discipline them, and to put them into good physical shape. The second was more a matter of psychology, for it turned individual men and women into team players who were able and willing to kill. Looking at Oglethorpe's account once again:

The second full day we were instructed on the Uniform of the Day, then lined up and were marched into a large building where we received an "orientation" and welcome to the Army, and assured us we would not be there long, and then proceeded to scare us all half to death with a litany of misdemeanors that could land us in the stockade.

After the orientation we took a long run. My boots did not fit well and I was, admittedly way out of shape, so the run was difficult. I was not sure I was going to make it. We had no more gotten back to the barracks area when I got sick and began to throw up the remainder of my field rations. A totally unsympathetic corporal, a man I later learned had received a Silver Star for courage, stood by me and shouted "Don't just lie there puking, do pushup." I did.[3]

BASIC TRAINING

Some men were sent directly from the induction center to a training camp and some were sent to reception centers. Those in the reception center usually did their processing, got their uniforms—one size fits all—and the initial shots, and were then sent off to a training depot.

Training schedules varied some from camp to camp, but generally would begin at 3:30 AM and run until 6:00 or 7:00 PM. In the morning, there was a short amount of time to make the bed, take a shower, and be ready for the march to the mess hall where there would be a long wait, with trainees standing in line from thirty to sixty minutes. The day could be much longer if the soldier had been selected to the Kitchen Police (KP) or furnace duty. And, on a rotating basis, a good many of the night-time hours were spent in security and fire watch. It was generally held that Sunday was a free day, but that only meant free from field exercise, and most of the day was spent in cleaning the barracks and one's own gear. Training was hard and the most consistent feeling was of sleep-deprivation. A large portion of off-duty time was spent asleep, even though recruits were generally forbidden to lie on their cots during the day. Recruits slept on the floor.

A training unit is a simplified and over-strength adaptation of a combat infantry unit. There were usually ten to twelve men in a training squad as against the combat size of eight to nine. Each unit was assigned a permanent cadre, almost always veterans of the Korean War, and recruits were selected for the lesser positions of squad leaders and platoon sergeants. These men were picked on the basis of prior military experience (ROTC) or size (the tallest, or shortest), or on what appeared to be leadership potential. The units lived in old World War II barracks with a platoon occupying one floor. At the end of the barracks floor was a private room where one of the cadres lived. The accommodations were rough but clean and in good repair.

To accomplish the first goal of basic training, the recruits were taught the elements of military behavior: discipline, to disassemble, clean and reassemble the infantry weapons in the dark, dry firing, live firing, how to dig a foxhole, how to throw a grenade, the basis of camouflage, bivouac in the field, running long distances, bayonet training, some simplified hand-to-hand combat training, and constant physical training. There was also classroom time where the soldier learned about hygiene, the Uniform Code of Military Justice, the ten General Orders, how to behave as a prisoner, and the nomenclature of several weapons. During basic training, almost every moment was spent in some sort of hands-on training. Field activities included close-order drill; instruction in the use of the rifle, mortar, and grenade ranges; mortar instruction; squad tactics; artillery spotting; running obstacle courses; and bayonet instruction. In addition to fieldwork, hours were spent in military subjects, often taught by a bored instructor to GIs desperately wanting to sleep. These classes included military courtesy, map reading, military justice, nomenclature of the primary weapons (M-1 rifle, 45 pistol, and BAR), and hygiene, including incredibly gross lectures and films on venereal disease.

It also meant learning to march, drill in unison, obey with unquestioned discipline, show respect for rank, depend on one another, think as a team, and drill in small units;

there were also indoctrinations about "Why We Fight." Basically, however, it was designed to stop the civilians from thinking too much and to encourage group thinking, all accomplished by keeping the individual so exhausted that the proper military response became automatic.

The second goal consisted of turning civilians into soldiers. It began immediately after being sworn in, and it was a well-designed—and usually well-executed—plan. It began with an alteration in the recruit's appearance, the ritual shearing of the head, the redressing in clothes which made everyone look alike, the yelling and harsh (very rarely cruel) behavior of the Drill Instructors (DIs). It consisted of being forced to deal with extreme and often totally irrational orders: bunk-making turned into an art, cleanliness to a degree of absurdity, uniformity driven to a fetish.

The second eight weeks of basic training for most new recruits was an extension of the first, advancing to more complicated instruction and based on group-operated weapons, as well as vehicles, tanks, and larger group exercises. For those assigned to the artillery, it was spent in fire direction control exercises, how to level and plot a gun (howitzer), the work of the forward observer. For others it meant transfer to a specialized school where the army's hundreds of tasks, from cooking to cryptology, were taught.

There was a lot of griping, about the DI's, the food, the training, the lack of sleep, but there was very little whining. There was too much discipline and, to a large degree, a fear of being pointed out, of being identified as a troublemaker. Everyone knew what they had to do—what they had been told to do—and few were anxious to get at odds with the command.

Some things were hard to learn. Some seem impossible to forget; the recruit's serial number, the number of the first rifle—most veterans even today can recite the General Orders required when walking guard.

In addition to daily training, there were numerous special activities designed to educate the recruits. Among these were the trips to the firing range. The firing range was a long way out from the barracks area and the troops usually went by truck. Once there, they were divided into two groups, one to fire and the other to pull targets. There was a wall made out of cement that the target pullers hid behind. The targets were attached to a pulley system that allowed the puller to raise the target when the group on line was ready to fire. After they fired, the target would be pulled down, the hits identified, and the target raised again so they could see. If the soldiers missed the target completely, and many did, a red cloth, not unlike a pair of women's underpants and called Maggie's Drawers, was raised.

After half had completed the firing, the groups changed. The positions were difficult to get into, and they seemed unnatural to most young men who had been hunting a good portion of their lives. The M-1 packed a major wallop, and if the recruit was not holding it correctly when firing, it would leave him with terrible bruises.

A rather significant amount of time was spent on bayonet training. The training consisted of a series of dummies—sandbags hanging on ropes—that the soldier was suppose to smash (penetrating the bag), slash (bringing the bayonet across the face of the bag), and stroke (a stroke which brought the butt of the rifle up against the bag. During this time, an appropriate amount of yelling and screaming was also in order.

Two special courses had to be satisfactorily completed. The first was the obstacle course. The courses differed a good deal depending on the natural terrain that was available. There was a lot of climbing, moving through and under barbed wire, a wall about eight feet high that had to climbed over while carrying a rifle, pits to swing over on a rope, barrels to run around and jump over, and crawling through natural or man-made mud.

A second was the infiltration course. Toward the end of basic training, each soldier moved through the course at least once. It was a rough area, often muddy, and stripped with barbed wire, through which the individual—with full pack and weapon—was to move. While the individual crawled through the course, live ammunition was fired overhead, at about three feet, to prevent him from standing up. Small explosions were set off to give the soldier the feeling of being in combat. Those who were in the know always managed to get pads—often Kotex—to tape to the elbows and knees to make the journey somewhat easier.

Sometime during the training, everyone took part in a field exercise, a week or so spent in the field. There the GIs learned to set up a two-man tent, each using their shelter half, eat field rations—often with a little dirt mixed in—enter into squad and company exercises, get along without enough water, and become accustomed to life in the field.

As something of a commencement exercise, there was the long march. Often the first eight weeks of basic were topped off by a march of twenty or more miles. The march was route (a nonsynchronized step), and the unit was stopped every fifty minutes when the troops were allowed to take a drink of water and "smoke 'em if you got 'em." Twenty miles with full pack and rifle is a long way and even the Army recognized this. The unit usually had an ambulance or a duce-and-a half (two-and-a-half utility truck) following along to pick up those that passed out along the way.

Physical Education

Basic to everything was physical education. It was a continuous effort. "Do not walk when you can run; do not ride when you can walk; do not sit when you can stand; do not rest when you can do exercises," with primary punishment being set out in terms of physical exercise. Physical training once or twice a day, testing and retesting of each soldier's ability to perform, all were built on the common theme of endurance.

Duties

One of training requirements was guard duty, which was primarily a training exercise for there was little to guard. The duty, which could come as often as once a week, required individuals to move into the guard hut where they served watches, two hour on and two off, during the night. Often it was around a small area of no value: buildings, sometimes the motor pool, or the empty parade ground. The duty was a twelve-hour shift. The change of guard was a carefully orchestrated event and every guard was expected to execute it perfectly. The relief of the posts required a ritual of marching, challenging, and then marching in a prescribed fashion during the tour. The officer or noncommissioned officer (NCO) of the guard often made the rounds, requiring the individuals to recite one of the general orders. No allowances were made the next day for the fact that the individual had been up most of the night.

Another activity known to all was that of the kitchen police (KP). KP, which is often considered the scourge of the military, was usually assigned on a rotation basis, or for unit or individual punishment. It consisted of getting up a couple of hours before everyone else and working for two or three hours after the evening meal. Some units worked their KP by meal (assigning only one meal at a time), but sometimes one would spend the whole day, missing whatever training was scheduled. If an individual was assigned KP, he would tie a towel to the end of his bunk, and the fire watch would wake him up in time to make it to the mess hall. For many, the loss of those extra two hours of sleep was a high price to pay.

Duties varied, the worst being the grease traps. In the 1950s, many cooks believed "if it isn't fried, it isn't food," which meant that someone had to clean up the grease after cooking 1.300 strips of bacon. It was a terrible job and usually reserved for someone on punishment duty, or for the poor soul who had disrespected the mess sergeant. The other duties consisted of dish washing, mopping, cleaning off tables, refilling sugar, salt, and pepper, working on the serving line, or cleaning up spilled food or milk.

The furnace detail was another of the never-ending assignments. If an individual was sent to a cooler climate for basic then, he would be involved, at some point, in furnace detail. The detail was responsible for seeing that the furnaces received whatever coal they needed, getting the coal from a central supply area, and keeping the barracks furnace area clean. Not difficult, hard work, but it continued on a twenty-four-hour basis.

Another duty given the troops was the fire watch. There was always someone awake in the barracks. Partly because it added to the training, but in part because the old wooden barracks were heated by a nearly uncontrollable coal furnace that made fire a continual possibility. Fire duty was perhaps easiest except for the loss of sleep, but it was the one that the NCOs watched most closely.

Supplies

One of the first NCOs a recruit met in the army was the Supply Sergeant. At times, he seemed to have more power that the company commander. He was responsible for the recruit's issue, but also for keeping track of what had been given. Early on, the army manages to convince most soldiers that they are personally responsible for everything given them, from caps to tanks, and that if they should happen to lose or damage one of these items, they would need to pay for them. To add to the problem, the Army had a special talent for selecting supply sergeants who seemed to hate to part with any single bit of clothing or equipment.

Everything was marked with the recruit's laundry number: the first letter of his last name and the last four numbers of his serial number: (E-5698). If it was not marked, it was immediately lost, and the "federal government would come after you." The initial clothing allowance for those entering basic included a bag, duffle; belt, waist, web (2); boots, service combat russet (2 pairs); buckle, web, belt, brass; cap, garrison, khaki (2); cap, garrison wool (2); cap, HBT (Herringbone Tweed) OD (Olive Drab) (2); drawers, cotton shorts (6); drawers, winter (2); glove-inserts, wool (2 pairs); glove shells, leather; insignia, chevron Army (14 pairs); insignia, collars, EM; jacket, HBT (Herringbone Tweed), OD (3); jacket, wool, OD (2); necktie, cotton, dark (2); raincoat, dismounted; shirt, cotton khaki (5); shoes, low-quarter; socks, wool (five pairs); trousers, cotton khaki (5); trousers, HBT (3); trousers, field wool (2); undershirts, cotton, quarter sleeves (6); undershirt, winter (2). The list is described in Special Regulation 32. (SR 32)

The assignment of a rifle, memorizing its number, and learning to carry it with efficiency was all a part of the early training. Many a soldier ended up sleeping with his rifle because he forgot the number or, worse, mistakenly called it a gun. A barracks ditty sometimes helped: grabbing one's crotch, men would be required to say:

This is my rifle, this is my gun.
This is for fighting, this is for fun.

Stored in rifle racks in the middle aisle of the barracks, the rifle became enemy and friend, to be cleaned, cared for, and considered with far more respect than one was allowed to consider for themselves. Usually old, often misaligned, and scarred, it was nevertheless the single most important piece of equipment for the rookie.

There were always exceptions, but the food during basic training was good, plentiful, and nourishing. Breakfast consisted of eggs ("anyway you want them as long as its scrambled"), bacon, toast, juice, sometimes a sweet roll, coffee, milk, or, more often than most wanted, a combination of creamed beef on toast (Shit on a Shingle) which, despite the stories, was often tasty and filling. Lunch was usually in the field and consisted of meat, vegetables, desserts served out of canisters. It did not vary much, but after six hours of marching in the heat, it almost always tasted good. Supper consisted of mixtures, casseroles, macaroni and cheese, potatoes, cabbage, canned peaches, hamburger, and something that the cooks called Swiss steak. In most units, the mess hall was always open and, on occasion, coffee, milk, and cookies were available if someone wanted to make the effort. Quite often, the first job of the fire watch was to go to the mess hall and get the cadre a bottle of milk and some cookies.

Escapes

Most GIs in training longed for a pass to get back to civilian life, if only for a short time. In most units, there were no passes for the first few weeks, but staff had a class A pass, which meant they could pretty much leave and return to base as they wished. Most of the rest were given passes for a particular time period: 24-hour, 36-hour, 48-hour or 72-hour passes. While, in theory, passes were available for trainees when they were off duty, the denial of the pass was often used as a disciplinary tool and few, indeed, could manage to get through a week without messing up at least once.

The next best thing to a pass was a chance to call home. This was a time before cell phones, and it was necessary to go to one of the pay phones on base. Sometimes, the unit would be marched to a phone and given a few minutes to call or, when off-duty, some cadre allowed individuals to walk over to the booths and make a call. But even in these cases, the calls were few and far between.

The one thing that seemed to be available without too much difficulty hassle was mail. Sometime during the day, often during the evening meal break, the First Sergeant would assemble the unit and call out the names of those who had mail. It is hard to describe how much those letters seemed to mean to the men at the receiving end.

Every once in a while, the troops were assembled for a partial payment called a "flying twenty." The rest of the pay, after receiving the "flying twenty," was either kept or sent home. The active duty pay roster of October 1949 lists the pay of a Private with less than two years of experience at $169.06 per month. By 1952, the pay was up to $175.81. It wasn't much, especially if the soldier were having an allotment sent home to the family, but, as a comparison, it is worth noting that Scottish troops were paid two shillings (twelve cents) a day.

There were a lot of training accidents, but most of them were minor. The men were pushed hard and there was very little of the emphasis on safety that exists today. If possible, the accidents were dealt with within the unit—cuts, bruises, blisters—or in a quick visit to sick call. While every trainee coveted a brief period of rest while sitting waiting for the dentist, very few trainees were willing to be sent to the hospital because that meant a transfer to another training unit and usually the need to repeat a week or so. While there was little to encourage close friendships during basic, it was far better to be working out the process with the devil you knew.

Cadre

Leadership at the training camp was stable and well organized along routine lines, though to the recruit it seemed that everyone was in charge. Following the usual platoon or company organization, there would be a commanding officer, an executive, a couple of staff officers, and platoon leaders. The man the troops saw the most was the field first sergeant, the NCO responsible for training. The first sergeant was the administrative NCO who pretty much ran the company. Most of the cadres were either corporals or sergeants with long service or combat experience. Usually, each barracks had an NCO assigned to live-in. Specialists would come in for some of the training, usually the troop information officer and the men who ran the firing range.

Later in the war, part of the basic training cadre was made up of those in the various NCO schools, who were identified by a UN blue helmet liner. They were called Blue Bonnets, and they were most often the most difficult of the instructors to deal with. Usually assigned for a period of two weeks, they did their best to prove to the permanent cadre that they were ready for stripes.

There was a great deal of difference between the officers, the warrant officers, and the NCOs, as well as considerable difference between the NCOs and the other enlisted men. There were several sources of commissioned officers: graduates of the military academies and recognized military schools, enlisted men or college graduates who successfully passed the Officers Candidate School (OCS), those commissioned out of Army Reserve Officer Training Corps, those directly commissioned as specialists of some sort: lawyers, doctors, nurses, veterinarians, and chaplains, of in unusual displays of valor and leadership enlisted men can receive a battlefield commission. Once qualified as officers, they were commissioned as reserve officers. On attaining the rank of major, they were appointed to the regular army with the consent of the President and the U.S. Senate. Commissioned officers were assigned to a branch of the service in which they specialized (infantry, engineering, etc.) until they reached the rank of brigadier general. By that time, it was assumed they were able to command soldiers of all branches. Once commissioned, the officers were sent through several levels of professional education to improve their service and to prepare them for higher command.

The warrant officer was a company grade officer but received some field-grade privileges when reaching the highest warranted rank, chief warrant officer four. The warrant officer was a single-track special officer appointed by the Secretary of the Army. There were far more warrant officers during the Korean War than there are today.

The NCO Corps was the first line of leadership. It was not until the late 1940s that NCOs started attending schools in preparation for their rank. The training sought to instill in them the self-confidence and sense of responsibility required to make them capable leaders of men. It is a cliche, but nevertheless true, that NCOs—particularly top sergeants—run the army.[4]

While NCOs have always been significant battlefield leaders, during the Korean War, the NCOs emerged more prominently as field combat leaders than they had during World War II. The reason for this was the increased role of small units. The steep hills, ridges, narrow valleys, and deep gorges often forced large commands to advance as squads, thereby placing the NCO in roles that might, under other circumstances, have been played by officers.

As basic drew to a close, there were the constant rumors about assignments. "The whole draft is going to Europe," the optimistic reported. "This draft is for Korea," was the more common rumor. There were the usual opinions that individuals who messed up in basic were automatically sent to Korea; but, in most cases, the drafts were used as fillers for vacancies in troops all over the world. During the Korean War period, there were still thousands of GIs coming out of training units and heading for France, Germany, or to the Philippines. But the majority, during the first year or so, went to Korea. It was the luck of the draw.

Because of the war, all the jobs had to be filled, and those sent to other commands made their contribution, albeit in somewhat better circumstances. But it was not an easy ride. Many hoped to be kept on in the training commands, but that was rarely the case as those slots were filled with men returning from duty stations. When trainees got their orders, during the final days of basic, they were usually provided with a few days (seven in most cases) leave or delay en route. For those whose final destination was a debarkation point, there was little hope of a "pushy" assignment, in a training command or stateside unit.

TRANSPORTATION TO WAR

In most cases, the newly trained soldier reported to a replacement depot, or disembarkation point, within two weeks. The first men assigned to Korea were so badly needed that many of them had to be flown, stretching the military's ability to the limits of its performance.

Flights to Korea

The first two companies of the 24th Infantry Division arrived at an airfield near the port city of Pusan just a week after hostilities had broken out and only three days after President Truman's decision to engage ground troops. This unit, later identified as Task Force Smith, had flown from Itazuke Airbase in Japan. After landing, they went by truck to the Pusan Railroad Station and then 150 miles to Taejon. They were in combat by the 5th of July. For the next few days, the Far East Air Force continued to airlift troops to Korea using C-46s, which did not damage the airfields as did the larger C-47s.

Getting troops to Korea fell on the shoulders of the Military Air Transport Service (MATS), which was in no position to meet the needs, especially in light of a shortage of aircrew (particularly navigators) and the need to keep up with other commitments.

Having dropped from its high of having transported equipment and personnel during the Berlin airlift, the MATS was neither strategically nor tactically capable of providing what was necessary. Within hours after the war broke out, MATS was ordered to support the air movement of two Strategic Air Command medium bomber wings to bases in the Pacific. It had also been called on, on the night of June 26,1950, to begin flying American dependents.

The initial problem was of aircrew. So, during the seventy-five days it required for the Command to recall and train personnel, the services relied on sixty-six aircraft and crew provided on contract from civilian airlines. Pan American World Airways, Transocean, Overseas National, United, Seaboard and Western, Flying Tigers, and Northwest were contacted. On June 30, a Transocean Air Lines carrier delivered a planeload of 3.5 bazooka rockets to Korea. Others were assigned to190 round-trips across the Pacific. Later, Alaska and California Eastern Airways were added. As of September, 345 trans-Pacific flights had been completed.

Because there had been no plan for combat operations in Korea, a logistical support system was developed piecemeal from emergency to emergency. At the beginning, the military services were in competition to contract these carriers, but in July MATS took over this function for all military needs. On July 18, infantry and artillery replacement began to go to the Far East by air. Actually, in August, the Air Force flew more than 10,000 replacements to the Far East Command.

By mid-September, MATS was ready to phase out the airlines and, in October, reduced them to 264 flights. By November it had dropped to 89. Other nations helped out, the Royal Canadian Air Force (RCAF) provided six Northstar transports, Canadian Pacific Airlines operated as a continuing contract carrier, and Belgium's Sabena Airlines furnished three DC 4s.

Once men and materials reached Japan, they were moved on by an airlift set up between Japan and Korea. This was organized as the Far East Air Force Combat Cargo Command (Provisional) on September 10, 1950. Within nine days of its creation, the Command was flying men and equipment to Korea. A significant illustration of this service is found in the Combat Cargo Command's airlift missions to the troops caught in the Chosin Reservoir. During the operation, airlifted supplies were the only means of keeping the troops supplied, and taking out casualties.

Men and cargo moved by air to the Far East from the United States amounted to less than 1 percent and that from Japan to Korean less than 5 percent. Nevertheless, the importance was to be found in the speed of getting personnel replacements and small quantities of essential supplies to units located in isolated areas.

Travel by Ship

Although some replacements continued to go by air, most of them went by sea. Despite the early pressure, the aircraft of MATS could not lift the necessary forces. It was easier and increasingly necessary for significant numbers of troops to be moved by sea. The Military Sea Transport Ships (MSTS), and those taken from the National Defense Reserve Fleet were called on to make the run. The early transportation was from Japan where occupation troops were put into immediate service. By the middle of July, the 25th Infantry and the 1st Cavalry Division were put ashore. For those coming from the United States, it was a long and difficult trip.

At the end of June, the Navy still had twenty-nine ships operating in the Army Transport Service and, by July, the Navy had chartered twenty ships and begun the process of taking more than forty from the mothball fleet. Most of these early shipments were quartermaster supplies being sent from continental reserves, primarily equipment from World War II. Shortages in supplying Browning Automatic Rifles, rifles, light machine guns, and 105 howitzers were overcome by rebuilding serviceable weapons left over from World War II, and withdrawing "canned" equipment from long-term storage.

The sea trip from the United States to Korea was long and monotonous. After basic, troops were collected at gathering points like Camp Stoneman Replacement and Reclassification Depot in California. As a ship was called, those identified would form long lines along the embarkation dock, the majority of them wearing the deep green of fairly new fatigues, helmets, carrying new rifles, and larger than necessary duffle bags. Once lined up, numbers chalked on their helmet liners, they moved onto the ship, and, as their last name was called out, responded with first names and middle initial. The line seemed interminable and many questioned whether the ship could hold them all. The ship would average about 1,500 men on each trip. On board, a dry-looking petty officer directed them to ladder wells where the lines moved down into assigned barrack areas, bunks piled four or five high with canvas mattresses strung on loosed ropes, men vying for whatever bunks they thought might be the easiest to get out of.

The advance party—kitchen police, cleaners, and the like—boarded ship ahead of the soldiers and were already working at the various jobs to keep the floating city active. The smell of the mixture of seawater, dock, and too many sweating men was added to the dull oil smell of the ship, as men tried to create some semblance of comfort in the cramped quarters. The deck holds were open and ran the width of the ship, except for the watertight doors that could be closed in an emergency. About 350 men were housed in each section. Barrack bags were stacked in one corner of the room and a man who felt the need to get something was in for a long search. There were no sheets and each had a single blanket. Some had pillows of sorts, but there were not enough to go around. Light, such as it was, came from open bulbs attached overhead. The deck was painted a bright red and the bulkheads, like most of the rest of the ship, a dingy, grey green.

Between each housing section ran a ship-wide latrine where waste was deposited in a sluice of seawater running from one side to the other. Some fresh water was available for washing, and showers (usually salt water) were turned on for a few hours a day. Not long enough for the majority of the men to take a shower.

Despite the confusion and the apparent lack of hurry, the ships would pull out pretty much on time and move out into the harbor by tug. The gentle rumble of the ships' propellers would provide a dancing vibration that would last the entire trip. NCOs and ships' crew moved through the mulling troops assigning, directing, explaining and, eventually, checking to be sure each man had a bed, and each of the areas had an eating assignment. Below deck it was hot and moist, the bottom deck almost slimy, as men stored their equipment, tried out their bunks, and maintained the chatter that was so characteristic of men facing unusual circumstances.

Other than mess detail, a few clean-up jobs, and an occasional assignment, there was little for the men to do. Some games were available but card games, usually for money, were the primary time killers. Technically, there was no gambling aboard the MSTSs but, depending on the captain, little was done to prevent it. In the evenings, a movie would be shown, but the area was usually so packed with men that the heat became unbearable. Rumors moved through the ship like a cold wind in Maine. Most of the time the men just waited, sat about, and sweated. Then, usually during the first hours at open sea, some began to get seasick, puking in their helmet liners, rolling on the resident decks in agony, some only making it to a meal every few days. None of the enlisted men, unfortunately, were allowed on deck so there was no refuge in fresh air.

For those who felt up to it, the primary attraction of the day was chow and it could well take up most of the day. The lines ran throughout the ship as men stood for hours trying to get the next meal. Most were patient, moving through the hatches, the compartments, and up and down ladder wells, leaning against bulkheads, reading or chatting. Some were silent, some even able to sleep. The line moved slowly, and most were aware that once done with their meal, they would simply move into the chow line waiting for the next one.

As the line moved into the mess area, tin trays were taken from a stack of these compartmentalized plates, and the men picked up some eating utensils. As the line passed before a window the cooks—they all appeared perpetually angry—scooped out meat and potatoes and canned beans, provided stacks of bread and butter, and ended it up with canned fruit, the juice of which quickly saturated the bread. At the end of the line were big handleless crockery mugs for coffee. After getting the food, the GI would move into the long porthole mess hall where steel tables were set up, bolted to the floor, and where the GI would eat standing up. In the most part the meal was tasteless and the coffee – the mud or the coffee called, joe – was awful. Then, after the meal, the trays were banged against the GI cans and stacked next to them. The poor man on KP would then dip them in boiling soapy water, rinse them in even hotter water, and put them back on line for the next man.

Twice during the first few days, the men were called to boat drill, where they learned their stations if anything happened to the ship. It was not hard to figure out that with all the men and the selected locations of the boats, it would be very unlikely if anyone would make it in the time allotted. Then there were fire drills, and the routine set in. And, as often the case in the military, time weighed heavily. Captains often used drills as a means of getting the enlisted men on deck for a few minutes.

On Sunday, services were offered and large numbers of the men attended. The ships carried a chaplain who offered several services in order to meet the demands of some denominations. With that many men on the ship, the chaplain's job was a busy one. Many of the men were away from home for the first time and felt the need to talk, and the chaplain made as much time as he could to see as many a possible. There were requests for communication with home, or fears to be faced, but in the main the men just wanted to talk. Sick call was also popular, many claiming minor ills, but the majority complained of colds, sore throats, heat rashes, and venereal diseases, resulting from the last days at shore. Some of the ships carried civilian nurses and, thus, sick call was simply a chance to be in the presence of a woman for a few minutes.

Sometime on the eleventh to fourteenth day, the first signs of the land to which they were sailing became apparent, and those with a chance to be on deck would report what they had seen. For many, the first indication they were approaching was the smell, a smell which was distinct far out to sea. The land to which they were headed used human waste as fertilizer for their fields and the distinctive smell, at least at first, was nearly overpowering.

As they approached, the ship changed directions, several times, sailing up a channel where other boats were seen. The process of disembarking began, and men were restricted to their bunks as the numbers were called off, then they would move to the deck and begin the departure process onto the Landing Ships, Tank, (LSTs) that were being used to ferry the soldiers into port. Once again, names were called out, and responded to, as the long line of servicemen and women began to leave the ship. As they neared the dock, they saw a line of service-painted cattle trucks, which were used for hauling troops, waiting. Some soldiers were moved off to a replacement depot, there to wait for their assignments, but some—generally those with some unit identity—moved up to line outfits. The vast majority arrived as replacements and were ferried out to the needed units within the next few days. Very little attention was paid to the training each had received, or the Military Occupational Specialty (MOS) they maintained, and men who had been together from basic soon found themselves moved off alone to some distant outfit.

Perhaps one of the saddest places in the Army is the replacement depot. There the soldiers are totally without purpose or direction. It is a place where they wait. While they wait, there are KP and details, harassment by the permanent cadre, and again the waiting for a call from the blaring speaker, sending them to a truck or a jeep that would take them on the next phase of the journey. Most of the cadres were men on their way back along the system and they had little or no patience with the newly arrived.

CONCLUSION

The job of training those who were called into service fell to the basic training units, where the recruits were taught the essentials of military life, the use of weapons, maneuverability, tactics, and endurance. In this process, the armed forces filled the ranks, prepared their forces for the roles they were to play in Korea, and slowly but carefully grew to meet the challenge that faced them. The job of turning young men and women into warriors was a difficult one, but carefully planned, and required the recruit to leave behind the essence of civilian life and embrace the hard, demanding, and focused life of the military combatant.

The methods changed little during the war, though the demand was high and facilities and cadre pushed to the limit. It was based on the need to prepare persons to fight and that required that they be both physically and mentally toughened. The physical training was accomplished by a constant push, seeking endurance through long marches, runs, exercises, physical strain, and competition. The mental toughness was engendered through strict discipline, aggressiveness, seemingly irrational demands, as well as pushing for diminished individualism, and the growth of team spirit.

In the course of eight weeks basic and six to ten weeks advanced training, a near mob of young individuals were turned into a team of well-disciplined men and women capable of joining the ranks of those engaged in the war in Korea.

NOTES

1. David Wilson, Center for the Study of the Korean War (CSKW), A 8977.
2. David Oglethorpe, CSKW, GU A. 1076.
3. David Oglethorpe, CSKW, GU. A. 1076.
4. *Army Regulations 350–90* (June, 1957).

5   LEARNING TO FIGHT
WITH WORLD WAR II WEAPONS

All of my means are sane, my motive and my object mad.

—Captain Ahab in *Moby-Dick*

While it is often stated that the Korean war was fought with leftover weapons that had been in storage since the close of World War II, it is nevertheless true that, with the exception of the 2.35 bazooka, they were primarily good weapons. This is also true for the communist soldiers, who fought with a wide variety of weapons of World War II vintage from several nations. The average American and UN soldier was equipped with weapons that had stood the test of time and which had, through years of combat use, been honed to a level of high efficiency.

PERSONAL WEAPONS

M-1 Garand Rifle

The M-1 was the standard weapon used in both World War II and Korea. Designed in 1933, it went through several prototypes and emerged in the 1940s with the more traditional gas port system. It was known as "the last true butt stroker," because the stock of the weapon was strong enough to deliver a lethal blow. About 3.8 million M-1 rifles were produced during World War II, primarily by Winchester and Springfield Armory. Production was interrupted at the end of the war, but the outbreak in Korea brought about a reintroduction, first at Springfield, then at Harrington and Richardson, and finally at International Harvester.

This basic weapon was a .30 caliber, gas-operated, semiautomatic weapon. It used an eight-round clip and weighed nine pounds. It had an effective range of 550 meters and could fire 30 rounds per minute. In the hands of a capable marksman, it could find a target at 1,000 meters.

It was considered an excellent weapon. For many, the great thing about the M-1 is that it used the ammo from the belt of a 30 caliber cal. machine gun, which could be used to reload the clips for the M-1 or the Browning Automatic Rifle. Carbine ammo sometimes was a bit of a problem, so a lot of men would trade off their carbines for an M-1. With the M-1, an extended target at about 1,000 yards could be reached. On some occasions, men considered them for sniper rifles, but the lack of a silencer made this less appealing.

The primary sniper rifle was a modified version of the M-1903, which was the basic infantry weapon used during World War I. A well-built bolt-action rifle, it was equipped with a five-round, nondetachable magazine and weighed about eleven pounds. When it was equipped with a telescopic sight, it was effective at about 900 meters.

Carbine

While many considered the carbine to be underpowered, many men carried it, especially company grade officers, noncommissioned officers, and support troops who needed a more manageable side weapon. There were both automatic and semiautomatic versions with 15- or 30-round magazines. Its effective range was only about 300 meters. Since the carbine was not very good for stopping anything farther than 50 yards, anyone close to the front wanted an M-1.

Pistols

The primary pistol was the .45 caliber M1911A1, which was carried by field-grade officers, gun crews, signal linemen, tankers, and those who needed to keep their hands free. As with the bayonet, there are more recorded instances of the use of the service pistol in Korea than are to be found in the records of companies during World War II. It was considered an effective killing weapon within a twenty- to thirty-yard range. It was a semi-automatic weapon that carried seven rounds in a clip. The .45 was the standard sidearm during both World War II and the Korean War. There were problems with the temperature, though. When it got below freezing, the .45 caliber service weapon occasioned frost lock; it had to be kept nearly free of oil and fired frequently if is was to be trusted in combat.

Browning Automatic Rifle (BAR)

Considered by many to be the backbone of the infantry, the M-1918A2 Browning Automatic Rifle (BAR) used the same .30 caliber ammunition as the M-1 Garand. It could be fired either automatically or semiautomatically. It used a 20-round detachable magazine and weighed 19.4 pounds when loaded. With an effective range of about 800 meters, it could fire 600 rounds per minute. It was fired both as a shoulder weapon and on an integral biped. One or more BARs were issued to each infantry squad.

Grenades

The kind of war that was fought in Korea determined that the hand grenade was one of the primary weapons utilized. S. L. A. Marshall suggests that while this was true, the training provided to troops heading for Korea did not prepare the men for this fact.[1] The result, Marshall says, was a great deal of wastage. Nevertheless, expanding on the theory that most Americans know how to throw a rock, grenades served the same purpose in the hill fighting as they had during the trench warfare of World War I. A strong man can throw a grenade from twenty to thirty yards with fair accuracy. In a daylight raid against dug-in positions along a mountain ridge, it is about the only thing that can provide a gap in the firing to allow infantry to advance. The UN either had, or assumed, the advantage because, as a general rule, it was believed that the Chinese were not as physically suited for their use. This idea has never been documented.

In times of extreme cold, the grenade can be dangerous to hold and use. As it gets colder, the pin becomes harder to extract and usually the mitten must be removed to accomplish it. The metal ring, if held in the hand a couple of seconds will freeze to the fingers. Sometimes, the difficulty in getting the grenade free from the hand resulted in premature explosions. Company officers often reported that the grenade was of little use when the temperature was below –20°F. Other than the deficiencies caused by the cold, grenades had an incredibly high percentage of not exploding. In the cold, up to 20 to 30 percent might misfire.

The troops reported that the serrated, modified, Mills bomb was far more practical for both offensive and defensive use; particularly, if the unit had available someone with baseball or football experience who could throw the grenade a particularly long distance. There is little evidence of the use of rifle grenades and, in many cases, it was discovered that the launchers had been discarded.

Bayonets

Though there are many cases of exaggeration, it seems to be true that there were several legitimate bayonet fights during the Korean War. No matter what its actual use, it is evident that the introduction of the bayonet into any report of combat, credits it with almost miraculous powers to consolidate the determination of the American fighting man. The need for a bayonet—a sharp killing instrument attached to the end of the rifle barrel—was highly important. There is no doubt that during the winters of defense, on the hilltops and perimeters, that the infantry companies were engaged at such close range that the bayonet, used as a spear, came into use. But not all troops were equipped with bayonets, and the story most often reported is that men whose weapons had run out of ammunition closed in on with clubbed rifles and bare fists. Many of the troops were simply not "bayonet-minded," and many who had lost or never been issued a bayonet did not make an effort to have the weapon reissued. Admittedly, the bayonet issued to the military forces in Korea were heavy, hard to sharpen, and surprising hard to get a penetration

The First Marine Division, believing that the bayonet made the men more aggressive, continued to issue it. The soldiers used it as a defensive weapon as well as to present a ribbon of cold steel to aggressors who might feel they could move through a line of weakening fire.

Perhaps, the most famous of the known bayonet charges was accomplished by Easy Company of the 27th Infantry Regiment, as they attempted to mount Hill 180. The attack, let by Captain Millett led to the death of eighteen enemy soldiers killed by the bayonets of Easy Company. The bayonet was necessary because of a shortage of grenades and ammunition and misfires but, nevertheless, this defense is an excellent example of the courage and emotional intensity required in fighting with bayonets.

Team Weapons

Most of the time, heavy weapons were operated as team weapons. They included machine-guns both light and heavy, rocket launchers, mortars, and recoil-less rifles. The light machine gun was the M-1919 .30 caliber, which was air-cooled. It has a reduced range, accuracy, and rate of fire, but it was still a formidable weapon. One or more were issued to an infantry platoon.

The medium machine-gun was an M-1917A1, developed during World War I, which fired a .30 caliber (the same as the M-1 and BAR) on a belt that allowed a rate of 400 to 600 rounds per minute. The heavy .30 was the water-cooled M-1917 A-1, which was tripod mounted. Each division had about 500 of them. During the long Korean winters, it often necessary to use antifreeze as the coolant.

The biggest gun was the M-2 caliber .50 which was generally a mounted weapon, either on trucks or was used as an infantry weapon. It was air-cooled, but the extra heavy barrel made it possible to fire about 575 rounds per minute to an effective range of nearly 2,000 yards. Each infantry Division was issued about 350 of them.

The bazooka (M-1 2.35 inch Rocket Launcher) was developed during World War II as an antitank weapon, but it was almost useless against the T-34 tanks that the North Koreans operated. During the early months of the war, their uselessness was exaggerated by the large amount of "dud" ammunition supplied. Before long, however, troops were equipped with the M-20 3.5 inch Rocket Launcher, an aluminum tube that fired an 8.5 hollow-shaped charge.

The mortars available were 60mm, 81mm, and 4.2 inches, and were primarily antipersonnel weapons. The closed-breech mortars were mounted on a baseplate and supported by bipeds. By definition, a mortar fires in a high arc, which made them ideal for the trenches, valleys, and defiladed positions favored by the North Koreans and Chinese.

The UN troops also had available the 57mm, 75mm, and 106mm recoilless rifles. They fired conventional artillery shells on a flat trajectory. The gases escaped through the rear of the tube, thus they had little or no recoil. The smallest could be shouldered, but the 75 and 106 were mounted and required a crew to operate. The most effective was the M-40 106 mm developed during the Korean War (T-170E1) and adopted in 1953. It was a two-man weapon that could fire about five rounds per minute and was effective to about 1,000 yards. It weighed about 250 pounds and was often fitted with a single-shot .50 caliber-spotting rifle.

ARMOR AND TRACKED VEHICLES

When World War II ended, the United States had only a single armored division and it was in Europe. There had been sixteen such divisions during the war. When consideration was being given as to what should be left behind for the South Koreans when U.S. occupation troops pulled out, it was determined that Korea was not a good place to deploy tanks. There was some fear, as well, that leaving anything too heavy might encourage Syngman Rhee to launch his own attack. Therefore, during the first few months, the U.S. infantry had very little to no armored forces. Military strategy had earlier assumed that the best antitank weapon was another tank, and the weapons available, primarily the 2.35 bazooka, were not successful.

Armor, though certainly effective in its primary role, was not used in the traditional fashion through much of the Korean War. This was particularly true after the war

Emplacement for 105 howitzer, under construction, Korea, 1952. (*Used by permission of the Center for the Study of the Korean War, Graceland University*)

settled into a stalemate. The terrain, full of mountains and valleys, flooded rice paddies, mud and ice, made it difficult to deploy tanks in unison. Most efforts to use tanks in concentration usually ended up with the tanks getting bogged down. Rather, both the UN and communist tanks were more often employed for long-range direct-fire against specific targets. Once the tanks were worked to the miliary crest, just over the ridge in order for it to provide some protection, ridge of a hill, they could be dug in, becoming a mobile pillbox, and used to fire on missions.

However, tanks were on the immediate supply list and, when they arrived, went into the field. Unfortunately, the most advanced tank available was the Pershing, which was an interim conversion. The Pershing (M-26) was a heavy tank with a crew of five and could attain speeds of up to twenty-five miles per hour. It had a 90 mm gun and two machine guns. Soon the more effective Sherman (M-4A3E8) was available. It was a World War II 35-ton tank armed with a 76mm main gun and two machine guns. The three more advanced tanks that had been in consideration from 1947—the T-41 light tank with the 76mm gun, the M-42 medium tank with a 90mm gun, and the T-43 heavy tank with a 120mm gun—were not made available for service. During the war, other tanks were available: in1951, the Patton (M-46), which was a converted M-26, in 1952, the M-48 and the Chaffee light tank (M-24) with a 75mm cannon. The primary ammunition was the T4 HVAP nine-pound armor-piercing round, the M-42A1 HE round, the M-62 APC-T. Armored Personnel Carrier (APC) ammunition could push its way through 90mm of enemy armor at 1,000 meters, and High Velocity Armor Piercing shell HVAP penetrated 132mm of armor, also at 1,000 yards.

The British brought the Churchill, Centurion (A41) and Cromwell tanks, some M-8 Greyhound and M-39 APCs, and the M-29C Weasel cargo carrier.

The anti-aircraft vehicles sent were, as in other cases, recast from World War II. These were anti-aircraft armored vehicles with wheels in front but tracks at the back. At first, the quad .50s mounted on the vehicles were seen as the best defense against potential enemy aircraft, but as the air war moved toward being a jet war, these became ineffective as anti-aircraft weapons. However, they soon took up the role as antipersonnel weapons, firing as many as 100,000 rounds a day against enemy infantry. The primary vehicle was the M-16 Multiple Gun Motor Carriage. The M-19 40mm Multiple Gun Motor Carriage mounted dual 40s on an M-26 tank chassis. They, too, soon became primarily an antipersonnel weapon. There were also fully tracked vehicles, which mounted twin Bofors 40mm guns, though they did not see a lot of service in Korea.

In the highly mechanized character of the forces in Korea, it was necessary to transport troops quickly. Two APCs were available. The M-75 had an open top and could carry about a dozen troops. It was a tracked vehicle, with a boxlike passenger compartment providing all-round protection. These arrived late in Korea. The M-59 used civilian components to control the costs. It had limited amphibious capabilities, and could hold up as long as it stayed in fairly calm water. In most cases, both the M-75 and M-59 could keep up with the tanks.

Other significant transport vehicles included the Landing Ship, tanks (LST3), Landing Vehicle Tank Armored (LVTA4), and the Landing Vehicles Tracked (LVT5), which were all upgrades of the original World War II LVTI. These amphibian tractors were used extensively by the Marines and to some degree by the Army. The LVT3 and LVTA4 had ramps in the rear so that vehicles could be loaded. The LVTA4 was open topped. The LVTA5, which came along later, had its ramp in front, was enclosed, and armed with a short barrel 75mm howitzer in a turret.

Once the war in Korea settled down, it became increasingly an artillery war. The early troops came equipped with a limited number of 105mm guns. The guns—105mm, 155mm, and 8inch (203.2mm)—consumed huge quantities of ammunition. The M-101A1 105mm howitzer had a range of about 12,000 yards (about seven miles) and could fire about 100 rounds an hour. It was mounted on a two-wheel carriage and called on a crew of eight. Nearly 20,000 rounds could be fired without replacing the barrel.

The M-114 155 howitzer had small crew-protection shields on both sides. It was mounted on a two-wheeled carriage towed by a truck. It had a range of about 18,000 yards (about ten miles) and could fire about 100 rounds an hour. It demanded a crew of eleven. Its big brother, the M1A1 155mm "Long Tom," was about the same size and was handled in the same way as the eight inch. It had a longer range, however, pushing a shell about 25,000 yards (about fourteen miles). The M1 eight-inch howitzer was mounted on a four-wheeled carriage and weighed nearly fifteen tons. It could fire up to 30 rounds an hour for 18,000 yards (about 10 miles). These guns were towed and had a crew of fourteen.

In addition to U.S. weapons, a few of the UN units brought their own. The best example was the British-made twenty-five pounders used by the New Zealand 16th Artillery regiment. The effectiveness of artillery shells was improved with the use of the proximity fuse developed during World War II. These shells used radio waves to detect targets and then exploded at a preset distance, rather than on target. This gave the shells an increased killing range.

ATOMIC WEAPONS

Something should be said about the role of atomic weapons during the Korean War. Obviously, the weapons were not used, and so the discussions and planning did not really affect the soldier on the line. It is important to note that one of the reasons the United States was so poorly prepared was because of a strong belief that control of the atomic bomb would prevent future conflicts. This was not the case, however, and the military considered the use of atomic weapons, even though the United States had very few that could have been used. In June 1951, the Joint Chiefs of Staff considered the use of these weapons and finally agreed they could be used only in case the U.S. ground forces in Korea faced annihilation. In September and October 1951, as a part of what was called Operation Hudson Harbor, plans were made and dummy bombs dropped secretly in preparation for their use. There is some belief that the threat to use atomic bombs in Korea was instrumental in bringing the communists back to the negotiations. Later President Eisenhower, in "Analysis of Possible Courses of Action in Korea," suggested the threat was one part of China's agreement to accept an armistice. The other part was the death of Premier Joseph Stalin.

In all honesty, the role of the atomic weapon had more value as a threat than it would have had in Korea. The essential character of the Korean landscape, and the diverse pattern of North Korean and Chinese troops, would make determining targets very difficult.

Nevertheless, a part of the Korean War period, and a significant participant in the war effort, was the Strategic Air Command (SAC). The mission of SAC was to maintain a global nuclear deterrent force, with the capabilities of conducting air operations on a worldwide basis and to support area commanders by attacks on tactical targets. It was established on March 21, 1949 as one of the three U.S. Army Air Forces. Operating on the assumption "we are already at war," the SAC base maintained an around-the-clock fifteen-minute alert system, with bombers and tankers combat ready and armed for nuclear combat. Soon, SAC would begin keeping a number of nuclear-armed bombers constantly in the air in case of attack. There was always a "Looking Glass" plane—an EC-135 that mirrored the command and control functions of the headquarters—in the air.

Life a the SAC bases was tension-filled as the mission continued day and night, leaving little time for rest. Crews were on both air-borne and standby alter in shifts that ran from eight to fourteen hours and, while in the air, the significance of the mission did little to ease the boredom of long hours at the controls.

COMMUNISTS' ARMS

When they launched the invasion "the North Korean People's Army (NKPA) was better armed and equipped than any of the other forces involved in the conflict. A large portion of the weapons available to them were of Soviet origin, but they were World War II surplus. The weapons used were simple and easy to use and maintain, designed for the, often illiterate, peasant that made up much of the army. They carried the Soviet-made PPSh-41, an automatic or semi-automatic weapon with a range of about 150 meters. It was one of the best such weapons developed during World War II and was designed with their strategic policy in mind: ground troops required a high rate of fire rather than accuracy. The UN troops called it the burp gun.

The North Koreans also carried the Tokarev 7.62 Semiautomatic rifle, a 7.62mm carbine, the Japanese 99 Long Rifle, the Tokarev 7.62 pistol and bayonets that were of little use. Used both as a sniper rifle and an antitank rifle, the PTRD-1941 was effective against soft-bodied vehicles. It was more than six-and-a-half feet long and weighed thirty-eight pounds.

The primary machine gun was the Goryunov SG-43 Medium Machine Gun with a maximum range of 1,500 meters and a rate of fire of 600 to 700 rounds per minute.

Home tent used by the Forward Observer unit, which was the eyes of the artillery units, Korea, 1951. (*Used by permission of the Center for the Study of the Korean War, Graceland University*)

Because of its 30.2 pounds of weight, it was typically mounted on a wheeled carriage. Their heavy weapons also consisted of 120mm, 82mm, and 61mm mortars. The 82 and 61mm mortars could fire American ammunition, and often did. They had no rocket launchers, but became very good at using the American weapons that they picked up or stole.

Unlike the U.S., the North Koreans and, later the Chinese, were well equipped with tanks. The most used and successful was the T-34/85 Medium Tank that was armed with an 85mm gun. It could reach a speed of thirty-four miles per hour. They also had several SU-76 self-propelled guns, a Soviet-made tracked vehicle armed with a 76mm gun. It was crewed by four soldiers. It was a mobile unit that could, at twenty-eight miles per hour, be brought into play quickly.

The Communist troops were supported by 122mm howitzers. The Soviet-made 122mm rifled cannon and 152mm howitzer were also available.

FIGHTING LOADS

There is, obviously, a natural limit to how much a soldier can carry. And, just as obviously, every effort was made both officially and individually to limit what had to be carried. The average infantry soldier in Korea, for example, did not carry more than two grenades, even though grenades were the primary aggressive weapons. The fatigue of the march was the determining factor in the load. Men with carbines usually carried four clips, men with M1s between 94 and 120 rounds. Usually, machine guns would have 3 to 4 boxes of ammunition per gun, and between 50 and 100 rounds of 60mm mortars were supplied. Men carrying Browning Automatic Rifles averaged between six- and eight-round clips. Riflemen on the march often carried extra ammunition for the BAR.

The load in Korea was approximately forty pounds. When it rose to nearly fifty pounds, there was a noticeable straggler effect. On a normal aggressive march of about thirty minutes, the additional weights would mean that the crew, mortar ammo carriers, and flamethrowers would arrive in a greater state of fatigue. Infantry, simply because of their individualized role in battle, will always have to be noticeably burdened. Yet men complained that they struggled and wore themselves out carrying things that were never used in the combat situation. Often these were clothing issues. When there was an impractical issue of items, it resulted in waste.

UNIFORMS

Uniforms play a number of roles. In addition to covering the body, they provide a sense of identity. They are also adapted to meet the needs of the environment. Because of this, the uniform in Korea was often different from that worn in basic training. The Army had learned early that adequate clothing is the most efficient method of dealing with the weather, especially the extreme colds found in Korea. In the beginning, the primary uniforms were the same as those supplied to American troops during World War II. For most of the first three months, the troops fought in cotton fatigue uniforms and in winter wore the World War II type olive-drab wool uniform with a wool undershirt and cotton underthings. Sometimes, a woolen sweater and field jacket were worn for warmth. Field overcoats and, eventually, wool overcoats were made available.

The mountain sleeping bag was a welcome item, though, at first, they were not available in adequate numbers, and men had to be happy with the "mummy" bags made of wool.

The difficulty of providing necessary clothing was increased by the different environmental background of many of the troops. For example, troops who came directly from tropical countries and were dropped into the cold and wet of Korean climates were uncomfortable. When the first Filipinos arrived in Korea in September 1951, they were soon "freezing" in the temperature that still held at 65 degrees. It was necessary for some to drape the blanket from their pack over their shoulders until additional uniforms could be provided.

Shortly before the war, in August 1946, the Army had considered adopting a blue uniform for all troops to replace the general service olive drab. It was considered important to give the soldier a little more class. While there was no basic change, however, when the Korean War broke out a light-blue scarf was added as were light-blue plastic discs that were placed behind the collar ornaments. But there were not many of these seen in Korea.

Supplying the South Korean with uniforms often proved difficult. Generally they are a smaller people, slender, and an average height of 65 inches. It helped a great deal that they did not consider size to be a problem. Shoes, however, were more difficult. The Army found it necessary to issue shoes and those smaller than 6H had all been issued to the Republic of Korea (ROK). The majority of the ROK troops wore a size 6 EE, with the smallest down to two 1/3 EEEE and the largest to 10 1/2 EEE.

The shoe pac, the leather military boot of WWII was not capable of standing up to the wet and bitter cold of 1951 and was replaced with thermal boots as quickly as possible. The new boot had an air space between the inner and outer layers of wool-pile insulation, both of which were completely sealed off from any contact with moisture by latex. The air space under pressure produced a vapor barrier such that heat could not readily escape when it was transmitted from the foot. The boots prevented frostbite even at −30 degrees F. The wearer of the boot supplied his own warmth as long as he remained active, and socks could be changed every twelve hours. Distribution of the new boots was completed by November 15, 1951. Called Mickey Mouse boots, their most distinguishable feature were their giant size and pure white color. The drawback was the weight and bulk adversely affected a person's ability to run, and they were not comfortable for long marches.

The basic equipment assigned was acknowledged by signing the Department of Defense form #782 gear. The term is now used to mean the load bearing vest to which equipment is attached. It , consisted of a haversack, knapsack, belt suspenders, cartridge belt, a bayonet with scabbard, oil and thong, meal can with cover, knife–fork–spoon, a canteen cup with cover, first-aid packet and pouch, a poncho, shelter-half—with pole, five pins, and guy wire—steel helmet with liner, helmet cover, a gas mask with cover, entrenching tool, and a grenade pouch. To this was added cold weather gear, the parka with a fur-trimmed hood, mittens with trigger fingers, mitten inserts, waterproof trousers, thermos boots, heavy socks, and other items like chemical heaters. By 1953, leggings were no longer in use.[2]

FOOD

If the old adage is true that an "army travels on its stomach," then the forces in Korea traveled fairly well. It must be acknowledged that the military was extremely successful in the task of feeding three meals a day to thousands of men and women, spread over a large area., Not that men were always able to get three squares, or even one in some cases, but that was because of the conditions they were in.

Writing in May of 1953, Lt. Colonel Coy W. Baldwin, QMC, offered the opinion and evidence that the troops in the Korean War ate very well. For instance "he ordinarily gets fresh meet (*sic*), and vegetable, salads, rolls once a day, pastry products several times a week, ice cream at least weekly, and even such items as bananas regularly." One must wonder where he was stationed. Although this is not the memory of most Korean veterans, it is not all that far from the truth for many of the troops.[3]

All of the foods served to the United Nations forces, with the exception of some nonperishable items issued by the British Commonwealth to their troops, were supplied by the Army Quartermaster. The supplies were the responsibility of the Eighth Army. The determination of foodstuffs was based on a sufficient ration scale per man, determined at the General Headquarters command in Tokyo.

The vast majority of the food supplied to the troops came from the United States. There was, however, some essential procurement from the Far East, particularly eggs, apples, fish, tangerines, and bananas. One significant source for fresh supplies were the American-operated hydroponic farms located in Japan. They provided both chemically grown and earth-grown vegetables. American medical authorities were leery of the Japanese practice of growing vegetables in areas fertilized by night soil (human waste).

Perishable items required the careful scheduling of shipments. Since the existence of refrigerated storage was almost nonexistent in Korea, items were delivered as close to use as possible. Later the Quartermaster Corps refrigeration spaces were erected at special supply depots.

During the summer months, garrison rations consisted of a diet of 4,350 calories each day. When troops are forced to rely on into B rations, the basic group-feeding

Chow line, Division Rear, Korea, 1953. (*Used by permission of the Center for the Study of the Korean War, Graceland University*)

ratons consisting of canned and dehydrated goods, the count drops to 4,250 calories. During the month, the average trooper was to receive fresh meat 50.5 times a month and canned substitutes 9.6 times. During the winter months, a supplemental issue raised the count somewhat and on the basis of a thousand rations it included 23 pounds of cereal, 15.7 pounds of dehydrated potatoes, 20 pounds of whole dry milk, 67 pounds of jam and jelly, 30 pounds of oleomargarine, and 60 pounds of bread, which provided an additional 450 calories. The above was possible only for those troops in areas where meal preparation was conducted in organized kitchens. For the man in the forward area or actually on the line, there was the promise of such food, but it was difficult to keep.

On line, or close to it, every effort was made to provide five-in-one ration (rations for five soldiers for a day). Among these appetizing meals were such items as "beef and gravy" referred to by its British name of Bully Beef, a pound of bacon in a can, crackers, little packets of powdered milk, jelly, and instant coffee. The meals also consisted of a variety of Spam meats, and pork cutlets braised over noodles.

When combat conditions or isolaton made it necessary, the soldier existed on C rations that featured canned food such as sausage patties in gravy, corn beef hash, beans and frankfurters that could, if one was lucky, be heated over a sterno flame. The rations also included candy, crackers, a cookie, instant coffee, cigarettes, sometimes canned fruit, toilet paper, and an ingenious can opener. Everything was used, even the oiled boxes they came in, which, it was discovered, made excellent toilets. While C rations filled the troops up and were certainly better than nothing, a prolonged intake would tend to cause diarrhea and gastrointestinal discomfort. When on line, a spoon was one of those things the men carried where it would not be lost. If no spoon were available, the bayonet or a trench knife would work.

It became obvious early in the war that the United States was also going to be responsible for supplying the ROK Army. Eventually they supplied most of the food for the United Nations Command. In doing so, the allotment for distribution was based on the United States B ration, providing for each person 1.75 pound of rice, six- tenths of a pound of fish, three-fourths of a pound of pork, biscuits, salt and red pepper. They were also given 500 Won (the Korean currency) in order to purchase supplementary food.

During February 1951, the Eighth Army asked that no more 5-in-1 rations be distributed. These rations were designed to be used by small detachments, crews and the like, but they did not prove satisfactory. Most of the men did not have their mess gear or heating equipment with them, and the 5-in-1 was difficult to break down. The troops did not want to cook when they could open a can of C rations. Besides, the army had decided there was not enough food in them and the Table of Organization and Equipment (TO & E) was changed to 4-in-1. The complaints were that there was too much fat and too much gravy with too little meat. The most appreciated items were the fruit and peaches were the most popular. Canned pudding and deserts were well received. The precooked cereal was considered poor until milk could be found.

The C ration was the most acceptable meal pack. Among the items, the most popular were the beans and frankfurters, beans with pork, meat and beans, ham and lima beans, spaghetti and meat, hamburger with gravy, pork sausage patties with gravy, meat and noodles, chicken and vegetable, beef stew and corn hash. The C rations had the advantage that they could be consumed cold, but for most of the men only the bean issues could be eaten cold. The noodles and spaghetti combinations were considered too dry and usually burned when heated. The hamburgers and sausage patties had far too much gravy for the soldiers. Most of the men disliked the chicken and vegetable. Their opinions about corn beef hash and beef stew were probably worsened because these items were held in great quantities. The abundance of these particular rations made them the spam of Korea. Beef stew was far too fat to be eaten cold.

Even the cocoa disc and the coffee were consumed, if not always as intended. The cocoa was often eaten as a candy bar. The chocolates and starch-jelly discs were popular but became too hard to eat during the cold weather. The most acceptable item was the fruit—and the C-7 rations were preferred to the C-6 because the former latter had a spoon. It was later determined that a plastic spoon was a must in every ration.

Few men carried their mess kits, which were noisy and easily lost. They were usually kept in kitchen trucks. Eating utensils were also kept in the chow truck, for despite the efforts of many to keep a spoon, most were lost in transport. What everyone did keep, usually attached to their dog tags, was one of the can openers.

While there were a lot of complaints about the food, and to the men the cooks seemed perpetually angry, the cooks in the forward area appreciated their position and in most cases did an exceptional job. Some divisions' policies required cooks to go forward once a week and spend twenty-four hours with the rifleman of their company.

The variety of food required by the United Nations Command was distinctive. The Turks required additional bread, vegetable oil, olive oil, salt, olives, and dehydrated onions. In their command, pork was forbidden and all meat had to be boiled regardless of later cooking procedures. They were also fond of potato balls made of mashed potatoes. The average Turk soldier ate two pounds of bread a day. The Filipinos did not take well to the rice grown locally, and so their rice had to be brought in from the Philippines. The Thais were great consumers of spicy foods and at first were issued large rations of Tabasco sauces. Later this was discouraged because the Thai officers claimed it increased the level of sexual desire among their men.

The Ethiopians survived quite well with normal rations, but required increased measures of rice, potatoes, and hot sauce. The Greeks, on the other hand, did not require large amounts of salt, flour, sugar, or shortening, asking instead for larger rations of bread, rice, potatoes, and macaroni. Forces from Puerto Rico, Colombia, and the Philippines wanted more rice and fewer potatoes. The Netherlands troops, as well as the French and Belgium, required more bread, potatoes, sugar, and evaporated milk. A special shipment of cognac was brought in for the French. The Canadians ate more bread than the Americans.

The British provided some Combo Pack meals. This ration contained the ingredients for fourteen men for one day and consisted of two cans—one of vegetables and one of meat—instant coffee, sugar and biscuits. Ham, turkey, and beans were the least liked among the English troops, but New Zealanders would trade cheese and butter for them. The British accessory pack included cigarettes, pipe tobacco, gum, razor blades, and matches. The British also made a special tea that was brewed for a long time. Heating a bucket of tea with a whole tin of Carnation milk and a pound of sugar made a drink that was referred to as "brew's up."

PAYMENT

Payment in combat occurred as often as possible. It usually happened on a "flying twenty" (leave), paid in whatever military script was being issued by the military, primarily to avoid dollars getting to the black market. The rest of the individual's money was either sent home or kept for them in a running account. The Combat Duty Act of 1952, which was passed in July, authorized payment, retroactive to June 1, 1950, of forty-five extra dollars a month to members of specifically designated combat units. Enlisted pay at that time, during the first two years of service, was $82.50 per month for the private (E-2) to $139.65 a month for the Sergeant (E-5). This does not sound like much and wasn't in the U.S. economy, but when compared to the 5,400 Won (at the exchange at the time an amount equal to $1.35 U.S. currency) received by a Sergeant in the Republic of Korea Army, it was a lot.

SUPPLIES

From the moment young people enter the military, they must be taken care of, and that involves a huge amount of supplies. There are no exceptions: The troops must be fed, given some sort of protection from the weather, be provided with adequate clothing, and given the opportunity to take a bath (shower) with some regularity. This is in addition to the equipment of war, from their individual weapons to team-operated weapons, and all the ammunition they require. All of this was the responsibility of the Quartermaster Corps and its local extensions, the infamous supply sergeant. It was a difficult task. Sometimes, those on the line came to feel that the logistics personnel, most of whom were in the rear areas, were generally insensitive to the needs of the fighting men. The charge that those in the rear kept the best things for themselves had some truth, but probably not to the extent it was believed.

CONCLUSION

It has often been stated that the Korean War was fought with the strategy and weapons of World War II. The strategy differed in some respects, but the charge concerning the weapons is basically true. It is also true of the uniforms, the equipment, and in some cases even the food. In the main, however, these weapons were excellent. And while many were old, some even in a poor state of repair, they performed well. Other than the rocket launcher, which had done well in World War II but was no match for the Soviet-built T-34 tank, most of the weapons available served well. The basic weapons of Korea was, as it had been in World War II, the M-1 garande and it was well used and appreciated by those who carried it.

Much of the equipment was, as well, old and of World War II vintage. A good deal of it had, in fact, been salvaged from European and Pacific battlefields and refurnished in Japan. Propellor planes were pulled out of Air Force graveyards and returned to battle. Ships, long kept in mothballs, were recalled and sent into service. Small arms ammunition, some of it in storage for five years—some of this proved unreliable—worked well in the majority of cases, as did artillery shells, mortars, and rockets.

The necessity of supplying not only American troops, but most of the troops of the Republic of Korea and United Nations meant that the U.S. had to draw commodities from all over the world and focus them through the ports in Japan and Korea. The variety of diets, uniform needs, and the like meant that the supply problem was exaggerated by the demands for variety. The fact that it was done so well, and in such a timely fashion, must be considered one of the great accomplishments of the American military during the Korean War.

NOTES

1. S. L. A. Marshall, "Commentary on Infantry Operations and Weapons Usage in Korea, Winter 1950–1951" (West Chester, Ohio, Nafziger Collections, Inc., 2002): 87.

2. *Guidebook for Marines,* 1945 edition, Government Printing Office.

3. Food: www.gmmuseumllee.army.mil/korea/food.

6 LIFE ON THE FRONT

We find it sad that war seems so delightful, so often, to those that have no knowledge of it.

—Veterans For Peace

The ultimate mission of the armed forces is to place men and equipment in the field to fight, and hopefully to defeat, the enemy. All of those in the huge pyramid that make up the base of the armed forces are directed toward the point, which is the combat soldier. How a war is fought depends on the individuals and the units that address the enemy in the field. It is also true, though, that the conditions at the front alter the manner in which a war is fought. In Korea, as in most wars, the basic experiences were the same. Any generalized comments about combat are, however, just that, comments. Each man or woman will remember a war differently.

There is some value, though, in making a few comments in general about combat. Surely the most constant theme in the soldier's reporting of his service during the Korean War, much like that of other wars, was fear. Bill Crum recalls: "During the fighting were we afraid? Yes, definitely afraid. Did we dwell on the fact that we might not come back? No, you always had that fear that you may not come back. This was in your mind because death was round you all of the time. Some of your buddies were wounded or killed while you were there."[1]

People were scared, but there was surprising little talk about it and the veteran's memories are different. Robert Johnstone wrote after the fact:

Scared? Of course I was scared. I was so scared I could hardly move. I was so scared I had trouble preventing my bowels from relieving themselves. The fear sat in my stomach but I could also feel it in my arms and legs. Almost as bad as the fear that pervaded any order to advance was the fear of fear. Some president said that, but the fear of fear was one of the most difficult things to deal with.[2]

It has been said that the primary difference between raw recruits and the seasoned veteran is not that the latter have engaged in combat. On the contrary, it appears that the longer a man is engaged in combat, the more superstition takes over. There are reasons to believe that the advantage enjoyed by the more seasoned men lies in the fact that they have learned to adjust, not so much to the conditions of combat, but to their reaction to those conditions. They have dealt with the primary question of their own fears—the degree of courage that they seek but do not know if they possess—and discovered that they can function. It is not so much that the individuals have come up with a cause, or a goal, that spurs them on, but rather that they have found a place among others, and conclude they can carry their own weight. Among those who fought, there does not appear to be any lack of fear, only a confidence that it can be deal with.

COMBAT ROUTINE

It seems an oxymoron to suggest a combat routine. During those moments of fighting, things seemed to take on a life of its own—movements, actions, reactions, all happened so quickly. Even when following a well-prescribed plan of action, things seemed to move in unexpected ways.

Every night, patrols went out to either test the enemy or attempt an ambush. While there were exceptions, most recruits did not go on patrol until they had been on the line for eight or ten days and then, under normal conditions, were assigned to a patrol about once every seven days. While there were usually several men in any patrol or outpost, the numbers were not enough to offset the sense of isolation, the sharp awareness of the space that surrounded the soldier, and the feelings that the space around, especially during the darkness of the night, was full of the enemy. Spooky, some men called it, but it was more than the fear of sounds in the night; it was the realization that the soldier was alone, all alone. Some soldiers would swear that if they were on patrol and were downwind of the North Koreans, they could smell them because the North Koreans ate a lot of garlic and pickled cabbage called *kimchi*. Sometimes, soldiers reported getting close enough to hear the enemy soldiers chattering while they dug fortification.

The nights were the worst. In most cases, there was a 50 percent alert where two men would share one sleeping bag, even though the bags were not always used, as more than 80 percent of the company's work was done at night. Sometimes, the most difficult was to simply stay awake at night. The idea was to alternate every two hours with others, which meant that even when asleep, soldiers got only snatches of it. Oliver Hampshire remembers:

> Sometimes when I was on guard, I had to think of the enemy entering the trench and killing us, just to keep awake. Other times I would count, often into the tens of thousands, or bite my hand in hope the pain would keep away sleep. Nothing seemed to work very well. Perhaps fear was the strongest incentive.[3]

When reading the memoirs of men who have been in combat, there seems to be a constant theme of intermingling fear and boredom. But there was far more to the

Keeping clean, catching up on washing in Battery Reserve, Korea, 1953. (*Used by permission of the Center for the Study of the Korean War, Graceland University*)

conditions of combat than these two emotions. Part of the fright was not knowing which day would bring the bullets marked for them. The men and women tended to entertain a lot of futuristic thoughts, thoughts about what they were going to do if they got out of it all alive. Seeing those around them losing pieces of themselves increased the awareness of the danger. It was a war of tough, deadly brawls, with men dying on the barren ground. During the fight there was little chance of a break and, during prolonged periods, the simple expectations of men went unheeded. One GI reported that one winter he had been on line for forty-six days without washing. When they were finally pulled off line, their clothes were burned. Everything required effort. "I was wet for seven months," wrote Jimmy James Wathlers.

> I got wet when the rains started and I was not able to get dry until the cold winds started. I was wet from sitting in an open trench, I got wet crawling through ground puddles, I was wet from the sweat that ran off me as I tried to climb the damn hills and cross the humid valleys. I was wet so long my stomach and backside was white and wrinkled like after your hands when you have been swimming for a long time.[4]

Even during combat, an effort was made to provide at least one hot meal a day. That of course was not always possible. On line, but when not involved in combat, and again when it was possible, hot meals were served at breakfast and dinner, with C rations served at midday. The Company jeep was used to bring up hot food in marmite cans from the mess gear. When that was not possible, 101 rations were issued on line, which consisted of razor blades, chewing gum, shaving cream, toothpaste, soap, even candy (five assorted gum drops), stationery, and self sealing envelopes.

But there was another side to it all. Sometimes, the food supplied by Army commissaries was often as old as the occupation itself. A check of stockpiled K rations of World War II vintage revealed that the ham-and-egg component had turned black. Especially at the beginning, there were no replacements for damaged tents and little wire of any kind; radios were in poor repair if they worked at all, and combat boots and vehicle spare parts were in short supply. Some of the weapons that had been condemned as inoperable during an inspection had not been replaced. Jeeps could not be offloaded in Pusan because the dock cranes there were inadequate to lift them. Since no one had expected a war, the litany of inadequacies was enormous and got worse. The first soldiers in action found the situation hopeless, as the Republic of Korea troops, for the most part, bolted. One American "heavy weapons company" had no armor-piercing shells.[5]

In a situation of self-defense, where soldiers realize that they are the targets of the enemy effort, there is a tendency to feel cold, turn pale, and get goose bumps; the pulse rate increases and the body begins to tremble. This is not the result of undue fear but the natural response of the body preparing to either fight or to run. The senses tend to become stronger and blood is pumped into the muscles preparing them for quick action. As the muscles receive this oxygenated blood, they quiver with energy and the legs shake. The roughness of the clothes and the exposure to damp, heat, and cold all contribute to the irritation of the skin, sometimes rubbing an area so raw it is almost impossible to move without pain—though usually of a more annoying and irritating variety. The same is true for cuts and bruises, easily accumulated and often unnoticed until the action has died down. Abrasions that, if at home, would be dealt with cleaning and a bandage, under the circumstances became sore and infected.

While food and water were often in short supply, it seemed to be water that was missed the most. And, as many have reported, there developed an almost unquenchable desire for cold water. Sleeping and eating, the essentials, were not all that difficult in the rear areas, but once up front it became difficult. Particularly when the weather was bad, or the air came in at −40 degrees F. Men reported eating what they called bean popsicle, cutting both ends out of a can of beans and pushing the contents out of one end.

Most of the time, those in a combat situation were exhausted. When at rest there was little chance to rest, and when on the move the conditions were such that they extracted a huge toll on the men's strength. In the summer, the heat and humidity turned any movement into a sweat bath with no place to cool off. While only half true, it seemed that the march was always uphill, sometimes as steep as 60 degrees. Then the troops had to move down through the ragged valleys and up another hill.

The attack on the emotions was massive. Rex Brown recalled: "It seems to be that I was irritated the whole time I was in combat. Everything upset me, every little miscue or mishap—like having trouble opening a C rations can—became a major problem. Others irritated me with their coughing, or quirks, or the comments they made. I did not say much, but I could feel my anger rising. The whole situation seemed so unfair, I suppose, that every little thing made it even worse."[6]

Alex Schultz comments on the feelings during combat. "I've heard a lot of men say that they remember combat as if it were in slow motion. I am not sure that is what I experienced. The word I would use was clear. I felt that the time I was in combat moved very quickly, but there were moments—like when taking aim at an advancing enemy soldier—that the situation felt very clear, the air around me sharp and the image at which I was looking almost highlighted, almost unreal. Perhaps that is what others have meant by slow motion."[7]

In Korea, the environment made the whole experience even worse. T. R. Fehrenbach describes it well:

> Under the sullen sun, the ridges shimmered like furnaces and there was almost no shade in the scrubby brush that covered them. And there is little drinking water, outside the brownish stuff in the fecal paddies. Short of water, lacking water discipline, they drank from the ditches and paddies developed searing dysentery. . . . They sweated until their shirts and belts rotted, and their bellies turned shark-white.[8]

In addition, the monsoon came like torrents, making the roads into bottomless pits of mud and slush. The trenches where the men waited were full of dirty water, sometimes up to their waist, resulting in crud and fungus in the summer, frostbite in the winter.

When not involved in combat, or preparing for it, much of the time was spent on guard duty in the trenches, maintaining the condition of a combat bunker or outpost during the night, the repair or building of more fortifications in the muddy or frozen ground, or erecting tactical wire along the slopes. Most of the time, the men lived in crude bunkers that had been built up of logs and stacked with sandbags. The bunkers were filthy and the men too were soon covered with dirt. Whenever the enemy shelled the position, the bunkers often collapsed, burying the men inside.

The wire strung at the front of the Main Line of Resistence MLR was littered with cans and stones to warn of an advance, and 55-gallon drums of napalm with a TNT detonator were set into the slopes at a 45-degree angle. Where possible, mine fields were set up including the dreaded "bouncing betties." If there was nothing going on, it was possible to get back for a shower about every two weeks. At that time, an exchange of uniforms could be made and, in most cases, meats, cheese, onion, butter, and bread for sandwiches could be gotten.

When the units were in constant motion, as they were during the early months of the war, it was difficult to accumulate any personal possessions or extra equipment. But as the line formed and movement was limited, the nature of the fortifications changed, and the time to build and strengthen provided for better protection. The bunker was usually big enough for six and, if carefully built, was basically waterproof. Bunks were made out of barbed wire stakes laced with communication wire to hold an air mattress and/or sleeping bag. Ammo crates made side tables, and they were lit by lanterns or candles. The lucky ones were heated by a Yukon or potbellied stove, fueled by a Jerry can of diesel oil, a hose, and a drip valve. The stove would often get cherry red and run the men out of the bunker. Occasionally, charcoal and wood stoves, sunk into the earth, were also used to keep the ground warm.

Often, as the areas stabilized, the question of extra equipment became a problem in some units. Extra clothing, additional weapons, wire, cooking apparatus, and the like, began to collect without anyone really knowing how. The disadvantage was that when it was necessary to move, the not essential materials either had to be discarded, or the unit had to take the time and provide the transportation to move it. Another factor was that junk—used C ration cans, cardboard boxes, ammo boxes, discarded clothing, and the like—began to pile up around bunkers. This not only added to the lice and rat population, it made it fairly easy for the communists to identify which bunkers were occupied.

It was also quite difficult to keep clean at the front. Water was made available when possible, but it was not always possible. When there was some extra, more than was needed for drinking, some of the men attempted sponge baths in their bunker. The forward posts maintained communication with the rear areas and, when things quieted down, they brought up some hot foot up to the chow bunker where small groups of men rotated down to eat. The rest of the time, when the heavy fighting went on for several days at a time, there were C rations. Many times, it was little more than a tin of spam or similar, but it was enough for most to make it until the fighting stopped.

Not everyone was happy with the situation in which they found themselves. Most Korean War veterans will tell you that they were prepared for what they found and that there was no shortage of heroism displayed. The second aspect of this belief is not as well supported, and may seem contradictory, but it appears that many were aware that the conditions under which they fought were limited by "poor generalship, poor equipment, poor preparation, poor replacement."

Historian Fehenbach suggests: "Generally unassuming, unaggressive, with no desire whatever to kill the man they called Joe Chink, when backed into a corner, or assaulted on their hills, these men showed the spirit of the Alamo was not dead."[9]

Bunkers

The bunkers were infested with lice and rats. Few of them were more than five by eight feet and awfully cramped and dirty. Plastic bags that came as packing for batteries were used for windows, straw when it was available served as the floor. During the spring of 1952, the Army and Marines began to use Lincoln-log type bunkers. It took a hole dug twelve feet square and seven feet deep to house a bunker. The design used tree trunks about eight inches in diameter, and a cover of seven to eight feet. It was about four feet of logs, and three to four feet more of rocks, sandbags, and earth.

Logs collected for making bunkers, Korea, 1952. (*Used by permission of the Center for the Study of the Korean War, Graceland University*)

By summer 1952, the Marines developed their own style, a prefabricated timber structure designed to fit into a hole eight feet square and somewhat less than seven feet. These bunkers could house a 50-caliber machine gun, the crew, and several riflemen. It could be made with no tools whatsoever, other than the entrenching tools. The greatest difficulty was the weight of the heavy roofing timbers, which were some eleven feet long, a foot wide, and more than four inches thick. On top of that was placed a layer, about two feet in depth, of sandbags, tarpaper, and four feet of earth.

Trenches

Whenever possible, trenches were dug, as they provided the easiest and quickest protection. In most cases, they were ad hoc but, as the pace of the war slowed down, they became more elaborate. The soil in much of Korea is hard and rocky and, when frozen, very difficult to penetrate. Besides, working up a sweat was exhausting in the summer and in the winter led to frostbite. But cover was necessary in the seemingly barren hills, and most troopers, aware of the presence of the North Koreans or Chinese, dug deep. At least deep enough to provide a man cover. As had been the experience during World War I, most soon learned that the trenches were quick to collect moisture and, soon after that, rats. In many cases, the trenches were basically simply facilities facing an outpost or in the line an enemy was expected to follow. Others were elaborate, connecting bunkers and outposts with lateral lines and widened spots for movement or passage.

American soldiers were considered poor at digging, and dug as little as possible. It was necessary for command to keep after them or they would be satisfied with a foxhole or a space just big enough to cover them.[10]

WHAT DO YOU DO ALL DAY?

The most honest answer to the perennial question, "What did you do in the war, daddy?" was to answer, "I waited." For, in fact, that is a good portion of what soldiers do during the day and the night. They wait for chow, they wait for transportation, they wait for patrol, they wait for entertainment, they wait for more beer, they wait for mail, they wait for the brief leave called Rest and Recuperation (R & R), they wait to go home. Those troops located in the states, or in rear echelon areas often spent their days much like any other working person, sometimes even having an eight-to-five workday, with little or no responsibility during the evenings. The further up you got, however, the more it was necessary to kill time between other activities. Even those on line who filled the trenches, the bunkers, and the foxholes, watched and waited to see what the enemy would do, or what assignments their units would be given. When they could, they slept, or played cards—poker, hearts, double-deck pinochle—talked with each other telling tall stories, or wrote letters, picked the lice off themselves, cleaned equipment, or perhaps brewed up some coffee.

Essentials were primitive, but that did not mean simple. The need to relieve oneself sometimes became a matter of life or death. The soldier usually dug a small hole near a tree and hung his butt over the hole while hanging onto the tree. Then, after he had finished, he covered up the hole with dirt. Or, sometimes, if it was too dangerous to leave the trench, he did his business right there, covering it up as much as was possible.

For a lot of the men serving in Korea, particularly those who were rotating in and out of the front lines, it seemed unnecessary to be continuously engaged in training activities. Nevertheless, this was an activity in which almost everyone took part. Part of it consisted of rehearsals for planned actions, sometimes a dozen different times. More than that, however, it was necessary to keep the men active.

The recovery of damaged equipment and the picking up (policing) of brass took up a lot of time and was a difficult but a necessary job. A great deal of this task was carried out by men on the line during periods of relative calm. The cost of shell casings was one significant reasons for the clean up, but there was also the possibility of their being taken and used by the enemy. One of the surprising things about an artillery bombardment was how many "cases" were left over, sometimes amounting to thousands—on some occasions tens of thousands—of rejected cases.

THE PHYSICAL ENVIRONMENT

The Heat

In the majority of cases, the men dealt with the heat by discarding as many clothes as possible and using towels or pieces of rag around their necks to control some of the sweating. Men constantly suffered from various degrees of heat exhaustion. In the heat, and the accompanying humidity, even sitting raised a sweat, but when called on to run, particularly uphill, the men became drenched in their own sweat. As long as the men kept their helmets and jackets on, they could avoid a lot of the sun, but they often saw the sun's heat as a proper substitute to the weight of their uniforms. The heat brought about a huge increase in the need for water and led many men, driven nearly mad by their thirst, to drink from creeks or even rice paddies.

The Cold

The U.S. military was ill-prepared for the cold winters in North Korea. As a result, many soldiers and marines fought in frigid conditions with inadequate equipment and supplies. Not only was there little winter clothing available at quartermaster supplies, there was also a shortage of wool and cotton. Even the synthetic materials used for field jackets and parkas were in short supply. Front line soldiers were identified to receive what came in, but battle conditions made the delivery most difficult. By October 1950, some winter supplies reached Pusan, but distribution was difficult and only slightly eased by redirecting supplies to Inchon. As the Chinese advanced in December, a great proportion of the cold weather supplies were lost. Lieutenant General Ridgway discovered that the 24th Infantry Division was without winter clothing in December and ordered supplies airlifted in. By the second winter, supplies were more adequate, but the distribution problem was not much better.

When it was really cold, equipment did not work. Men became incoherent. Even the gases used to propel the bullet from the chamber of the M-1 was so weakened that it was hardly strong enough to drive the projectile. The stock became so brittle it broke easily. Grenades sometimes failed to explode and simply fizzled harmlessly. Artillery pieces fired but did not rebound. The ground was too hard for entrenching tools and men working to try to control their equipment soon found that they could freeze to death in their own sweat. C rations froze in the cans and the auxiliary packs became a solid mass. Food had to be warmed in the mouth before it could be chewed, and water froze in the cup if it was less than ten feet from the oil stove. Blood froze and plasma became useless; morphine had to be kept warm to be of any use.

Unidentified soldier wearing the "Pyle Cap" with flaps down. (*Used by permission of the Center for the Study of the Korean War, Graceland University*)

Stanley Sandler recalls a night when the temperature dropped from 49 degrees to 8 degrees below zero, with a wind of 35 miles per hour. "In the next two or three days, some men of the tough 7th Marine Regiment collapsed from the cold and were hospitalized; stimulants had to be applied to many cases to revive depressed respiration."[11]

Soldiers had to change their socks at least once a day, as the perspiration would freeze and frostbite would develop. This was such a danger that for some time platoon leaders were given letters of reprimand for their 201 File (permanent personnel record) if one of their soldiers got frostbite.

When the weather was extremely cold, the troops were advised to drink half a quart (half canteen) of water with each meal and before they went to sleep. An additional half-quart was to be taken every hour during the workday. Field rations contained a much smaller amount of water than garrison food, which had to be taken into consideration. A total of five to six quarts of water per day was necessary. There were further difficulties in supplying water, and the fact was that at −10 (F), the standard canteen froze. Unmelted snow, which might appear to be a solution, wasted more body heat, warming it up.

Dehydration was a problem. Generally, the troops would not feel the thirst until they were already significantly dehydrated. Men were encouraged to monitor their own dehydration by watching the color of their urine. The lighter the color, the better off they were.

Weapons in Cold Weather

The extremely cold weather that the American troops encountered took its toll on both men and equipment. The various weapons reacted differently, but the primary concern was to what extent a weapon could be counted on. During extremely cold weather, the mortars did not do well on the hard ground. Lacking the cushioning effect, there was a great deal of bucking and the cracking of both base plates and firing pins. The difficulty was the greatest among the 60mm mortars.

Machine guns became more difficult to operate when the heavy frost formed on the unfaceted parts, and it was necessary to do warm-up firing before it was put into operation. The Browning Automatic Rifle (BAR) stood up well though there would be some frost-lock that was freed (as the story goes) when the men relieved themselves on the lock. Primarily, however, the BAR was a good cold-weather weapon.

The M1 rifle worked well in the bitter cold. The most common problem was broken firing pins, and the frost locked the piece if it was not worked occasionally. The incidents when the weapon failed to operate were very minor. However, if the carbine became sluggish in subzero cold, it often required five to ten warm-up shots before it went automatic. When it was fully automatic, it tended to be hypertensive. In hot weather, even small amounts of dirt or water caused a misfire. During the cold, it was more sensitive to frost than other weapons. Nevertheless, it was a handy weapon for those whose duties did not require sustained fire. The Marines complained about its inaccuracy following the Chosen Reservoir operation. The kind of warfare going on called for marksmanship, and the accuracy of the carbine just did not meet the requirements.

Another aspect of the cold weather was that it produced shock. It numbed the senses, muddled the thoughts, and promoted forgetfulness about what had been learned about cold-weather fighting.

It was not just the cold, however, but poor maintenance too that produced a good part of the trouble. In a fire fight, there is little time or inclination to keep a weapon clean. If the soldier recognized a fault in a weapon, he might well throw it away and pick up another one. If it blocked during a firefight, the soldier, being nervous and hurried, would not clear the weapon well. The conditions under which the soldiers fought made it nearly impossible to keep the weapon clear. Lubrication was also a problem, and the question of how and when to lubricate a weapon was never clearly answered.

Darkness

For many, the darkness was a problem. Not only did it provide cover for advancing enemy troops, it also served as a frightening event to be dealt with every night. One of the first things a new replacement noticed about life in Korea, especially in advanced positions, was just how dark it was. Without much electricity, few villages, and limited traffic, the extent of the darkness was shocking. On a clear night, the star patterns were totally visible, and yet the phrase "can't see your hand in front of your face" took on real meaning. Because it was so dark, the shine of a single light was immense and could be seen for long distances. The sight of lights moving in the distance was frightening in itself, for it announced the presence of the enemy.

Noise

It seemed that sound on the battlefield went from a deathly silence to an almost unbelievable clamor of numerous and mind-chilling explosions. The silence was frightening in itself, and every sound was taken seriously—noises could or could not mean intervention—for it was usually very hard to see at night. When it came, mortars, artillery shells, mines exploding, and air strikes, it numbed the mind, making conversation impossible and reducing everyone to a tight defensive position.

Unused to the sounds, the average American soldier reacted to the Chinese use of traditional communication instruments such as shepherds' horns, rattles, and bugles with anxiety. When these instruments were used, often in night attacks, the effect of it was unnerving because of their mysterious qualities. While there was no evidence the noise-makers greatly affected the fight, there was considerable evidence that the noise was frightening—"they made our hair stand up on end." As they became accustomed to the noise, there was little attention given to the details; there did not seem to be any "tune" to the calls, few remember any sequence to them and, in the main, just remember the noise in terms of its source: bugles, shepherds' horns, bronze whistles, drums, and the like.

The Chinese, and occasionally the North Koreans, used noise-making instruments as a means of communication to control their own forces, but there is little doubt that the communists were also aware of the fear factor created with these mysterious sounds echoing across the night-time battlefield. By 1951, however, whatever fear factor they retained was against those men who were on the line for the first time.

Rate of Fire

As compared to those involved in World War II, there was a radical increase in the percentage of individuals who fired their weapons when involved in a firefight. It was determined that during the day, even when the infantry was moving in a single line and only the front troops had occasions to fire, it was more than double that of World War II. At night, in perimeter defense, the vast majority of those involved participated. Several things might have contributed to this.

One was the increased danger of envelopment and fractionalization caused by the manner in which the communists fought, which tended to promote a better fire discipline. A second was that many of the troops seemed to be aware of the fire involvement percentages, and personnel were aware of their fire delivery. And third, during training, the role of the individual and his weapon was greatly emphasized. A fourth reason might better be discussed under the topic of morale, and that was the Army had begun to yell. Both in the attack and the defense, there was more noise, cheering, strafing, shouting of orders, increasing both the team character of the unit, but "talking it up" emphasized the unit's dependence on the individual.

The effective fire of infantry weapons is about 200 yards. But, in Korea, more than in previous wars, the battle was often fought at less than that range. Often the two sides would close to within 150 yards before firing opened up. In the case of the Army, there are numerous reports of the heavier guns running out of ammunition, leaving the soldiers to hold off until their fire from the lighter weapons could be more effective.

It became increasingly apparent as the war went on that the best defense against the Chinese Communist Forces was the use of automatic fire combined with slow fire. Not only were the semiautomatic weapons conservators of ammunition but, in the hands of a good marksman, they were of inestimable value, especially in the last hours of a fight when both sides were exhausted.

CONCLUSION

"Everyone has to be someplace, and everyone has to be doing something," says the old response. For those during the Korean War, the "someplace" has been well defined. Not so well know is the "doing something." It is easy to consider the military person in Korea during the fighting, we all seem to know—or think we know—what that means. But even in the most hostile of situations, battles do not last long. There are hours, and days, and even months, between confrontations during which those on the line and in support in the garrisons wait. They wait for everything. Their days are filled, as are all days, with twenty-four hours during which they must prepare, perform, and occupy themselves.

It is hard to believe that in a combat area boredom would be the most common experience, but that was often the case. And yet the time was filled. There was training, preparation, cleaning of equipment, patrols, maneuvers, details, personal needs, letters to be written and read, and hours of individual reflection or casual comradeship. Essential, of course, were those military duties and the preparation that was required to perform them, the concern for equipment, but also the need to defeat the extreme heat or mind-numbing cold. When talking to veterans, few remember what these things were, for the memory tends to remember the unusual or extreme events. But doing what had to be done was as much a part of the life of the soldier in Koreas as was their assignment there.

NOTES

1. William Crum: www. Koreanwar-educator.org/memoirs/crum_bill.
2. Robert Johnson: CSKW, GU RG 9 A.005.
3. Oliver Hampshire: CSKW, GU RG1 A 0178.
4. Jimmy James Walhlers: CSKW, GU RG 7. B.0016.
5. Stanley Weintraub, "How to Remember the Forgotten War," *American Heritage* 51 (May/June 2000): 100.
6. Rex Brown: CSKW, GU RG 1 A. 2100.
7. Alexander Schultz: CSKW, GU RG 1. 069.
8. T. R. Fehrenbach, *This Kind of War* (Washington, D.C.: Brassey's, 1963), 105.
9. Fehrenbach: 423.
10. Fehrenbach: 329.
11. Stanley Sandler, *The Korean War: No Victors, No Vanquished.* (Lexington: University Press of Kentucky, 1999), 121.

7 CARE OF THE WOUNDED AND THE DEAD

Our duty hours were as long as we can keep standing.

—Oree George Michael, GI, 1950

From battalion sick call during basic training to advanced surgical care following a serious wound, the American serviceman and woman generally received the best medical care available. And, in comparison to the men and women of the opposing forces, the United Nations soldiers were very lucky indeed.

Although it sounds callous, the ultimate purpose of military medicine is to keep the troops on the line. The soldiers, sailors, airmen, and marines who are on the front lines are the assets of the military command, and when one is injured or wounded or unable to fight because of sickness, injury, or exhaustion, the mission of the medical command is to get them back into the fight. "Healing them was comparable to repairing an aircraft or a ship. Getting them back into the war zone was paramount to mission," wrote Frances Omori, then a U.S. Navy Commander, in her book *Quiet Heroes*. "While this was the overall mission, the process involved the best possible care for those who have been hurt and this mission was accomplished with extreme efficiency and kindness."[1]

The Medical Department of the U.S. Army was as unprepared for the outbreak of war as were the rest of the armed services. Arriving only five years after the end of World War II and the rapid reduction of the military services, the war in Korea during most of 1950 was fought with the supplies left over from the world conflict. At first the U.N. forces depended on stored medical supplies that were housed in Japan, with resupply from similar sources in the United States. The rapid depletion of the available stock during the early months required the military to seek the aid of the Japanese manufacturers, who drew upon local cottage industries to provide substitutes for what was needed. These items, as supplied, were of variable quality, and one medical officer reported it produced "needles that wouldn't penetrate the skin, sterilizer gaskets that would blow out at the slightest pressure, and operating tables that would buckle and collapse under the weight of an average American soldier."[2]

Many of the supplies, therefore, were procured from hand labor in scattered, independently owned shops and were absolutely necessary as, from June 25 to September 15, almost no bulk medical supplies were received from manufacturers in the United States. It was not until the first of October that supplies began to arrive in any reasonable quantities. During this early period, when the casualties were very high, the Army's reserve supplies were supported by Navy and Air Force stocks.

The Navy was not a lot better off. Lieutenant Omori pointed out that when the Korean War broke out, the system that was in place immediately overloaded. In some cases, as the wounded arrived in droves by ambulances of all kinds, there were as many as 5,000 patients in a hospital at any one time. "The book went to hell overnight! A 100-bed hospital had to be converted to accommodate 5,000 patients. They stacked the patients on bunk beds, sometimes three tiers high."[3]

The Army had its own corpsmen and litter bearers who served with a great deal of skill. These men, assigned to a unit, followed it into combat and saw to the soldiers' wounds and injuries. Two decorations were provided: the Combat Medical Aid Men, provided by combat medics and corpsmen in the marines, and the Combat Medical Badge, the combat medic's equivalent to the Combat Infantryman Badge CIB.

The Bureau of Navy Medicine and Surgery provided hospital corpsmen for the U.S. Marines in the field. There has always been a special bond between the corpsmen and the Marines, who lovingly referred to their corpsmen as "doc."[4] Lieutenant Helen Fable at the Navy Hospital at Yokosuka wrote that she was very impressed with the professional training that the corpsmen had received in surgical procedures. "The corpsmen with the Fleet Marines were good," she wrote.[5]

In her book, *War in Korea: 1951,* War Correspondent Marguerite "Maggie" Higgins tells of a time when the influx of wounded was so large that she found herself helping. The aid station had been set up next to a mortar company, and bullets were hitting the shed where the doctors were working. At one moment, the number of casualties was so large that there were not enough hands, and when a medic needed to leave a patient to get more plasma, she offered to "administer the remaining plasma and passed about an hour there, helping out as best I could."[6] Many things added to their difficulty, but the cold was a major problem. Dr. Lessenden, remembering his own Chosin ordeal, told a reporter, "Everything was frozen. Plasma froze and the bottles broke. We couldn't use plasma because it wouldn't go into solution and the tubes would clog with particles. We couldn't change dressings because we had to work with gloves on to keep our hands from freezing. We couldn't cut a man's clothes off to get a wound because he would freeze to death. Actually, a man was often better off if we left him alone. Did you ever try to stuff a wounded man into a sleeping bag?"[7]

At times, the forward aid stations were scenes of half-controlled chaos. Medics and sweating Korean laborers, at gunpoint, hauled litters. Stragglers and walking wounded wandered in by themselves, often preempting litters needed for more serious cases. Medics stripped the wounded, tossing clothes and armored vests alike into growing piles of ruined equipment. Sometimes, they turned up grenades with half-pulled pins.

The conditions among the wounded were dismal. Infection was a fact of life, for most wounds were grossly contaminated with dirt from the field, bits of leaves and rice plants, and crumbs of human excrement plainly visible in some cases. The wounds were frequently infested with maggots.[8]

PREVENTATIVE ACTION

Clean Water

Probably the most necessary item for the man or woman in the field was water. From the beginning, the supply of water was to be a major difficulty. The problem belonged to the Corps of Engineers but the Medical Services worked closely with them. The advancing North Korean Army was destroying water stations and water-processing plants, making local sources nearly impossible to locate. Halazon tablets (a chlorine base), issued during World War II to make the water drinkable, were not working. The heat in Korea in July and August was almost unbearable and the terrain—one hill after the other—made water a necessity. Tormented by thirst, the soldiers would fill their canteens from the pools of water in the rice paddies, water that was filled with human excrement. The Halazon tables, added to the canteen, had lost most of their potency during the years of storage and did not help. The result was attacks of dysentery, which soon affected nearly a quarter of the men of the divisions.[9]

The water problem came up again following the invasion at Inchon. Whatever supplies of drinking water were available in Inchon became contaminated once the fighting started, and there were no distillation units available. In one effort, the military

Honey-bucket carts, used to collect human waste, Korea, 1951. (*Used by permission of the Center for the Study of the Korean War, Graceland University*)

decided to transport water from Japan in oil tankers. The containers were scrubbed out and covered with a cement wash. Then filled with lightly chlorinated water. During the trip, however, seawater and oil leaks from the ships invaded many of the tankers. The lack of water caused many hardships among the troops, and the chief cause of illness was gastroenteritis, an inflammation of the stomach and bowels.[10]

Preventive Medicine

Preventive medicine, so necessary for the overall health of the force, was nearly impossible during the weeks of withdrawal and defeat. The largest problems arose from the heat and a multiplicity of insects, and impure water was an obvious source of disease. From the beginning, everything that could be reached was dusted with DDT. An effort was made to maintain some standard of personal hygiene, but the hygiene of the Korean KP worker who labored in the mess halls was judged extremely poor. During these early months, diarrheal disorders formed one of the greatest single groups of medical disabilities.

A second problem arose from the supplies and locations of litters and blankets. The procedure was based on a standard chain of evacuation. In theory, the blankets and litters were exchanged on a one-on-one basis, so that as they came into a station they were sent back to the units of origin. But during this early phase, so many of the wounded were sent forward along the Medical Evacuation Chain on litters and with their blankets that the supply system did not work. Blankets and litters accumulated where they were not needed.

Supplies were always a problem. During the period when Corps X and the Eighth Army worked as separate commands, however, it seemed that Corps X was so well supplied that the Eighth Army team referred to them as the Gilded Lily. In some of the front line areas, in the 8076 Mobile Army Surgical Hospital (MASH) for example, resupply was so bad that sponges and bandages had to be washed and used again. Yet, they had a steady and sufficient supply of blood.

EVACUATION

The Medical Evacuation situation in September 1950 was as follows: The first aid and evacuation from the field to a battalion aid station, from there to the Regimental Collecting Station (often a MASH unit), then to the Division Clearing Station (also sometimes a MASH unit), from there to the Evacuation Hospital at Pusan, then on to planes for flights to Japan where they were located in one of the Army hospitals there—most often to the 118th Station Hospital at Fukuoka—or then on to other Army hospitals in Japan. For those whose recovery would require more than 120 days, they were flown out of Haneda International Airport, Japan to Tripler Army Hospital in Hawaii, where they were stabilized, and then on to Travis Air Force Base in California and eventually to one of the Army hospitals in the interior.[11]

Helicopters, referred to as air ambulances, were introduced early in the war and were quickly put to use to evacuate the wounded from the battlefield to MASH units. The Bell H-13 was the primary helicopter used for Medevac (medical evacuation). Two patients were transported on skids placed outside each helicopter, limiting the treatment they might receive during transport. Medical Services Officers were the primary pilots, in 1953, and were chosen for their ability in transporting the wounded.

Helicopter landing to pick up passenger, Korea, 1953. (*Used by permission of the Center for the Study of the Korean War, Graceland University*)

Because of a lack of doctors and the under-strength units, triage and transportation took the place of physicians and beds. By frequent sorting of the wounded, the more serious cases were moved on quickly to available hospitals in Korea and Japan. This imposed a disproportionate burden on medical transport of all kinds to move the wounded to stations where they could receive adequate aid.

The evacuation process was very difficult for all involved. In the first place, the enemy was indifferent to the Western etiquette of war, and attacks on medical personnel, medical vehicles, and tents turned out to be the rule rather than the exception. The aid stations were often the first targets of the North Korean artillery, and enemy riflemen used the red crosses on ambulance vehicles as bull's eyes. In some cases, the wounded had to be evacuated by tank. At one point after the battle at Chochiwon, medics painted out the emblems on their equipment and, on some occasions, armed themselves.[12]

Even in the more routine cases, there were still nearly insurmountable problems. Maps were critically short and many ambulances lost their way in blackout trips over precarious mountain passes. A number of ambulances had been destroyed by enemy fire. North Korean tactics of infiltration and envelopment often cut off the wounded from the evacuation route. Snipers would often shoot at ambulances and evacuation vehicles as they moved through the darkness of mountain roads and rainy trails. The roads were rough, extremely narrow, sharply winding, and steep in ascent and descent. The bad roads and overuse broke down the sturdy ambulances. The broken terrain separated the fighting units from the units that supported them.

One response to these problems was the introduction of the helicopter as an evacuation vehicle. The helicopter, which the Air Force had begun to study, was designed for rescue operations, picking up downed pilots. However, as these rescue missions decreased, the helicopter was used more and more in evacuation. General MacArthur, seeing the value of the helicopter, agreed that they should be a part of the Table of Organization and Equipment (TO & E) of a medical unit and be used as was an ambulance. By October 8, 1950, four detachments of four helicopters were sent for use in Korea.

The helicopters were so scarce and fragile that they were not authorized for routine evacuations from battalion aid stations or even some regimental collection stations. Their vulnerability to small-arms fire made them too much of a target. However, they were assigned to bringing out the worst patients, usually those with head, chest, or abdominal wounds that made travel by field ambulance less satisfactory.

In fact, the helicopters have achieved a reputation far in excess of their use. The dramatic nature of their flights as well as the dramatic arrivals and departures led many to believe that the helicopter was the most-used method of evacuation of combat casualties. Add to this the much-publicized scenes from the movie and TV program *MASH,* which gave the impression of more use than was realistic. In fact, the vast majority of the wounded was transported by ambulances.

The "Doodlebug," a gasoline-powered railroad car that shuttled from Chochiwon to Taejon, made the thirty-mile trip in about forty-five minutes, carrying seventeen litters and fifty ambulatory patients on each trip.

Battalion and Regimental Aid Stations

The MASH units reflected the Army's emergency reaction to the problems found in Korea. Established in 1948, they were created to provide temporary missions and were not intended to see extended service. None of the original five saw service in Korea. The units were generally numbered in the 8,000 series to reflect their assignment to the Eighth Army. In early July, three MASH units were activated: the 8055th, the 8063rd, and the 8076th. The Eighth Army Surgeon selected MASH units because these units, and their backups, the semi-mobile evacuation hospitals, had their own transportation. Certainly understandable during the mobile war, but it is interesting to note how long they continued in service after the war stabilized.

At Pusan, MASH unit 8063 occupied a schoolhouse building, which was determined to be singularly venomous. There, seventeen nurses slept in a single room that was shut tight in the stifling heat to prevent rats from coming in. By the close of the first year of the war, the regimental companies, the MASH units, and the evacuation hospitals had all become veterans and were able to work and move under most conditions.

The *Medics War* provides a composite picture of an aid or MASH unit, stressing the difficulty of dealing with the conditions as well as the limited equipment. The array of antibiotics—not only penicillin but also streptomycin, aureomycin, and chloromycetin— was limited, but available in medical chests. There would be a blood drip for the man on the table and others waiting for transfusion. All this time, more and more wounded would be coming in. Later MASH nurse Captain Oree Gregory wrote: "I've never seen such patients. Blind, or with legs or buttocks blown off. Many died despite skilled surgery," She also commented on the July heat and the swarms of "green large, and heavy flies," that were everywhere.[13]

It is significant to note the degree to which these MASH units were, in fact, mobile. During the month of October 1950, the 8063rd advanced from Chinju near the Korean

Strait, by way of Taegu, to Taejon, then Ascom City, on to Pyongyang—some 300 miles by air, but much further by winding road. As it turned out, several of the MASH units were required to support more than one division, and the range of the patients expanded as members of the United Nations joined the fight.

The official medical history of the war recounts the problems of the medical department during the retreat from Chosin. During this withdrawal, the wounded lay across the fenders and the hoods of vehicles. Ambulances were filled by piling dead bodies on top of the wounded, aiding in keeping them warm. Intravenous solutions froze in the flasks, diesel fuel for heating would not flow unless mixed with kerosene, space heaters burned out, ice formed in gasoline and caused electric generators to fail. Surgeons worked by the light of potbellied stoves and hand-held flashlights. Boiled water turned to ice before the instruments could be washed, and the bodies of the wounded steamed when opened, making it difficult for the doctors to examine the wound.

From the beginning of the war, it had been found necessary to abandon the non-transportable wounded to the mercies of the enemy. In more than one case, corpsmen and physicians waited with the wounded and spent years in captivity.

On July 6, 1950, the 8054th Evacuation Hospital Semi-Mobile arrived to set up shop in a Korean schoolhouse. It opened a blood bank in Japan, and the first shipment of sixty-nine bottles of whole blood arrived on the night of July 7. Most of this came from servicemen and their dependents stationed in Japan.

Hospital Ships

A major stop along the evacuation route was the hospital ship. The first such ship that was available was the Royal Navy HMHS *Maine*. She would be the only hospital ship in British history to receive a naval battle honor. She arrived on July 14 in Pusan and, for the next two months, the captured Italian liner carried 1,849 casualties to Fukuoka. It was quite crude in terms of what would be available later. She had only one air-conditioned ward and the temperature below decks could rise as high as 100 F. Nevertheless, she saved many lives. Later, supported by troop carriers USNS *St. George D. Keathley* and *Sgt. Andrew Miller* in tossing Landing Ships Tanks (LSTs) and Chinese junks, the wounded endured a tedious but successful journey. The Danish ship *Jutlandia* arrived at Pusan in October 1950, where it served as an evacuation hospital. She served a second tour of duty after a helicopter landing deck had been attached. She returned to Denmark in October 1953 after the cease-fire was signed.

The USS *Consolation* was diverted to Pusan when the war broke out and reached Korea in August. At 15,000 tons, she was spotlessly clean, well equipped, one of six ships built during World War II. The USS *Haven* served at Inchon during 1950 and at Pusan in1951; the USS *Repose* saw service but all quickly turned from evacuation ships to floating hospitals. As the Eighth Army pulled back following the Chinese entry into the war, the USS *Consolation* was anchored offshore at Inchon for the evacuation of the wounded. Their efforts were complicated by the extreme nature of the tides, which caused long periods of waiting.

The USS *Repose,* called the "Angel of the Orient," had been taken out of action, but was recalled. She was accepted by the Military Sea Transport Service, Pacific Command (MSTSPAC) on August 26,1950, and sailed with a civilian crew on September 2. She served on station at Pusan. In November, she was stationed at Inchon where she provided hospital service until recalled in January. Returning in June, with a helicopter deck in place, she served to transport patients from Korea to Japan. She received nine battle stars for her service during the Korean War. During the Vietnam War too, she served several tours.

The USS *Haven* was an 11,141-ton hospital ship decommissioned in July 1947 following distinguished service during World War II. Following the collision and sinking of the USS *Benevolence* in August 1950, she was recommissioned and sailed for Korea. She served along the west coast where she supported U.S. forces primarily from Pusan and Inchon. On return for maintenance, she was fitted with a helicopter flight deck.

Addison Terry, who was wounded, recalls his return to the United States. While in considerable pain, he obviously enjoyed the trip on the C-47 taking him to Tokyo. "All the patients were given shots of some kind, and we slept until there was a jolt from the wheels hitting the runway at Johnson Air Force Base outside of Tokyo. The air base hospital was like a rest home. Clean sheets, clean latrines, nice people, and great food. . . . This was the first time I had been in a bed for two-and-a-half months."[14]

Army Hospitals in Japan

Even before the war, the Army regularly evacuated those whose hospitalization was expected to be more than 120 days. During the first six months, evacuation was about 223 persons a month, 91 percent by air. As the war progressed, it rose dramatically, 513 in July, 1,269 in August, 5,014 in September. During September, 1,400 were moved by ship as an emergency measure. After a brief rest stop and a hot meal at Midway Island, Military Air Transport Service (MATS) evacuation planes flew nonstop to Hickam Air Force Base (AFB) in Hawaii. After a stay of about forty-eight hours, during which patients were stabilized, they were flown on to the Zone of Interior (ZI).

In the United States, they were sent to Travis Air Force Base in California. At that point, if they were able, they were flown to one of the Army Hospitals in the interior, usually as close to their homes as possible.

THE SPECIAL RISKS IN KOREA

When the United Nations soldiers reached the Koto-ri plateau during the first winter of the war, the men were not ready for the cold weather. Medical officers reported numerous cases where men were suffering from what they identified as shock brought on by the terrible cold. Many of them were crying and appeared to be very nervous. Most recovered after they were thawed out, and platoon warming tents, heated by camp stoves, were set up wherever possible.

As the first winter of the war approached, and the fighting was close to the Yalu River, two programs were printed and distributed to the troops. The first was a pamphlet called "Cold Facts for Keeping Warm," and the second was a common letter that listed preventive measures. Nevertheless, many men were disabled by the cold.

The warm clothing did not keep up with the advance, and many men were still fighting in their summer garb. In the advance MASH unit at Pukchon, men had received the necessary warmer gear, but the nurses had to make do with men's uniforms, sometimes wearing two or three pairs of socks to fill the large boots they were issued.

Cold war injuries in Korea are generally given at 7,285 with a hospitalization period of 255,835 days. Blacks were six times more at risk of being injured due to the cold as whites, and it was more severe when it happened. Southern-based soldiers were 1.6 times more likely to be effected than were greater than northern-based soldiers.[15]

It was discovered that the movement of troops from tropical countries to the wet-cold climate of Korea created difficulties. When the Filipinos arrived in Korea in September 1951, they found they were "freezing" in the 65-degree weather. Some of them broke into their packs and had blankets draped over their shoulders.

Shells that hit frozen ground were the greater danger than those that hit the mud. More of the former's fragments fly on the horizontal. Direct fire was more dangerous than indirect fire.

Of the immediate problems facing the medical department, environmental difficulties played a major part. Among these were the massive numbers of men who suffered frostbite. It was not hard to get. The duration of exposure varied from a few minutes to sixteen hours in ambient temperatures ranging from 20 to −80 degrees F. Prior to the Korean War, only one official medical directive (TB Med 81), dated August 4, 1944, existed that pertained to the prevention and management of cold-weather injuries. Most of it had to be learned on the job. Frostbite is particularly hard on the soldier for the simple reason that most armies still travel on their feet. Care of the feet was a major concern. On the other side of frostbite was trench foot, a condition that was the product of wet feet. The duration of exposure varied from two to fourteen days in temperatures ranging from fifty to 20 degrees F with wet ground conditions.

Korea was ripe with disease. The soil, fertilized with human waste, made the smallest exposure deadly. One of the major problems was bacillary dysentery. This was particularly bad after the first recapture of Seoul, when it became a near epidemic. Dysentery is not only disabling physically, making it nearly impossible for a man so cursed to fight, it also played heavily on the individual as a disgusting and embarrassing problem.

Another significant problem was malaria. When war broke out, the military was afraid that malaria would be a major problem. The primary strain in Korea was the *Plasmodium Vivax,* with a latency between attack and relapse of six months. One response was insect repellent, and one division quartermaster had a nine-month supply of four bottles of repellent per man per month in storage. The suppression, however, was provided by taking a quinine prophylactic tablet, Atabrine, each day, and chloroquine in dosages of a .5 gram tablet per week. Ample supplies were available and troops were ordered to take them once a week. It reduced the impact of malaria to the point that the anticipated problem did not arise. When a change in the tactical situation separated the troops from the wet reservoir area, the problem got even smaller.[16]

Yet another of these diseases waiting to attack the men of the UN command was hemorrhagic fever. It was not nearly as common as the other two, but because of the stories told about it, was perhaps the most feared. An unexpected, near epidemic broke out in late 1951, when UN troops settled down in a defensive line near Seoul. Hemorrhagic fever was a highly contagious summer-time disease spread by mites. Troops would arrive at the hospital in shock, often comatose, their bodies covered with small red dots. With proper care, most of the men recovered, but a large segment of those affected did not. At first, the fatality rate was nearly twenty percent, but after the establishment of a specialized treatment center with the 8228th MASH unit, the percentage dropped to about five. The only protection the staff had was to put rubber bands on the cuffs of their trousers and sleeves.

Napalm burns were hard to identify. Nurses put the wounded men in tubs of magnesium, and the skin sizzled where the napalm had hit them.

One other problem had to be faced. Neither the Chinese nor the North Koreans were sticklers for the protocol of Red Cross protection. Attacks on medical units, hospital tents, and hold areas, as well as on ambulances were common. While evidence does not suggest these areas were deliberately targeted by the Communist military, many individual riflemen, as well as artillery and mortar men, seemed to consider the evacuation vehicles and aid stations as available targets. After being hit several times, many ambulance men painted out the red crosses. Some of the medical personnel began to carry weapons.[17]

PSYCHIATRIC DISORDERS

The pressures of combat sometimes get to a soldier. Why this is true of one person and not of another has never been adequately explained, but the medical forces were aware of this difficulty, and dealt with it. Sometimes, those in battle suffered psychiatric breakdowns. The symptoms were numerous but, generally, included a lessened sense of reality, apathy, and jerking of the body. During World War II, it has been learned that those "with the thousand-yard stare" were often more easily helped if they were treated, and kept, close to the line. When those suffereing from battle fatigue were moved out of the area, or sent home, it tended to suggest two unwanted thing. It made the soldiers believe they were in worse shape than they really were, and it encouraged those who were faking the illness. However, the lesson learned with such difficulty was not well learned and, during the early months, failures by commanders and medical officers to take this into consideration meant that many men were lost who could have been returned to duty after a few days' rest, a sedative, and a hot meal.

During the fight for Pusan in July 1950, the psychiatric admissions ran to about fifty cases per thousand men on line. During the month of August, these admissions rose to 258 cases per thousand men. From July to December 1950, the 8054th evacuated 85 percent of its neuropsychiatric patients and were able to return only about 15 percent to duty. Later, following a program that kept the disturbed men close to the action, they were able to return 71 percent of the neuropsychiatric patients to active duty. The average stay for neuropsychiatric patients was only a few days.

On those occasions when a man broke, it often became apparent in a moment, quite often in a reflexive act. During the softening up phase of the battle for Hill 355, as an example, eleven men had to be evacuated for neuropsychiatric breakdowns. One man stood up, shot two enemy soldiers who were approaching, and then went completely out of his mind, running hysterically down the hill never to be seen again.

Self-Inflicted Wounds

Sometimes, the situation became just too much for a serviceman. The "million-dollar wound" (the wound that sent you home) had not happened, and they felt they couldn't go on. When this happened, one type of psychiatric response was the self-inflicted wound. With all the firing going on, many an individual soldier felt that there was no way anyone could tell who did the shooting, and fired into his own arm, leg, or foot. Common enough to have its own acronym, SIW (self-inflicted wound), the problem was, nevertheless, fairly rare. It existed among all armies and was dealt with as a medical problem, at least until the wounded man recovered. It existed among the other armies fighting under the UN banner and among the members of ROK Army. Commonwealth troops suffered the same problem. No Canadians were ever court-martialed for this offense, but the Canadian Inspector General was disheartened to learn that eighty-three soldiers were undergoing treatment for such wounds. The highest recorded rate, a condition that has never been explained, was among the troops from New Zealand in which, at one time, seventy-five percent of their medical admissions were for self-inflicted wounds.[18] There are no records to indicate if soldiers of the North Korean or Chinese armies took this way out.

THE MEDICAL TEAMS

Young doctors had a hard time adapting, many complaining they were unqualified for the work they were given. A large portion of the doctors who served in MASH units, for example, were residents, and this would continue during the war, as the Surgeon General reached into teaching hospitals to locate officers for the forward posts. In July 1950, most of the MASH units were down to two or three doctors. The 1st Cavalry and the 24th and 25th Infantry Divisions went into combat with only fourteen medical officers each, instead of the TO&E regulation of forty-two. During 1950, the number per division never rose above twenty-five per division.

Another problem that developed unexpectedly was that the early emphasis on professionalism among the enlisted men meant that many of them were deeply trained in rather narrow fields. The wide cursory knowledge demanded during the high-pressure situation as combat casualties came in was lacking. Because of the shortage of personnel, the experienced were more valuable than those with extensive technical training.

Nurses in the forward stations were not sent back when the danger increased. It was determined that the forward units could not operate without them, and they agreed to stay at their posts. Fifty-seven army nurses arrived at Pusan on July 5, 1950, and on the 8th Twelve Army nurses moved with a MASH unit to Taejon. By August, more than 100 were on duty in South Korea in support of the United Nations troops. During the first year, the number increased from 3,460 to 5,397. The nurses served in twenty-five medical treatment facilities. During the war, no Army nurses were killed in action, but several were killed as the result of action-related accidents.

Captain Lillian Kinkela Keil, Air Force Nurse Corps, was one of the most decorated women in the U.S. military. She flew more than 200 air-evacuation missions during World War II, and then returned to service and flew more than 100 in Korea.

Several things can be concluded in terms of the effect of the medical team for the fighting man or woman. The ratio of all battle deaths, including MIAs declared dead, to surviving wounded plus battle deaths were higher in Korea than in the European theater of World War II, though lower than in the war as a whole, and much lower than in the Pacific theaters.[19]

Another insight had to do with the effects of the cold. A study conducted at Osaka discovered that black soldiers suffered more than whites, even in those units fully integrated. It was also discovered that the lower ranks (private, PFC, corporal) suffered more from the cold than the higher ranks. Line units suffered from frostbite more than support units, and that those under the age of twenty-five were more susceptible than those twenty-five or older. The investigation, however, did not offer any evidence that veterans were less susceptible than the replacements, or that tobacco was a factor.[20]

The remarkable fact, of course, is that the doctors and nurses did as well as they did under the circumstances. Rear Admiral Lamont Pugh, the Surgeon General of the Navy in 1952, spoke of the ability of those involved. "You would need to go to Korea," he said, "to appreciate the essentiality of service doctors being psychologically gile, emotionally stable, professional, genuine, and physically able and tough."[21]

Medical Innovations

During the course of the Korean War, some highly significant medical innovations and discoveries emerged. Among these was what was called Force Reaction Medicine. It came about because the huge numbers of casualties forced the medical teams to keep the patients moving. What they discovered was that getting the patient up and out as quickly as possible was far better for the patients than a long bed rest.

Again, growing out of necessity, the idea of triage developed, where the order of patients' care was determined on the basis of medical need. Less time was spent working on a patient who did not have a chance to recover, and those with wounds that were not life-threatening could wait while the most seriously wounded were taken care of. Triage was initiated at battalion aid stations, where nurses and general medical officers were responsible for deciding whether to evacuate a wounded soldier or return him to duty after minor therapy. Many deaths occurred at battalion aid stations. The MASH triage dictum was "life takes precedence over a limb, function over anatomical defeats." There were numerous cases requiring pre-operative care and anesthesia.

Another significant development was the concept of debridgement and delayed closure, which meant that wounded soldiers could be stabilized in a MASH unit before they were sent on for more serious surgery. The wounded received whatever aid was needed to get them stabilized, so that they would have the chance to live long enough to reach better-equipped units. Also, the effectiveness of adequate debridgement of devitalized tissue became evident during the Korean War.

The artificial kidney was developed and, in March 1952, used for the first time at a forward hospital, where many of the functioning difficulties were worked out. Other significant innovations included grafting, the forward-area clinical innovation of 1952 that allowed for the rapid improvement in arterial repair. In World War II, the arteries were tied off hoping other veins would aid recovery but, in most cases, that did not work and, eventually, an amputation was required. In Korea, arterial materials were taken from corpses and grafted into large gaps, which allowed the medical teams to save a large number of limbs that might otherwise have been lost. The discovery of open exposure for burn victims, worked out in Korea, meant that men badly burned healed far more quickly than they had previously when burns were covered.

Some techniques and processes were also worked out that improved the medical service provided. One was delivering blood in plastic containers so that the patient in need could be force fed if necessary. Also helpful was what came to be called litter integrity—that is, keeping the wounded man on the same litter all the way through the process. The fewer times he was moved, they discovered, the better off he would be. Another innovation (rediscovery, rather, for it was discovered in World War I and then forgotten) was the importance of artificially warming the injured patient. One way to do this was the use, starting in 1952, of the casualty bag, which increased the comfort and survival chances of the wounded.

Three more significant improvements came about during the war. One was the development of insulated footwear (called Mickey Mouse boots) to protect the soldiers' feet from frostbite. Very effective, it cut down on the cases that needed to be treated. Another was the armored vest designed to protect the mid-body and groin area. The armored vest made chest and abdominal wounds much more rare, but peripheral wounds became proportionately more common. The third was the development of the Jamesway, a weather-tight insulated tent stretched over a semicylindrical frame, which proved to be an excellent shelter and greatly improved the conditions in the surgical and medical area.

Air Force Medical

When the U.S. Air Force was established in 1947, it was agreed that the Army would provide medical care for two years. On July 1, 1949, the Air Force (AF) got its own. During the first months of the war, the Army and Marine preferred rail and sea evacuation, but it soon learned that aeromedical evaluation was good. In 1950, to cope with the rush of casualties, AF H-5 rescue helicopters went into action in the front line in medically equipped crafts. C-47 crews of the 315th Air Division flew into most forward strips to evacuate casualties under enemy fire. The 801st Medical Air Evacuation Squadron evacuated more than 4,700 casualties from the Chosin Reservoir.

While at the start of the war, the Army and the AF had not reached an agreement on a division of aeromedical responsibilities, by December 1951, the AF agreed that the Army and Marines should assume primary responsibility for forward medical evacuation and acquire their own aeromedical helicopter. The AF would supply longer-range evacuation. In December 1953, the AF was also given responsibility for organizing and staffing aeromedical facilities, and the medically designed C-131 Samaritan joined the AF fleet in 1954.

ENEMY MEDICAL SERVICE

The North Korean Medical Service was based on the Soviet model and was, at least on paper, well organized and efficient. But, in reality, they suffered a great deal from a lack of qualified personnel, necessary medical materials, and transportation. Supplies were mixed, coming from captured American and Japanese supplies, as well as some Soviet materials.

Evacuation was limited and the ability to move men back to better medical facilities was poor. In the North Korean Army, there were often clashes between doctors, who apparently considered themselves a higher class, and the cultural officers, who were trying to maintain at least the image of a classless army.

When the North Korean Army invaded, they looted South Korean medical facilities even though these facilities were very limited to begin with. More than 2,000 doctors were impressed into the invading army. For the North Korean soldiers, the lack of immunizations accounted for the 75 percent cases of tetanus among POWs who reached the 8054th. UN soldiers suffered very little from this infection. Most of the wounded North Koreans brought into aid stations had had their wounds dressed with leaves and old paper.[22]

CARE FOR THE DEAD

Part of the problem in dealing with those killed in action was identification. Battle tends to disfigure and dog tags are lost. During the Civil War, 42 percent of the casualties were buried without being identified. By World War II, this had been reduced to 3 percent (856 remains). It would be harder to do much better. But some difficulties remained. Most of the identification processes during the Korean War consisted of fingerprints and dental records, but not X rays.

At first the Graves Registration Units had no fingerprint kit, but it was soon discovered that a regular stamp pad would work. Every man buried in the UN cemeteries was fingerprinted, regardless of whether he was identified or not. Each body was carefully examined in order to make a note of all identifying marks, scars, and tattoos.

Since the war, the Joint POW/MIA Accounting Command (JPAC) has maintained five different teams whose responsibility it is to locate those 8,100 Americans who have not yet been accounted for. From the end of the war until early in 1990, the efforts to account for missing Americans provided few results but, in 1990, the North Koreans unilaterally returned more than 200 sets of remains. Because of the complications of commingling remains, few have been identified. Since 1996, with increased cooperation from the North Koreans, more than 170 sets have been returned. Most are believed to be Americans. By 2000, more than seventeen had been identified, while others were still being researched. One of the problems with identification is the poor quality of Korean-era dental records, which were not very detailed and thus of not much use in identification.

The JPAC is located at Hickman Air Force Base in Hawaii. Working in conjunction with the Department of Defense, every scientific effort is being made to locate and identify those American servicemen who have still not been accounted for. The JPAC meets every year, with families of those missing bringing them up to date on what has been discovered.

Claiming Remains

The lack of a consistent front, especially one that on occasion needed to withdraw, made it very difficult to claim all the American dead. Young men and women who fell north of the 38th Parallel were often left behind, their whereabouts unknown.

The armistice agreement signed in July 1953 included a provision for the exchange of military war dead on both sides. A final plan was signed by the Allies and the communists in July of 1954 and "Operation Glory" (Op Plan 14–54) on the 22nd. The KCOMZ Quartermaster Graves Registration Corps proceeded with the disinterment of the enemy dead and by August 30, 1954 began to deliver the bodies to the communist representatives. The communists did the same. On September 1, 1954, the UN received the first 200 remains. The exchange continued daily until September 21, when the communists turned over 123 remains and said that was the last to be discovered. A final total suggested 4,023 remains had been returned. At a meeting on October 11, both sides agreed to continue searching and to return what was found. For the United States, the search for the missing dead continues in 2006.

Cemeteries

During World War I, the remains were buried throughout Europe in one of the eight permanent cemeteries established and maintained by the American Battlefield

Monuments Organization. About 47,000 remains were returned to the United States for interment. During World War II, more than 250,000 U.S. soldiers were buried in temporary cemeteries, and many remain in more permanent locations.

In Korea, there were few cemeteries. It was quickly determined that it would be inadvisable to establish any permanent cemeteries in Korea. The order was given that all American casualties were to be returned to their homeland. There were several reasons for this. The main one was that the United States was not sure of being able to maintain control of an area that might be quickly overrun by the enemy. A second reason was that, at the time, unlike during other periods of combat, it was easier to bring them home.

Some temporary cemeteries were set up. In the beginning, it was determined that the most likely place for a cemetery was within 400 or 500 yards from the class I and class II supply points. The first interments occurred on July 23. Some thirty-two or thirty-three bodies were interred at Kwan-ni, only two of which were unidentified. "Some bodies were brought to the area by their regiments or companies. Others were evacuated through medical channels, and occasionally a driver would find a body along the road and bring it to us."[23]

Since the graves were temporary, there were no regulations to provide for beautification. Three flags flew, however: the United Nations at the front entrance, the United States in the center, and the Republic of Korea toward the rear. Sketches of the gravesites were forwarded to the Eighth Army graves' registration section.[24]

One illustration of the process can be found in the manner in which the 7th Division processed battle fatalities. Major Jacob W. Kurtz, Graves Registration Officer, had determined early that the casualty rate would be high and that the availability of supplies would be limited. In anticipation, he requisitioned 5,000 mattress covers, hundreds of identification tags, enough burial forms, some temporary grave markers, personal effects bag, burial bottles, a fingerprint kit, and an addressing machine. When the 7th Division arrived at Inchon, however, casualties were evacuated directly to naval craft and his section did not begin its work until the division headquarters had been set up at Pukchon.

A temporary cemetery was established there about half a mile south of the town. When a body came in, it was encased in a mattress cover. Each body was identified by unit and was given an emergency medical tag. Personal effects were then inventoried and put in bags for shipment. The graves were dug by Korean laborers who received two canteen cups of polished rice a day. Then the body was lowered into the grave face up and the burial bottle–which contained a report of the internment—was placed under the left arm. The grave was closed and a temporary gravestone was put up. Unless there was a chaplain available, there was no ceremony. In most cases, ceremonies were held after the grave was closed. A memorial service for those interned during the week was performed on Sunday.

CONCLUSION

The troops who served during the Korean War received the best medical treatment available. The goal of military medicine is to save as many of the wounded as possible, and to return men to active duty. In fulfilling this goal, the medical personnel during the Korean War could take advantage of the tremendous progress made during World War II. They also witnessed the emergence of evacuation systems and care provided faster than ever before. The recognition of speedy evacuation, aided considerably by the emergence of the helicopter, immediate care provided by up-front medical services, such as MASH, and the development of new methods of treatment for injuries and burns gave the wounded a far better chance of recovery than previously experienced. From treatment received by the corpsmen, to the hospital ships floating in the harbors, to every precaution taken to diagnose injuries, the object was to begin recovery as quickly as possible.

Dealing with the wounded and the injured under the most difficult of situations were doctors and nurses with little battlefield experience, but who learned quickly, performed majestically, and saved thousands of lives.

Considerable care was also taken for the recovery, identification, and dignified care of the dead. The rapid movement of the war, especially in the early phases, made it impossible to always recover the dead but, whenever possible, the military took on this task and that of clearly identifying the bodies of those who had perished. Often buried in temporary sites, they were, nevertheless, all brought home for final interment. This project continues even now, after more than half a century, as the remains of men lost are recovered and brought home.

NOTES

1. Frances Omori, *Quiet Heroes: Navy Nurses of the Korean War 1950–1953, Far East Command* (St. Paul, MN: Smith House Press, 2000), 10.

2. Albert E. Cowdrey, *United States Army in the Korean War: The Medics' War* (Washington, D.C.: Center of Military History, 1987), 134–136.

3. Frances Omori, *Quiet Heroes: Navy Nurses of the Korean War 1950–1953, Far East Command* (St. Paul, MN: Smith House Press, 2000), 6.

4. Omori: 6.

5. Omori: 38.

6. Marguerite Higgins, *War in Korea* (Garden City, NY.: Doubleday and Company, Inc., 1951), 28.

7. Joseph C. Goulden, *Korea: The Untold Story of the War* (New York: Times Books, 1982), p. 363.

8. Albert E. Cowdrey, *United States Army in the Korean War: The Medics' War* (Washington, D.C.: Center of Military History, 1987), 87.

9. Cowdrey: 74–75.

10. Cowdrey: 98.

11. Cowdrey: 151.

12. Cowdrey: 76.

13. Cowdrey: 83.

14. Addison Terry, *The Battle for Pusan: A Korean War Memoir* (Novato, CA.: Presido Press, 2000), 219.

15. Albert Cowdrey, *United States Army in the Korean War: The Medics' War* (Washington, D.C.: Center of Military History, 1987), 117.

16. Irvine H. Marshall, "Malaria in Korea" Paper presented 29 April 1954, Army Medical Services Graduate School, Walter Reed Army Medical Center, Washington, D. C.

17. Albert E. Cowdrey, *United States Army in the Korean War: The Medics' War* (Washington, D.C.: Center of Military History, 1987), 76.

18. Watson: 107.

19. Albert E. Cowdrey, *The United States Army in the Korean War: The Medics' War* (Washington, D.C.: Center of Military History, 1987), 194.

20. Cowdrey: 117.

21. Lamont Pugh, Paper presented before the Association of Military Surgeons of the United States, 17 November 1952.

22. Albert Cowdrey, *United States Army in the Korean War: The Medics' War* (Washington, D.C.: Center of Military History, 1987), 87.

23. John Westover, *Combat Support in Korea.* U.S. Army in Action Series (Washington, D.C.: Center of Military History, 1987), 144.

24. Westover: 181–182.

8 AWAY FROM THE FRONT LINES: DIVISION REAR AND THE TRAIN

They also serve who only stand and wait.

—Anonymous

DIVISION REAR

Division rear was located a considerable distance from the front line. Here, the Division Administrative Center dealt with the administrative duties of maintaining the division. It included the officers and men who were responsible for all personnel status changes, assignments, reassignments, rotations, awards, and promotions. It also provided the Post Exchange (PX), the postal system, and an officer who worked as a liaison with the Korean civil government. They controlled the hiring and firing of Korean personnel and screened those for potential use in the military service. It was here that legal arguments were settled, security was provided for warehousing, troops were paid at the end of each month, and personnel records were kept current. It was here that the replacement company and Division Rotation Center was located.

Most soldiers who were assigned to the rear areas lived better than those on the frontline. They seldom had to eat prepackaged food. They had the advantage of well-constructed latrines and "outhouses" that were quite sanitary and filled with lye to disperse odor and kill bacterial growth. The most familiar latrine was known as the "piss tube," an ammo sleeve of impregnated cardboard that was stuck in a small soak pit. Latrines were very much like those used in the American West for nearly a century, only usually made larger. A four-, six-, or eight-hole latrine was not unusual. There were always stories around about the result of such facilities being hit by North Korea rounds.

Four-holed latrine, constructed at Division Rear, Korea, 1953. (*Used by permission of the Center for the Study of the Korean War, Graceland University*)

Rear-echelon forces made up about 67 percent of the military personnel and they served an average of 18 months. Those who experienced frequent combat made up the other 33 percent.

While the ultimate goal of the military was to keep a well-trained, well-equipped soldier on the line, keeping him there was an immense job that took the efforts of thousands of other soldiers, sailors, airmen, and marines. This included workers from the GI who kept the pay records to the major-general who operated an immense staff of specialists. The armed services, like the government, is a massive bureaucracy. Little is done without proper paperwork and the innumerable "endorsement here-on" that verified and cross-checked each significant activity. The business of moving troops from one place to the other was almost as difficult in the United States as it was on line, for the orders, chits, memos, passes, TDY (temporary duty, yes) forms, and leave papers all had to be prepared.

Each soldier had to be paid, bathed, clothed, replenished, healed, transported, equipped, and kept track of. The "morning reports" were enough to occupy fully the time of many men who might otherwise have been on the line. Starting with procurement elements all over the world to carrying supplies to the men on the line, vast numbers of GIs were kept at work buying, sorting, moving, protecting, repairing, replenishing, and serving the forces. Each of these men or women was doing a significant job the service considered necessary, and in doing so each man or woman contributed to the successes in Korea.

While there was no way to cover all the military occupational specialities represented by those in the rear—from division rear back to the United States—there is some merit in talking about several of them. They are listed in alphabetical order.

Air Crews

The services all had and maintained aircraft for a variety of purposes. These ranged from the Piper used for messenger service and reconnaissance to the sophisticated helicopters used in rescue and evacuation. These planes had to be maintained and flown, as well as used for the related jobs at air stations and landing fields.

Band Members

Often not thought of when one considers an army in the field, bands played a significant role in Korea as they have always done. On June 30, just days after the war began, the 124th Army Band was attached to the Headquarters, Special Troops, Eighth Army. It accompanied the Eighth Army Headquarters to Korea on October 8 and was re-designated as the Eighth Army Band on November 8, 1950. It consisted of two warrant officers and sixty-eight enlisted personnel. On November 18, the 8th Army Honor Guard, 8230th Army Unit was activated. This unit's mission was to provide security for the Eighth Army Command Party and visiting VIPs, as well as furnishing troops for the ceremonial formations. It was awarded the Republic of Korea Presidential Unit Citation on January 19, 1953 for its contribution during the period April 22, 1951 to 89 July 1, 1952.

Chaplains

Concerned with meeting the spiritual needs of the serviceman, the armed forces have always maintained chaplains in the service. When there was almost no response to the volunteer call-up of reservist chaplains at the beginning of the war, it became necessary to initiate an involuntary recall. Beside those already called by virtue of the activation of Reserve and National Guard units, 240 company-grade Chaplain Reservists were individually ordered to active duty. Many chaplains were bitter after being "Johnsonized" (released as a result of Secretary of Defense Louis Johnson's cuts), but they returned and moved into positions to be with the troops. Boston's Roman Catholic Archbishop Richard J. Cushing told his people "Mass must be said within the sounds of the cannon. From now on, our priests will have less freedom and more work and can no longer afford to be spiritual millionaires while our men are dying in Korea."[1]

Clerks

The Army may run on its stomach, but every level of army life is constantly recorded by clerks. The vast amount of paperwork that the armed services maintained was primarily done by hand or on out-of-date typewriters and, generally, with numerous copies. It was a massive job and took the time of many men and women. From the company clerks and the ever present "Morning Reports" all the way up the line, just about everything the services did—from assignment to burial—required someone somewhere to fill out forms. These men were basically fighting men, and the number of times they were called from their clerical duties to occupy a position on the line, was significant. The diversity of their assignment covers the spectrum of human activity, including personnel clerks, financial clerks, supply clerks, and transportation clerks.

Communications

One of the most difficult jobs for the fighting men was that of communications (Commo) whose job it was to make sure that communication links were not snapped regardless of what was going on, either incoming or outgoing fire. It was a very hazardous

Setting up temporary communications camp, Korea, 1952. (*Used by permission of the Center for the Study of Korean War, Graceland University*)

job because the soldiers often worked exposed to enemy fire—not only small-arms-fire, but also artillery. They were armed with carbines and when possible wore flak jackets and helmets. The carbines were light and carried in case they met a Chinese patrol, but generally were not much defense. The flak jackets would protect them partially, but there was nothing to protect the rest of the body, the legs, and face.

Cooks

A lot is said of the Marines, where every man is trained as an infantryman and, on more than one occasion, this fact became very important. In several cases, cooks dropped their utensils and picked up their M-1 to take a stand. This happened often enough to bear out the importance of recognizing each man as a fighting man. The same was true, of course, for army personnel, for they too had undergone basic training as an infantryman, and there are several recorded occasions when the cook joined ad hoc units to fight as infantry. Their main duty was feeding the troops and, despite the grumbling, they did that quite well.

Engineers

The role of the combat engineer was somewhat unique, with many men coming into the units with specific skills already learned as civilians. They were builders and fixers. But they were also trained to fight and did so on many occasions—Yongsan, for example—just as they guarded the facilities they had created, and served as the rear guard defense as other soldiers and Marines moved back. In November 1950, the 2nd Engineers held while elements of the Eighth Army withdrew from Pyongyang. During the fighting in Korea, three engineers—Sgt George Libby, Corporal Dan Schoonover, and PFC Melvin Brown—all received the Medal of Honor, posthumously.

The job of the engineer was sometimes frustrating as, on more than one occasion, they would build a bridge in order to allow the UN forces to advance, then destroy the same facility during a withdrawal. "It didn't make much sense, but that's what the Army needed" reported Ray Miller of the 62nd engineers.[2] When they could, they would construct airstrips, POW facilities, and training areas; develop sewage and drainage systems, replace electrical grids, set up water systems and towers; and rebuild destroyed railway and port facilities. During the war, the engineering units suffered 2,706 battle casualties, including 850 deaths.

Fumigation and Bath Platoon

Certainly not the job most would have considered when enlisting, or being drafted, in the Army, but it was a vastly necessary and important responsibility in the constant battle to keep men clean and free from the many diseases waiting for them. While few men gave it much thought as they enjoyed a rare bath or were being debugged, they appreciated the outcome of this work.

Graves' Registration Units

There was also the unpleasant but vastly necessary role played by members of the Graves Registration Units. Since graves' registration is a wartime activity, the services were quick to disband them once World War II came to a close. At the time of the North Korean invasion, there was only one unit, composed of about thirty men, located in the Far East. It was immediately necessary to create temporary cemeteries for the internment of those who, it would quickly prove, had to be moved as the enemy advanced. As long as the line was moving, it was necessary to collect the bodies of those who had fallen, and as quickly as possible to avoid being overrun. Often, it was necessary to send out patrols to locate a missing man and bring him back alive or, if that was impossible, at least to bring back his body. The bodies were collected at a series of points, some buried quickly, only to be recovered when there was time to move them. Once located, the bodies were sent to Japan in refrigerated rail cars and ships where the Central Identification Unit, located at Kokura, Japan, made every effort to identify any bodies that were shipped home. It is estimated that 97 percent of recovered American bodies were identified.

Intelligence

The old joke about army intelligence being an oxymoron is only partially true. Considering the difficulties under which they worked most of the time, the intelligence officers and associated enlisted men did a fairly remarkable job. These responsibilities included the interrogation of prisoners, interruption of photo-reconnaissance, etc., and production of a great deal of intelligence about the enemy's intentions. While the intelligence operations at the highest levels—MacArthur's failure to anticipate the nature of the Chinese response is still being questioned—were not always successful, many of the smaller units showed important results.

Medical Personnel

Other than dealing with the wounded or seriously ill, the army had to provide whatever preventive and corrective medicine they could. Perhaps most appreciated, if not necessarily liked, were the dentists, who managed to work on patients suffering from tooth problems. Other services included the oculists who, with a tray of lenses, could fit you for a pair of GI glasses in no time. Another role consisted of improving personnel hygiene and sanitation, as well as the delivering the shots required to meet one crisis after another. There were also large numbers of enlisted men working at the medical facilities, dealing with everything from service as orderlies to X-ray technicians.

Military Police

The military police units provided a wide variety of services, playing a vital role behind the UN lines. They protected vital roads and junctions, installations, equipment, and supplies. They also worked at crime prevention, apprehension of absentees, accident prevention, and investigation. A major mission that evolved for the military police (MP) was the control of prisoners. By 1951, there were nearly 150,000 communist prisoners in a variety of camps. Disturbances in the camps were common and in October 1952, the 8137th Military Policy Group (Provisional) was established to control the growing difficulties in the camps. Military police were also ordered to conduct search-and-kill missions against North Korean guerillas. The 728th Military Battalion was awarded two Meritorious Unit Citations for maintaining the security of thousands of miles of roads and bridges during the war.

Motor Pools

The UN Command was a mobile one and required the services of thousands of vehicles, from tanks to jeeps. These machines had to be kept track of, serviced, maintained, repaired, replaced, and generally kept available for those who needed them.

Personnel

These men and women were responsible for dealing with the needs and the records of those who were serving. Among them, the legal officers provided legal aid to the serviceman and also served as the legal department for the service. It also included men and women working in finance, and who were responsible for keeping track of individuals' pay, making payments, and identifying allotments.

Ordnance

The nature of war makes the ordnance corps especially important. The acquisition, storage, supply, and recovery of ordnance, or the weapons, ammunition, vehicles, and related supplies, required a large number of men. They staffed the ordnance maintenance units, a recovery platoon, ordnance depots, as well as reclamation and classification units. Associated with them were members of the ammunition recovery platoons.

Quartermaster

In June 1950, the Quartermaster Corps geared up quickly to supply the armed forces with what they needed. This amazing large-scale logistic effort was conducted under trying conditions and the essential need to get what was needed to the troops as quickly as possible. Members of the Corps, both the highly qualified managers and specialists and the grunt at the warehouse, contributed to the almost overwhelming task of collection, allocation, and delivery of supplies to the soldier in the field. The variety of what was needed made up an inventory of supplies and equipment far in excess of the largest civilian distribution systems, and included everything from providing toothpaste to returning the bodies of the dead.

Recreational Personnel

The military was well aware of the value of recreation, especially when men came back from the lines for limited times. The most popular consisted of sports. But there were also other kinds of entertainment provided: card and board games, movies, music, an opportunity to write home or—on an extremely rare occasion—put through a radio call to the United States. All this was put together by officers and enlisted men given this responsibility.

Replacement Companies

As difficult as it was to locate replacements, it was made more difficult by the processing the services required. Troops coming into or leaving Korea were processed

Volleyball game in progress, Korea, 1952. (*Used by permission of the Center for the Study of the Korean War, Graceland University*)

through the replacement companies—dull, drab areas where the chief occupation of the replacement or person rotating was waiting. Behind the scenes, however, it was necessary to get the soldier ready to be placed in a unit or, in the happier scenario, on his way home.

Signal Battalion

Because of the nature of Korean roads and terrain, as well as the distance and speed with which communication was needed, the use of wire was limited. The Signal Corps VHF radio became the backbone of tactical communication through the war.

Troop Information

While the news was generally old, and often bad, the military did make an effort to keep the troops informed. This included the preparation and release of unit newspapers, the distribution of the *Stars and Stripes,* and the broadcast of the Armed Forces Network. All of these required large numbers of men and, sometimes, women. The counterpoint of this service included those who worked in mis-information and who created, printed, and distributed propaganda materials, administering psychological war programs against the enemy.

Veterinary Services

Despite the fact that the cavalry was no longer a basic unit in the army, there were animals at war that required medical treatment. There were dogs in service during the Korean War and they needed treatment. The military also used some mules and horses and these animals needed constant care. As the war went on, horses and mules were captured from the Chinese and the North Koreans and were used as highly effective pack transportation. One famous mule was discovered to have a U.S. Army, Preston Brand 08Ko. He was one of the mules shipped to the China–Burma–India theater during World War II and had been commandeered by the Chinese Army.

And More

There were many roles that have not been identified but which were just as critical to the success of the military effort. However, to catch something of the diversity of the assignments, one must look at the chemical and chemical decontamination units; pipeline companies; maintenance and construction battalions that seemed to be constantly rebuilding; topographical map services; linguistic and cryptology sections; a vast variety of engineering units, including a Treadway Bridge Company; men of the battery searchlight companies; jail keepers; quartermaster, reclamation and maintenance; as well as laundry units; transportation units for light, medium, and heavy trucks; a cement unit; vehicles and their drivers for half a dozen service vehicles; railway transportation crews; signal battalions; and radio relay companies. There were also hundreds of men involved in work as stevedores to load and unload the massive amount of supplies being delivered.

NAVAL TRAINS

In the Navy, those ships and men who carried the responsibility for supply and service were called "The Train." In addition to the ships identified as "fighting ships,"

ships that were involved in the complexity of keeping the military machine moving were the ships of the train. On each of these ships, officers and men carried out their duties, dealing with everything the situation could send: bad storms, freezing water, mines, as well as tedium and hard work. Among these ships, on which men served long hours, were fleet oilers, hospital ships, landing ships (dock, men, rocket, tank), minesweepers, patrol craft escorts, picket ships, repair ships, supply ships, general and ammunition, tenders (general, aviation, seaplanes, submarine), attack transports, ocean tugs, as well as underwater demolition teams, and amphibious construction battalion, fleet activities units, and Naval beach groups.

Some ships bridged both worlds, providing service but also involved in the fighting. Among these would be the APDs, or "High Speed Transports." These ships provided the core for multinational raiding parties that struck North Korea's railway systems. The most active were the USS *Horace A. Bass* (124), *Diachenko* (123), and *Wantuck* (125).

Picket ships, often destroyer escorts, served to warn the United States if the Chinese or Soviets decided to commit their fleets or planes in any aggressive manner. These pickets were to provide the first warning. Other ships would include communication relay ships, reefers (insulated or refrigerated cargo space), combat stores, weather, and search and rescue ships. Tenders were designed to provide support, including repair and maintenance, to the crafts assigned to them

Replenishment at sea (underway replenishment) was an art difficult to recapture. A severe shortage of auxiliaries required for this demanding task meant that warships had to retire to port in order to obtain fresh supplies of ammunition or provisions. Because of the intensity of the action, this often meant a return to Japan every five or six days. If the warships could be kept close to the Korean shore, they were far more available for whatever action was required. By autumn, replenishment at sea was again the routine undertaking that it had been in the heyday of World War II. The new ability meant that the carriers and gun ships could replenish every few days while remaining near the Korean coast to supply firepower when needed.

Naval Construction Battalions

When the war broke out, the strength of the naval construction battalions was at about 3,300 on active duty. The number peaked at about 14,000. The Seabees supported the U.S. Marines in Korea, especially in the area of airfield maintenance and construction. The shortage of native skilled labor made the work even more difficult. Several events during the war reflect the duties as well as the skill and courage of these men.

In September 1950, as UN troops landed at Inchon, the Seabees, in what was known as the "Great Seabee Train Robbery," moved behind enemy lines and captured some abandoned locomotives to help relieve the bottleneck at the harbor. These same men were responsible for putting the operating ports at Inchon and Wonsan back in business. In 1952, called on to create a runway on Yo Island, they managed to finish the 2,400 yard airstrip in only sixteen days.

CIVILIAN SUPPORT GROUPS

While there were many ad hoc groups of civilians that provided support to the troops in Korea—blood drives, letter writing, etc.—the vast majority of this service was provided by one of two groups who made significant contributions to the welfare of the GIs.

The Red Cross

Ever since Clara Barton, in 1861, came to the aid of servicemen and their families during the American Civil War, the Red Cross has played a significant role during times of conflict. Basically, the Red Cross provided a broad variety of services. For the battlefield, they supplied blood and plasma and thousands of surgical dressing. They provided a lot of personal care items, including ditty bags and sweaters, and million of envelopes and sheets of paper.

The Red Cross provided immunization for the members of a serviceman's family, emergency communication with family members, and aid for both the serviceman and his family in case of financial emergencies. They also provided inquiry, information, and indemnification services for family and friends. For troops on the move, the Red Cross provided hospitality services and canteen-type facilities. All sorts of morale-boosting efforts were provided for the serviceman and their families. For those wounded, or held as Prisoners of War (POWs), they provided stationery and a free first call home.

At the request of General MacArthur, the Red Cross expanded its emergency mobile recreation services, enabling it to give service not only to American troops but to all UN forces. By November 1950, the Red Cross had opened a center in Pusan and started a subsidiary mobile canteen and club services for isolated military units, combat returnees, military personnel moving by troop ship, flying personnel, ground crews, and air-evacuation patients. By spring of 1951, there were twenty-four Red Cross operational locations in Korea. In 1951, President Truman established the federal blood program, designating the Red Cross as the blood collection agency for defense needs. Overall, between 1950 and 1953, the Red Cross collected and procured nearly five million pints of blood for the armed forces.

In 1953, the Red Cross played an active role in Operation Big Switch, the exchange of some nearly 12,000 prisoners. They facilitated POW repatriation and provided badly needed supplies and comfort articles to released prisoners in North America, who had been denied them during captivity. Upon the POWs' return, the Red Cross provided free telephone calls to the families and other morale and welfare assistance.

Every month, in 1953, 18,000 Gray Ladies (Red Cross volunteers) served in military hospitals around the world. Each year, an average of 1,100,000 servicemen received Red Cross assistance at camps and hospitals, at home and abroad. Two Red Cross workers gave their lives during the Korean War.

Salvation Army

The Salvation Army was involved in Korea and, though it took a low-key approach to its service, is gratefully remembered by many of the men and women who served in Korea. Providing just about everything the GI might need for comfort, from spiritual support to hot coffee and doughnuts, and available remarkably close to the line, the Salvation Army's presence was very significant to those they served.

YMCA

In the 1950s, the YMCA operated under the YMCA Armed Services Department. The YMCA had offered some voluntarily provided relief service to Americans during the Civil War. They established their first permanent Army YMCA 1889 at Fort

Monroe, Virginia, and sent more than 500 volunteers to Cuba, Puerto Rico, and the Philippines during the Spanish American War. In 1917, it launched a massive program providing welfare and morale services, eventually serving more than 90 percent of American military forces in Europe. It was the largest voluntary support of American troops in history. During World War II, the YMCA and five other units (National Catholic Community Service, Jewish Welfare Board, Salvation Army, and National Travelers Aid Association) joined together to form the United Service Organization (USO). The USO deactivated in 1947 and the YMCA assumed responsibility for its twenty-six branches. In 1951, the USO was reactivated in Korea, where it served as a major agency of welfare and moral support for the armed forces.

United Service Organization

By 1947, the USO had all but disbanded. In 1950, when the United States entered the Korean War, Secretary of Defense George C. Marshall and Secretary of the Navy Francis P. Matthews once again called on the USO to provide support for the men and women of the armed forces. During the years 1952 and 1953, not a day went by without a USO providing service somewhere in Korea. By the end of the war, more than 113,000 American USO volunteers were working at 294 centers at home and abroad.

Bob Hope, who had entertained the troops so well during World War II, was in Korea at the end of 1950 and 1953. When he came to Korea in December 1953, he brought actress Terry Moore with him. She created quite a stir when she appeared in a two-piece ermine bikini. The reaction, from columnists and clergy, was that Terry

USO show seen, as most GIs saw them, from a distance, Korea, 1953. (*Used by permission of the Center for the Study of the Korean War, Graceland University*)

Moore had to be sent home. GIs argued that she should stay, saying that if she had to go home they would go with her. She stayed.

Many other stars came to perform, some very well known and others just up and coming in their careers. Marilyn Monroe came in March 1953 after her marriage to Joe DiMaggio. The list of the performers included Jack Benny, Errol Flynn, Danny Kaye, Al Jolson, Robert Merrill, Rory Calhoun, Mickey Rooney, Piper Laurie, Debbie Reynolds, Marilyn Maxwell, Frances Langford, Jayne Mansfield, and many others.

REPLACEMENTS AND ROTATION

In an effort to deal with the problem of low morale of men too long on the line, the Army developed a rather successful system of personnel and unit rotations. Moving men up and back provided some relief, and the mere fact of moving broke the routine of life on the line. On the line or at company level, many units established "warm-up-tents" just behind the line, where a soldier would get warm, read, write a letter, or even get a haircut. Sometimes units were pulled back to Division Rear, so they could get twenty-four to forty-eight hours rest, change clothes, maybe even get a shower.

The stay in reserves was about forty days. When the beer came in, everyone got three cans. Movies were on a makeshift screen and the seats were sand bags. One time the beer tent caught fire. The strong-backed tent was a total loss, but not a can of beer was lost. There were times when a USO showed up for an evening of entertainment, which was greatly enjoyed. To the men in the military, the girls looked fantastic in their dance costumes.

It worked all the way up. While companies would rotate platoons on line, so did the battalions, regiments, divisions, and even the corps. The Army also operated a rather extensive replacement program in order to rotate men from rear echelon positions to more active units.

In early 1951, the Department of Defense issued instructions for its rotation program, designed to increase individual morale and to soften some of the public criticism of the war. The system was based on four points, where those serving in a line unit (other than artillery) were granted four points a month. Artillery, as well as those who moved up and back to the front (transportation units, for example), received three points. Those who remained in the "rear or safe areas" received two points a month. A wounded man received four points a month until returned to his outfit. On achieving thirty-six points, the soldier was eligible not only for return to the United States but for discharge. The rotation system was simple and, according to its goal, effective. In theory, combat troops were sent home after they had completed a year in service, but this was often delayed because of the lack of replacements.

While it sounded good to the soldier in the field and provided some bit of hope for those facing the enemy, there were some distinct problems generated by the process. In the first place, it added to the need for men and an additional 1.2 million men were required to be drafted and trained. It also increased the demands for transportation to move an increasing number of men. By 1952, nearly 35,000 men a month were being rotated. The rotation of men also meant that experienced men and NCOs were being replaced by those who were just coming into the service.

In a less tangible sense, the promise of rotation and the identification of a date at which an individual's service was over produced "short timers" with a level of efficiency that was far less productive. Men who knew they were close to being discharged took fewer chances, tending to hold back and protect themselves as their due date grew closer. It also had the effect of disrupting the cohesiveness and effectiveness of units as long-term relations were fewer and movement with a unit shortened, giving men a sense of temporariness and less identification with the unit. Lack of strong attachments produced an effect that was later identified by the term "empty battlefield," which suggested a far less sense of comradeship than was enjoyed during World War II. Some of the friends made along the line lasted a lifetime. Many of those that the soldier expected to maintain ended when one or the other rotated home. But the ties seemed to be less pronounced than they had been in earlier endeavors. "Most of them never developed any feeling for a division in which they had not trained, in which they merely had put in their time."[3] Explaining, perhaps, the lack of reunions that are identified with the Korean War.

CONCLUSION

The military has about as many occupations as the civilian world, and men and women had to be trained to perform these duties. Divided between their particular skills and their role as fighters, all who were involved performed a necessary task in keeping the giant machine, the military, functioning well and efficiently. For every man on line there were dozens, even hundreds, of men and women performing the tasks necessary to keep them on the line.

These were the men and women who brought the supplies, cared for the wounded, kept records, trained recruits, maintained communications, supported the well being of the troops through entertainment, information, and education. They delivered mail, prepared food, fitted uniforms, repaired vehicles, calculated points, provided movies, printed newspapers, maintained contact with families, payed the troops, policed the area, and guarded the facilities.

Each and every one of them was essential for the proper conduct of the mission and, as such, all are Korean veterans who can well be proud of their service.

NOTES

1. U.S. Army Chaplain Center and School, "Remembering Our Army at War in Korea," www. usachcs. army. mil/korea/battleforkorea.htm.

2. Gary Turbak, "Engineers in Combat," *VFW Magazine* (November, 2002): 2.

3. T. R. Fehrenbach, *This Kind of War* (Washington, D.C.: Brassey's, 1953): 361.

9   VIEW OF FRIEND AND ENEMY

It might be said of Korea that it was a war of 1950 fought by armies of 1945 using tactics of 1916.

—James L. Stokesbury, *The Korean War*

ALLIES

While the United States provided a major portion of the military that fought along with the Republic of Korea (ROK) Army in Korea, other members of the United Nations made important contributions. The most significant contribution in terms of numbers came from Great Britain and her commonwealth allies, Australia, Canada, and New Zealand. The British responded immediately with a naval force that arrived shortly after the war began and stayed until the firing ended. The First Commonwealth Division, which was eventually formed, was certainly capable of fighting independently, but in the main they fought in conjunction with the other nations, and most often under United States command. The Commonwealth forces, in addition to British and Canadian ground troops, consisted of armored units, artillery, engineer, and medical units. Air units included carrier planes, a Royal Australian Air Force squadron, and planes from South Africa.

Other nations that were involved sent troops, usually of battalion size or less. The Belgian Battalion, including Walloon and Flemish companies, arrived in Korea in January 1951; the Luxembourg's Detachment of forty-eight men was with them; Colombia sent a frigate and a battalion; the only Latin American ground troops to serve with the United Nation forces; Ethiopia provided a battalion made up of volunteers from Emperor Haile Selassie's Imperial Guard; France sent the frigate *La Grandiere* and a battalion despite the fact she was involved in her own war in Indochina; a reinforced battalion came from Greece along with the 13th Transport Flight; the Netherlands provided a destroyer and an under-strength infantry battalion as well as some nurses; the Turks sent a military unit.

There were, as well, several nations who sent personnel to support the UN effort, but who did not send combat troops. Among these nations was Norway, whose Norwegian Red Cross supplied a mobile hospital, "Normash," with more than 100 medical personnel. Denmark sent the hospital ship *Jutlandia* and the *Bella Dan.* India sent a medical team. Sweden also provided a medical team, the first to arrive, and operated a field hospital until long after the armistice was signed. Even the Italians, who were not a member of the United Nations, supported a hospital unit at Yongdungpo.

Other nations that could not send troops nevertheless supported the UN cause by providing support in terms of money and materials. These efforts were often political rather than military, as nations sought to align themselves with the United Nations, but they were still valid contributions. These countries included Argentina, Brazil, Chile, Cuba, Ecuador, Lebanon, Liberia, Mexico, Panama, Nicaragua, Pakistan, Paraguay, Peru, Uruguay, and Venezuela. The contributions consisted of cash, (a much-needed commodity), canned goods, frozen meat, sugar, alcohol, blood, rice, cod liver oil, medical supplies, rubber, beans, shoe soles, and blankets.

It is not our purpose to report on these various commands, but the story of the American soldier in Korea cannot be told without some reference to the manner in which they worked and fought together.

Military forces from fifteen nations served in the United Nations Command. Five noncombatant nations provided hospitals or ambulance trains, and a good number sent supplies. The nations sending ground troops were the British Commonwealth, Belgium, Luxembourg, Colombia, Ethiopia, France, Greece, the Netherlands, the Philippines, Thailand, and Turkey. Eight nations supplied naval vessels—totaling more than 100—both fighting ships as well as supply and transport. Australia, South Africa, Canada, Greece, and Thailand provided aircraft, some fighters, and other transport and supply. Denmark, India, Italy, Norway, and Sweden provided medical units.

The Soldiers' Attitudes toward the ROK and the Allies

However else they may be described, the relations between the GI and the ROK troops were uneasy and often hostile. There was not a lot of respect for the ROK as fighting men even though there is considerable evidence that they fought hard and with great courage. Separating them was not only language but also culture, and a sense of mistrust that rose from the fact that most GIs could not tell a North Korean from a South Korean.

Interestingly, most American soldiers were remarkably humble about what they had done and were doing, and quick to acknowledge the service of the armed forces of contributing nations. Most officers and men maintained a deep respect for what they considered the "professionalism" of the other allies who fought with them. "Their praise of the allies—the French, Thais, Turks, and Abyssinians—was far removed from the grousing about allies that had marked most previous wars. Most Americans, privately, would admit the UN Troops were better than they were." This is interesting, as historian Fehrenbach pointed out, because captured Communist Chinese Forces (CCF) intelligence documents suggest the Chinese, at least, considered them (the USA) the best.[1]

Inter-Service Rivalry and Cooperation

There was always a little inter-service rivalry going on, even unit rivalry in the various services, each feeling they carried a greater part of the load. Certainly, the competitive spirit was encouraged.

During the war, there was a strong disagreement between the U.S. National Guard and the Regular army, primarily about the National Guard officers' ability to lead combined arms activities. This was true with Oklahoma's 45th, the Thunderbird Division, where guardsmen comprised about 22 percent of the strength, but held a vast majority of the senior ranks. Coming as they did during the latter part of the war, there was little chance to test this, but the feelings persisted. The conditions under which they were fighting may well have had more to do with the "inadequate performance" than any lack of training or ability on the part of the Guard.[2] There was a particular problem, however, that created a certain amount of hostility between the Army and Marines, hostility that surfaces sometimes even today. It came to a head following the battle of Chosin Reservoir, in which the Marines blamed the Army and Army leadership for some of the difficulties there. The Army, on the other hand, felt that the Marines preempted their prominent role during the time, and discounting their contribution. Much of that disagreement is reflected by the division between the survivors of the Chosin retreat into Army and Marine groups.

Most of the UN troops got along well. There were some tensions. The British and the French maintained some of their life-long mutual suspicions. The Americans and the British carried on in a good-natured, but sometimes stressed, friendship. South Africa refused to serve with the Commonwealth Division. But in the main, the nations worked closely, and carefully, together.

THE REPUBLIC OF KOREA MILITARY

It is important to remember that though the United Nations contingent fought effectively from 1950 to 1953, the significant portion of the brunt of the war fell on the Korean soldier. And despite the nearly overwhelming problems they faced, the South Korean soldier, sailor, and marine, fought with valor and sacrifice. It is somewhat difficult to see these men and women in any complete light, for the records that substantiates much of their growth and performance were never well kept, and those that were have either been lost or are incomplete.

Basic to the armed forces was the army. South Korean President Syngman Rhee had at his disposal a poorly trained army with little or no experience. When the Korean Military Advisory Group (KMAG) began to operate in late July 1949, the strength of the ROK had reached a bare 100,000 men. Most of these were in various stages of their early development. The ROK Minister of National Defense had determined, in the light of the build-up of troops and resources in the North, that a defense force of 400,000 was required to defend the nation. He envisioned a standing army of 100,000, an additional 50,000 in reserves, 50,000 in the police or constabulary, and 200,000 identified reinforcements. They were nowhere close to this size in force. The artillery consisted of about a hundred 105-howitzers, and there were no tanks available. Not only were they lacking in manpower but also in equipment and ammunition. President Rhee had complained to President Truman that while his KMAG advisors were saying that the ROK Army had ammunition for two months of combat, his own men had reported it would

Two Korean Service Corps workers, Korea, 1952. (*Used by permission of the Center for the Study of the Korean War, Graceland University*)

be enough for only about two days. The force they had available was composed of eight divisions, only four of which were of full strength. When the war broke out, some of the ROK units were still armed with Japanese rifles, but no ammunition had been manufactured for them since the end of World War II, and they were soon discarded. Ammunition for American weapons had, during the intervening years, been kept at a minimum by the Americans.

While in occupation, the United States had made an effort to create a force capable of providing protection and internal security and, in August 1948, this small force became the ROK Army. During the brief period between the time foreign troops were removed and the invasion took place, the KMAG, left behind to train the South Korean Army, had worked on the problem but, in all honesty, had not been all that successful.

Having fought with limited equipment for some time, the South Korean soldiers were very good at making the best use of what they could find. Addison Terry in writing about ROK soldiers at the battle of Pusan remembered, "The ROKs were literally loaded with captured rifles and burp guns, each man with two or three plus his own weapons. They always brought back any enemy equipment they could get their hands on, while our troops were doing well to hang on to their own gear."[3]

At first, Major General Chae Pyondgok, a veteran of the Japanese Army and a very aggressive leader, was given command of all South Korean forces. By the end of June, however, Chae lost command and was replaced by Major General Chung Il Kwon, who was more willing to withdraw in an effort to save those under his command.

The Armored Forces consisted of about twenty-six armored cars with a small-bore 36-mm cannon designed primarily for breaking up demonstrations. There were no tanks and few antitank weapons.

The ROK Navy was very small. Following the early occupation, the ROK worked on building up the navy, which, in the first instance, consisted of about 6,000 men in the Korean Coast Guard. This limited force had some experience, having been called on to put down the Yosu-Suchon Rebellion. By February 1,1949, the ROK government had increased its fleet to four flotillas which included a training unit. It also made an effort to update the warships and replace some of those passed on from the Coast Guard. Most of what they had were minesweepers.

The United States had promised to provide several ships, equipment, and spare parts during the latter half of 1949. As the promised help came in, they were able to equip each of their ships with .37-mm guns and machine guns. The navy also established a naval operation system.

To further their effort, the Koreans set out on a full-fledged fund raising effort and, eventually, raised enough to travel to America, where they bought four pursuit craft (sometimes referred to as sub-chasers). The first of these arrived on April 10, 1950. The ships were equipped with a 3-inch gun and antisubmarine equipment.

At the outbreak of war, the ROK Navy consisted of one U.S.-made 105-patrol craft (frigate) and a few small miscellaneous craft—primarily Landing Ship Tank (LSTs)—which tended to put them on par, or slightly ahead, of the North Koreans. The ROK Navy fired the first shots of the war several hours before the actual North Korean invasion. It spotted, fired on, and sank a former Japanese Navy transport as it approached Pusan Harbor. The sinking destroyed a battalion of the North Korean 766th Independent Regiment whose mission was to secure the port of Pusan.

After the American troops entered the war, it became the American War. Today most English texts largely ignore the highly significant contribution of the Korean soldiers. Their casualty figures have seldom been discussed. The ROK units fought for every bit of ground until they reached the Pusan Perimeter. By the end of 1952, ROK soldiers made up three-fourths of the front line troops and an estimated 53 percent of the total UN casualties were borne by the ROK.

As the navy began to grow, it recognized the need for some form of a naval combat team. In response, on April 15, 1949, a battalion-strength ROK Marine Corps was established to support naval landing operations. It got its first taste, and experience, when dispatched to the Chinju area on an expeditionary mission and later to Cheju-do on a mission of counterinsurgency. Advised by the U.S. marine personnel, it was organized by volunteers from the Navy and Coast Guard. The three battalions were organized as the 1st Korean Marine Corps Regiment.

The ROK Air Force consisted of a handful of light support aircraft and did not play a significant role during the war. The force amounted to twelve unarmed liaison planes and ten North American Texans, T6, primarily a training plane. At the time of the invasion, the Air Force consisted of about 2,000 men. As the North Koreans crossed the parallel, there was a group of Koreans in the United States training to fly F-51 fighters, and they returned to Korea in 1951 to deploy at Kangnung on the east coast. They formed two more F-51 fighter groups in 1952 and 1953.

Another group of ROK personnel to be considered was the KATUSA (Korean Augmentation to United States Army). On August 15, 1950, the Eighth Army was ordered to employ Korean recruits in the American divisions serving in Korea. The 7th Division, which was preparing for disembarkation to Korea from occupation duty in Japan, was included in this plan. This program, known as KATUSA, determined that each battery or company was to receive 100 Korean soldiers. These men were to remain a part of the ROK Army and were to be paid by them, but supplied by their assigned units. The KATUSA were to be paired with a "buddy" who would help with the adjustment into the American units. The 7th Infantry Division received 8,625 KATUSA.

While not without documented successes, there were several problems with this program. In the first place, the young men assigned were often raw recruits, some of whom had quite literally been taken off the streets, and their military training had consisted of being issued a uniform. They were unprepared for combat and were easily demoralized. In the units that followed the buddy system, it worked a little better than where they were placed in separate platoons. The reluctance among American units to accept KATUSA prevented the program from reaching its potential, but by the end of the first year of warfare, there were nearly 13,000 so involved. A new goal, 27,000, was set and reached by the end of the second year.

When isolated as separate units with American command, KATUSA tended to be most effective in specialized tasks: the guarding of an area, patrolling, and scouting. They also were helpful in the movement of heavy weapons in the tough Korean land. When properly trained, supported, and equipped, the KATUSA solder performed well, but the inequality of the preparation led to an inequality of contribution. The program continued during the war and is still in effect among American troops stationed in Korea. In 1998, the KATUSA Memorial was dedicated in Kapyong, Republic of Korea, sponsored and paid for by the members of the Association of 40th Infantry Division (California National Guard) Korean War veterans.

Finally, some consideration needs to be given to members of the Korean Service Corps. South Korean men who proved unsuited for military service were drafted into a labor force that was organized along military lines. It seems almost paradoxical, for these men, and sometimes women, often worked harder than what was required in the military. Their job was to carry supplies, food, ammunition, and building materials to the front when necessary. And when necessary, they returned with the wounded. When possible, they wore the same uniforms as the soldiers, but they did not carry weapons. For most, however, their uniform consisted of a light cotton shirt and trousers, an outer jacket and cap, and Japanese sneakers. They generally had a wool blanket of either Japanese or American issue. They were assigned a load of fifty pounds to be carried on an A frame, sometimes for as far as ten miles. Although many of these men served reluctantly and required careful supervision to accomplish their task, the vast majority worked hard, and played a major role in the effort to keep the troops at the front supplied with what they needed.

In addition to their portage duties, Korean service workers cut timber and aided in the construction of the fallback positions at the Wyoming and Kansas Lines, where they repaired and strung barbed wire. On the Jamestown Line, for example, men of the Korean Service Corps, sometimes numbering as many as 5,000, formed human pack trains that helped support the 1st Marine Division and evacuated the wounded. A significant number of patrols were accompanied by a team of Korean stretcher-bearers, who were vital to the evacuation of the wounded. It was a dangerous job; four men standing to carry a litter made an obvious target. Nevertheless, many lives were saved by these men who sometimes moved to the rear while a corpsman administered to the man they were carrying. They also moved through the deserted battlefields to bury the enemy dead and retrieve abandoned weapons.

Yet another group to be considered was known as the Partisans. The term was used rather widely at first to mean North Koreans who, having gotten away from their country, were willing to fight against the Democratic People's Republic of Korea. Eventually, these fighting men and women were identified as the United Nations Partisan Infantry Korea. It began with anticommunists who, in trying to avoid the North Korean advance, fled to the hundreds of islands on North Korea's west coast. They decided to fight and were given aid and weapons by the Eighth Army. By January 15, 1951, they had been organized into the Guerrilla Section, Eighth Army, G3 Miscellaneous. These units were dedicated but, in the long run, not all that successful.

The organization of these groups, and their American advisers and comrades, are best described by Ed Evanhoe in his excellent book on the Army Special Forces, *Dark Moon*. There is still a good deal to be learned, some of it will probably never be completely known. On the one hand, it appears that many of the archives dealing with CIA activities in Korea have been "misplaced." On the other hand, it is known that there was a good deal of unconventional warfare going on, and the CIA was involved in one way or the other. Most of the activities were carried out by North Korean nationalists, many of them very young, and were carried out under such names as Blue Boy and Donkeys. In total, there were probably some 23,000 involved.

In addition, there were efforts by American, British, and Korean units to penetrate enemy lines in order to gain information, conduct raids against selected targets, provide rescue missions, and to try to recruit more guerrilla groups. A good deal of the effort of these clandestine groups took place on the numerous islands that were located along the west coast of Korea, and included rather large raids on such places as Changsa-dong (on the southeast coast), Yonghung-do, and Taemu-do. After the end of the war, stay-behind missions by "Camel" and "Beehive" finally ex-filtrated from southern Hwanghae Province.

A related group consisted of those identified as "line crossers," who walked through friendly lines and mined areas to report on military activities in their areas. The enemy had its line crossers as well.

THE COMMUNIST FORCES

North Korea

The distinction between the combat-experienced North Koreans and the South Koreans was perhaps most dramatically seen in the leadership. Kim Il Sung was a military veteran with several years of combat experience behind him. Syngman Rhee, however, was a scholar-politician, and his primary commanders were, often as not, political rather than military officers.

During the summer of 1950, North Korean Premier Kim Il Sung had under his command an army of about 135,000 men. Many of the troops in the North Korean Peoples Army NKPA, about one-third, were veterans of the Chinese Civil War that had led to the formation of the People's Republic of China, in 1949 and many others had fought against the Japanese during World War II. The force consisted of 8 fully manned infantry divisions, a couple of under-strength divisions, 2 independent infantry regiments, 8 regiments of artillery (attached to a division), an armored car brigade with 120 Russian-built T-34 tanks, 4 brigades of constabulary, about 180 airplanes, and a small navy composed of a few surface boats.

The North Korean Army came under the control of the general headquarters at Pyongyang. The front headquarters usually consisted of three or four divisions. The infantry division used the triangular design and consisted of about 11,000 men. This included the staff at headquarters, three rifle regiments, an artillery regiment, signal, antitank, and training battalions, as well as reconnaissance troops, medical services, veterinary, transport, and supply.

The personnel at headquarters consisted of a major general and his staff and a senior colonel who was the political leader and supervised the politico-military activities. They also had the job of reporting any difficulties or deviations. The North Koreans broke with the communist tradition of avoiding permanent rank. In Korea, the officers were distinguished by red piping on their sleeves.

The division artillery was a regiment of about 1,000 men with two 76-mm gun battalions, a 122-mm gun battalion, a signal platoon, and a headquarters company. Each battalion had three firing batteries with twelve artillery pieces. Personnel carried the M1938 carbine. There was also a self-propelled artillery battalion consisting of three batteries with sixteen pieces (SU-76).

A rifle regiment was made up of three rifle battalions (about 2,500 men) and artillery. The battalions included three rifle companies, a heavy machine gun company, a mortar company, antitank gun platoon, signal, medical, and supply platoons. There were four squads in a rifle platoon, also headquarters staff, and a heavy machine gun section. Squads had light machine guns, a submachine gun, Soviet M189/30 rifles, and each rifleman carried two grenades. The Air Force consisted of about 200 planes and attack bombers, most of them Soviet-made Yak-9 and Il 10.[4]

China: The People's Volunteer Army

Although the U.S. forces had superior firepower as well as complete control of seas and skies, the Chinese People's Volunteer Army (PVA) foot soldiers performed very well during their first encounter with the modern U.S. Army. In terms of the number of troops, the forces during the first campaign from October 28 to November 5, 1950, were about equal. The same was true during the second campaign, which began on November 25 and lasted till Christmas Eve, 1950. The total strength, at the time, was about 150,000 men in 13th Army Group and 120.000 men in 9th Army Group. Lieutenant General Walker's Eighth Army and General Almond's Corps X had a combined strength of about 240,000. The U.S. intelligence assessment of the PVA at the time of the outbreak was at about 40,000, which was a massive miscalculation.

The Chinese troops first appeared on October 25, 1950, and only sustained combat until about November 5 of the same year. During this time, they were the cause of some 15,000 casualties. After this brief campaign, the PVA pulled back and broke contact with the UN forces. At first, this mystified most field commanders, leading many to believe that it had been a one-time effort. Later analysis suggests it was a message to the UN that if the latter would hold up, the PVA would not attack. Or, others have suggested it was simply an effort to lure the Americans further toward the Yalu River.

In the second campaign, Mao had reinforced the PVA by sending Song Shilun's 9th Army Group. The 13th Army Group was to counterattack the Eighth Army on the west and the 9th Army Group was to take on Corps X on the eastern front. On November 25, PVA forces shattered the ROK 7th and 8th divisions and exposed the right flank of the Eighth Army. On the 26th, facing the possibility of encirclement, the Eighth Army began its withdrawal. The 113th Division moved deep across UN lines in a forced march of forty-five miles in fourteen hours by foot to capture Samso-re. To avoid the growing trap, the UN forces broke out westward along the route of the 24th and 25th Divisions. By December 1, UN forces were ordered south of the 38th Parallel. The UN forces, mechanized, moved faster, and only a small group of the PVA followed the retreating forces.

There is considerable support for the belief that the soldiers of the PVA could move at extremely high rates of march. On more than one occasion, chroniclers reported that PVA units marched up to eighteen miles a day, and did so for a period of eighteen days at a time. When they moved, they did so mainly at night.

The Chinese People's Liberation Army (PLA) Air Force was organized in 1949 and by the outbreak of war had about 100 planes. By December, through purchases from the Soviet Union, the number reached 600. Of this number, it is estimated that 250 were conventional and jet fighters, 175 ground attack planes, 150 conventional twin-engine planes, and 75 transports.

The PLA Navy consisted of a light cruiser, twenty or so frigates and destroyers, some light landing craft, and a few hundred gunboats and speedboats.

The PLA field forces were organized as four field armies—the First to the Fourth—and some separate units known as the North China Independent Unit. In each field army, were army groups and divisions. Of the six armies, each was equipped with three infantry divisions (about 30,000), two artillery divisions, a cavalry regiment, and two truck regiments. Officers of the PLA did not have nominal ranks as did UN commanders, but held provisional ranks of about the same equivalent. The commander of a regiment was a provisional commander and his staff officer executive had the rank of assistant regimental commander.[5]

When the Chinese had to move supplies by road, they did so mainly during the night and without headlights. It was the custom to place spotters on the hills to warn the drivers of approaching aircraft and allow them to take cover. When they moved supplies by foot, they could slog across the hills, moving through the steep terrain, across primitive trails, and through roadless valleys. The PLA operated along the lines established by the guerilla warfare doctrine of Mao Tse-tung and articulated in his work *On Protracted War.*[6] It is important to remember that only a fraction of the PLA entered Korea. The total number under arms was close to two million.

Morale

At first, the morale of the PVA was high, but after 1951 or so it seemed to have dropped. The victory, promised by their leaders, was slow in coming and very costly. Discipline was strict but surprisingly moderate, punishment was more inclined to be a matter of reeducation, and even deserters were sometimes let off. The discipline carried over in their treatment of the Korean civilian population, where troops were directed to treat the Koreans with respect. Some Chinese units offered special awards for those who performed some heroic action in respect to the population, and units even raised money for famine relief during some periods of the war, mainly the floods of 1951.

The Chinese soldiers had many problems and as an army faced considerable difficulty. The other side of the equation was that they were tough, combat-experienced, and were led by confident officers. And, they had the advantage of fighting an enemy that seriously underrated them.

The recruiting officers located potential "volunteers" and arranged for them to join. The first order of business, once enlisted, was a vigorous indoctrination program that was more political than it was military. They underwent what the Chinese called "hsinao," a form of what the UN called brainwashing. The new recruits then, in turn, became part of the political "spy system" used to keep the troops ideologically pure. Most of the young men and women came from poor families and had lived with cold and hunger most of their lives. They were strong, used to hard work, long walks, and carried heavy burdens, and while the army life included discipline, it was not all that different from what they were used to. While the Chinese tended to mistreat the individual soldiers, beatings were not uncommon; most of the young soldiers did not find that the military service differed a great deal from their lives as peasants.

Another aspect of the Chinese Army worth noting was the tendency to organize their units along ethnic lines. Some units of even battalion size, and occasionally divisions, were pulled from the same general area, with replacements drawn from that area, so such units tended to have a sense of unity from the beginning. Another aspect of the Chinese soldier that worked to the advantage of their commanders was that there was no provision for the individual soldier to be discharged. Once they had "volunteered," they were a part of the Army until no longer capable of service. A soldier could be released because of wounds or disease and, eventually by virtue of age, but there were no "rotation points."

Arms

The North Korean military was the creation of the Soviet Union. At first, they carried a few Japanese rifles, which they discarded when the ammunition ran out. Most of the Soviet issued weapons, but not all, were left-over World War II weapons. One of the great disadvantages faced by the average member of the communist forces was the varying type of weapons available. It was not uncommon to find a variety even within a given regiment or battalion. Many carried Japanese weapons confiscated after the end of World War II. The communist army had captured a large number of American arms from the Nationalists during the Chinese Civil War. A surprising number of Chinese soldiers were armed with M-1 rifles and Thompson submachine guns. They were particularly well supplied with American 60-mm mortars. Some arms were furnished by the Soviet Union, mostly submachine guns, recoilless rifles, and some mortars. Also, there was a variety of weapons taken from UN troops— British, Czech, German, and Canadian. The primary disadvantage was the logistics of supplying ammunition. The Chinese, however, were often able to pick up what they needed from the UN troops.

Armor

The communists had the T-34 tank, which many authorities consider to be the best tank to come out of World War II. They also had available the BA-64 armored car. The T-34/85 was equipped with a 76-mm gun. The North Koreans were reported to have 150 of these weapons.

Food

The accounts of Chinese soldiers living on "a pound or two of parched grain-meal in a cloth roll . . . with no water" may be somewhat exaggerated, but not by much. Supplies were slow in coming, and most of these peasant-born soldiers suffered from insufficient calories. However, they were hard men and learned to live in difficult situations. They quickly became used to the fact that they often fought with inadequate supplies of ammunition, food, and clothing. Most of the time they were forced to forage for food, taking it when it could be found. A good deal of the time these Chinese soldiers moved forward into battle, tired and hungry, and often aware of the necessity to preserve what supplies of ammunition they had.

Clothing

Most of the Chinese soldiers wore a uniform composed of a two-piece reversible mustard-yellow and white costume made of quilted cotton. They were equipped with a heavy cotton hat that, in most cases, had fur-lined earflaps. On some of these hats, there was a string attached to pull the flaps close over the chin. The "winter" uniform was often worn over a standard issue summer uniform and many of the troops wore every piece of clothing they owned. What few gloves they had were, in fact, mittens. Many carried a shawl-like blanket in which they wrapped most of their personal belongings.

For shoes, they were equipped with a canvas shoe that had a rubber sole. As the war went on, the Chinese appeared with some half-leather shoes and, occasionally, a leather boot. Footwear was often taken from dead or captured UN troops, but there was always the problem of size. If forced to, a coat that is too small or too large can be worn, but that is particularly hard with shoes.

THE UN VIEW OF THE ENEMY

During the early phase of the war, the capabilities of the army of the Democratic People's Republic of Korea (DPRK) and the People's Liberation Army (PLA) were frighteningly understated. The DPRK army, and at one time the PLA, was talked about in terms of a "peasant army" for which there was little early respect, if in fact the comments were not downright racially stigmatizing. General MacArthur often referred to his enemy, the North Korean leader Kim Il Sung, as "Kim Buck Too." Presidential envoy, General John Church, included sentiment in his report on the outbreak of the war; "a few white soldiers will scare the shit out of the gooks and the war will be over in no time." Even the well-regarded Marine, Chesty Puller, is reported to have commented that "There aren't enough Chinese laundrymen in the world to stop a marine regiment going where it wants to go."[7]

These sentiments arose out of a time and a place that was neither well informed nor politically "correct." More than anything, they represented a dangerous lack of appreciation for the strength of the enemy they were to face. It did not take long, however, for those involved to realize that the communist soldiers were tough, well-supplied, and well-led.

The tough North Korean soldiers soon earned the respect, if not the admiration, of the GI on the line. They turned out to be a capable enemy and, particularly at first, their military determination was frightening. The Chinese, despite all the potential warnings, came as a surprise to many.

There were several reasons for the UN failure to anticipate the Chinese attacks, two of them worth noting here. One had to do with the fact the Chinese were able to cross the Yalu and remain unidentified by rigid march and bivouac discipline, movements under the cover of darkness, and the fact that few UN reconnaissances were operating in the area. The second had to do with a sort of "code" used by the Chinese in identifying their units. The most difficult was the Chinese use of battalion for division. This and other disfigured designations led the UN intelligence officers to acknowledge the presence of twelve Chinese infantry divisions across the Yalu, when later information proved there were nine armies, consisting of thirty infantry divisions. Nevertheless, at one point, the myth of Chinese superiority had grown to such a proportion that, following an attack on Hill 355, the Commonwealth Division Headquarters found it necessary to circulate a memorandum reminding its troops that the Chinese soldier was not a superman.

Many of the myths, both supportive and frightening, were simply not true. The first was that the Chinese were all very small, and then that they were all very big. In fact, they were in about the same variants of size as the other men on the battlefield. Another myth was that they did not know how to shoot their weapons. It is true that neither the North Koreans nor the Chinese spent a lot of training time on individual target practice. Instead, they operated on the theory that a cheap automatic firing weapon would be much more effective. But the communist troops could shoot.

Neither is there much truth in the myth that the Chinese suffered less from the cold. The communist soldiers had a great deal in their favor, including a previous lifestyle that was full of poverty and discomfort. They were tough and hardened, and they did not expect as much in terms of comfort as did the UN troops. The U.S. official history suggests that the "grounds on which the communist forces could endure the cold were in their inborn adaptability, spirit to overcome poverty and shortage, and strict discipline."[8] But they suffered cold, desperately.

It was also true that their equipment and clothing provided far less protection from the elements than did that of the UN forces. In 1950, the PVA, 9th Corps, suffered one-third of its troops out of action through frostbite over a four-week period.[9] During the severe winter of 1951, they did not have enough supplies or heating apparatus and were often ordered to hide in the shaded areas to avoid air detection, spending the entire day dealing with the cold as best they could.

ENEMY ACTION

There were some common characteristics to the CCF movements on the attack. They almost always approached at an oblique to the northwest, facing the American perimeter and usually followed streambeds, or roads parallel to them. They approached in solid columns and usually moved forward at double time. They carried their own supplies so as to make each man capable of individual action. They generally appeared fresh. Generally, when an attack was made, it was along the whole front with several offensive movements going on at the same time. When they were in the retreat or tactical retrograde, they would withdraw by means of the low ground.

The Chinese used a great deal of diversionary tactics. While a unit would attack the line, others, supported by tanks, bugles blowing, arrived at the flanks, hitting with direct fire. It often appeared to the UN soldier that they were attacking in every direction at once. They would advance, often yelling and screaming as they did (thus initiating the commonly held belief they were on drugs) using hand grenades, guns, mortars, artillery rounds, rifle, and machine gun fire all at once. Unless they could be stopped, they kept coming, moving into the trenches, the bunkers, and fox holes. Often such attacks ended in hand-to-hand fighting.

On the defensive, both the North Koreans and the Chinese Communist were committed to fighting from strong fortifications when possible. Once the temporary cease-fire line had been established, the Communist forces, which had only been able to build up its positions during the night because of UN air and artillery bombardment, found they could work on the effort day and night. What they accomplished was the creation of a line stronger than the French Maginot Line. In order to deal with the superiority of the UN fire, they constructed underground tunnels and trenches on the reverse slope large enough to accommodate all their men. In rear areas underground forts along the line from the east to the west coast had connecting tunnels to bring supplies and reinforcements to their forward positions. In the building of their fortifications, they utilized lumber, rock, and sand. They did not have access to as much concrete as the UN forces. But they built large areas: one mess hall discovered was big enough for a platoon.

It was the communist policy to dig foxholes as soon as they took an area. They then would construct bunkers on the tops of the hills from which they could keep track of their own forces as well as those of the enemy. Often they dug from the back of the mountain and, on arrival at the far side, would develop trench works with various gun mounts in all directions. They set up barbed-wire fences in multiple belts around their positions and laid numerous mines. They also prepared mine holes so that mines could be laid in front of a second defense line, if they were forced to retreat.

Something of the significance of these fortifications policies can be seen in the careful manner in which Communist command kept track of their activity. The Chinese Communist officially published history of the conflict lists the construction of 7,789 trenches that were 198.7 km long; 750,000 covered shelters and covered and uncovered foxholes that ran 3,420 km long. The North Koreans were responsible for 1,730 trenches 88.3 km in length, and 260 km of foxholes.[10]

In a Chinese evaluation document, "Primary Conclusions of Battle Experience of Unsan," an evaluation is offered about the troops they were facing:

> When cut off from the rear, American soldiers abandon all their weapons, leaving them all over the place and play opossum . . . Their infantrymen are weak, afraid to die, and haven't much courage to attack or defend. They depend on their planes, tanks, and artillery. At the same time they are afraid to advance further . . . they specialize in day fighting. They are not familiar with night fighting or hand-to-hand combat. If defeated they have no orderly formations. Without the use of their mortars they become completely lost. At Unsan they were surrounded for several days and did nothing.[11]

After the battle, it was necessary to bury the dead. Because the communist soldier did not wear dog tags or means of identification, there was no real benefit from giving them separate graves. It was determined early on to bury them in groups of thirty-five to fifty. The burial was done with no ceremony and with little attempt to identify the gravesites.

CONCLUSION

In many respects, the war in Korea was a world war. More than thirty nations were involved, many actively supporting troops. The difficulty of the task—fighting a determined enemy—was magnified on both sides by the differences of those involved. For the Communists it was the conflict between Chinese and North Korean leadership, the supply confusion of differing weapons, and the low-key but pressurized involvement of the Soviet Union. For the United States, fighting as the United Nations, it was the difficulty of dealing with nearly twenty nations, all with their own ways of doing things, all with different agendas, sometimes with different weapons, and demanding different supplies.

On the UN side, there was also the problem of diverse languages, cultural backgrounds, and racial attitudes. Generally, the UN countries represented got along well with little real difficulties, sharing the common goal with as few problems of nationalism and cultural identity as possible. The Americans got along with the other nations but, because of the predominance of American command, there was some resentment. There were disagreements among the Commonwealth nations, some problems with the placement of South African units, but, in most cases, respect and dependence on one another won out. In general, the Americans and the ROK troops got along, shared mutual respect, even though there were some concerns among the Americans as to the dependability and fighting endurance of the ROK.

The Americans seemed to have a great deal of respect for the abilities of the Asian soldier once they came face to face with the reality rather than the myth. While they considered North Korean soldiers to be less efficient and more cruel than the Chinese, they nevertheless respected the abilities and the determination of the Communist troops. The Chinese were considered more professional and provided better treatment for their POWs than the North Koreans.

Certainly, the ability to keep a wide variety of nations working together in the Korean War is one of the high points of the leadership there.

NOTES

1. T. R. Fehrenbach, *This Kind of War* (Washington, D.C.: Brassey's, 1963), 422.

2. William M. Donnelly, "Thunderbirds in Korea: The U.S. 45th Infantry Division, 1950–1952," *Journal of Military History* 64 (October, 2000): 197.

3. Addison Terry, *The Battle for Pusan: A Korean War Memoir* (Novato, CA: Presidio Press, 2000), 197.

4. John Gittings, *The Role of the Chinese Army* (London: Oxford University Press, 1967), 141–142.

5. DA PAM 3051 *Handbook on the Chinese Communist Armies,* September, 1952: 75–76.

6. Allen Whiting, *China Crosses the Yalu: The Decision to Enter the Korean War* (New York: MacMillan, 1960), 132–133.

7. Thomas W. Smith, Jr. *Alpha* Brovo* and Delta* Guide to the Korean War* (Indianapolis, IN: Alpha Books, 2004), 103.

8. Korean Institute of Military History, *The Korean War* 3 (Lincoln: University of Nebraska Press), 274.

9. Stanley Sandler, *The Korean War: No Victors, No Vanquished* (Lexington, KY: University Press of Kentucky), 121.

10. Korean Institute of Military History, *The Korean War* 3 (Lincoln: University of Nebraska), 271–272.

11. T. R. Fehrenbach, *This Kind of War* (Washington, D.C.: Brassey's, 1963), 200.

10 MEDIA, MORALE, AND MYTHS

I only know what I read in the newspapers.

—Will Rogers

The key to understanding much of what was accomplished in Korea has to do with the attitudes of those who fought the war, whether they were on the line or manning the Post Exchange (PX. This attitude was fed, as well as adjusted, by the myths that grew up around what they were doing, and by the media's reporting of their story to the world. The attitude among the military, and what is constantly being gaged, is their morale. Thus, there is a connection between these topics, which all play a part in constructing the military mind of the men and women doing the fighting.

NEWS MEDIA COVERAGE

The military was ill prepared to deal with the correspondents who emerged on the scene during the early days of the war. In the space of only five months, correspondents serving in Korea moved through a period of reporting censorship, to accepting voluntary censorship, to trying to report with full-field censorship. Almost immediately there were concerns that an uncontrolled press was providing information to the enemy and, perhaps more important, were undermining the morale of the American and UN forces. Military commanders justified the progressive restrictions they imposed on the media on the basis of operational security. While the correspondents seemed to believe that the restrictions were designed to protect the public image of the military, the Overseas Press Club nevertheless asked the Pentagon to provide a set of standard guidelines.

Very quickly, however, General MacArthur imposed his own censorship. He forbade reporters from criticizing such things as military reserves, the failure of U.S.

equipment, or the performance of ROK soldiers. He also banned any article that was critical of his leadership. When his successor Lieutenant General Matthew Ridgway took command of the UN forces in Korea, he virtually banned any press coverage of the ongoing armistice talks.

Since the U.S. Army Signal operated the only telephone exchange that connected Japan and Korea, the military was able to control the flow of information in any manner they wished. Some journalists, however, were able to get rides to Japan and then delivered their text by sending it home with someone heading for the States.

All in all, there was little critical reporting during the Korean War. What there was tended to support uncritically the stated U.S. policy, which meant, as Bruce Cumings suggests, that the war was not so much forgotten as it was unknown. This was true because the mainstream media failed to provide an accurate account. The skepticism that journalists acquired in Korea of U.S. military leaders' motives would come back to haunt the generals in Vietnam. Battlefield conditions and new communications technology virtually ruled out any form of censorship during the Vietnam War.

Television

The Korean War was the first American war to be covered by television. Television was in its infancy, however, and very few viewers had access to a television set. In 1950, fewer than 10 percent of U.S. homes owned a television and at the war's end, it had only risen to 40 percent. The physical problems of overcoming technological obstacles in the field of battle served as an unintended censorship of what was filmed. More important, however, was the fact that because there were no satellite services, television film had to be transported physically and by the time it arrived, its value as news was gone. Because of this, newspapers and radio remained the primary source of news coverage.

Radio

In general, there were few on-site radio broadcasts. Not only was there heavy censorship imposed by the military, but an almost total lack of communication facilities available to the broadcasters. There were some correspondents in the field, however. Lou Cioffi was wounded in action and awarded the Purple Heart while reporting live. Edward R. Murrow did some radio broadcasts from Korea, following much the same pattern that he used in his reports from London during World War II. The retreat to the Pusan Perimeter was pretty well covered by the press.

Some reporters called Korea a "censorship without a war." Jack James, manager of the Seoul United Press bureau, was the first to report on the war. Bob Bennyhoff used a field telephone rigged by the Army Signal Corps to report live to New York (by way of Tokyo) on a tank battle at the Naktong River in 1950. He also reported the Capital Division's crossing first into North Korea. When the armistice was signed in 1953, only one reporter, LeRoy Hansen, was present and reported using a field telephone.

MORALE

There is always a period of excitement, maybe even euphoria, at the beginning of a war. There was, in Korea, a certain arrogance as well, for many officers passed on to their men that they were involved in fairly simple tasks, and an exercise that would end soon. Surely, it was believed, the appearance of Americans would slow down, if not completely stop, the North Korean advance.

This was not the case. For many Americans, the first encounter with the communist forces was "disturbing, confusing, demoralizing, brutalizing."[1] Under the pressure, and unprepared for appropriate action, some men turned and ran. War correspondent Marguerite Higgins of the New York *Herald Tribune,* generally friendly to the GI, reported during the first days of the war, "I saw young Americans turn and bolt in battle, or throw down their arms, cursing their government for what they thought was embroilment in a hopeless cause."[2]

At home, the situation was just as involved. Most Americans accepted the idea of the Korean War as part of the containment of communism, and simply an aspect of the otherwise cold war. The war, in their mind, was a shadow of the much larger fear of the Soviet Union and the prospects of World War III.

There is a great deal of disagreement among historians about the morale levels of GIs during the Korean War. It might be stated, however, that morale tended to be correlated to the conditions under which the soldiers fought. There is evidence that, in the early stages, most American troops were under the impression they could "lick" this enemy quickly and were not disillusioned of this fact until they came face to face with the determined and capable soldiers of the Democratic People's Republic of Korea (DPRK). During the initial defeats and the defense of Pusan, morale began to drop and was at its lowest point just prior to the end—around invasion at Inchon. After that, and during the advance toward the Yalu River, morale rose only to be hit hard with the Chinese intervention and the drastic defeats and retreats. Despite the efforts by General Walker to encourage his troops, morale was perhaps at the lowest at the point when Lieutenant General Ridgway took over command in December 1950.[3]

Defeat and retreat is always hard on any unit, and for the retreating Eighth Army, it was no exception. Much can be said for the argument that a significant factor in the low esteem of the Army during this bleak time, was its failure to properly measure its own strength and ability.

As the war settled into a static war, troop morale was considered level; that is, neither very high nor disastrously low. There was little doubt that the GIs in Korea hated the war and disliked being there, regardless of their assignments, and they were generally unable to comprehend either the political goals envisioned in Washington or the concept of the limited war they were soon expected to fight. It appears, however, that once the war settled down, there was little evidence of the swings of morale suffered during the early months of the war. There was, however, a strong sense of fatalism among troops, not unlike the case in other wars, where men placed themselves in the hands of fate assuming their life or death was determined (already) by events beyond their control. Addison Terry wrote: "although the policy makers in Washington had published statements of polity that might be acceptable to party supporters at home, I knew that the same statements would sound might[y] hollow in this valley where the smell of death was so heavy."[4]

There is no doubt that the moral of the Eighth Army Command was seriously damaged by reports and false rumors that the Army was in the danger of defeat. News reports such as that by Drew Pearson, whose basically fictitious report was printed in January 1951, accused the 2nd Infantry Division with running way in the face of the Communist Chinese Forces (CCF) advances. In many cases, the success of the army in Korea was severely threatened by the lack of any objective knowledge about what was being done. There is no doubt that by December 1950, the Eighth Army's spirit was dragging bottom. There was, curiously, an almost total lack of effort on the part of the high command to restore the confidence of the troops.

But once combat began, there was a fairly quick reverse, for the men faced the fierce realization that they were fighting a monstrous enemy. Part of this was a growing, and vastly exaggerated, notion about the ability of the North Korean.

In phase two, which began with the Chinese entry into the war, war correspondents appeared to be working overtime to magnify the enemy's presence and ability. And, in doing so, they portrayed the new enemy as a force of unimaginable hordes of Chinese soldiers, attacking with no regard to life or limb, probably advancing on the influence of some drug. This, of course, was not true and led to such questions as "How many Chinese does it take to make up a horde?" The Chinese were good fighting men, but though they were often strong in numbers, they had a deficiency in weapons and in experience with their use. The Chinese had fielded a powerful army but not an invulnerable one.

In a secret report filed by British General Leslie Mansergh to the British Chiefs of Staff, one of the difficulties was identified: "They [the Americans] do not understand locality defense in depth or all-around defense. They do not like holding defensive positions. They have been trained for very rapid withdrawals. Americans[s] do not understand infiltration and feel very naked when anybody threatens their flank or rear."[5]

Officers were aware of the difficulty. Lieutenant Colonel George Masters wrote: "We had the conceited opinion that we were trained soldiers. Yet what we did in Korea, as we do quite frequently in our history, was to try and use civilians as soldiers and expected them to be combat-effective. We are usually disappointed."[6]

The national and United Nations cause in Korea came close to bankruptcy, not because the Army and the Marines were inherently weak, but because in good measure they were operating under the limitations imposed by a blindfold. Certainly, President Truman's description of this event as a police action evoked considerable cynicism from the average serviceman.

"Unfortunately, many American soldiers came to despise Korea and its people—their customs were incomprehensible, their land stank of human feces and truth to tell, the methods of ROK law enforcement seemed little less brutal than what they heard of the "Reds"—on the other hand many Americans gave freely of their time, money and energy to build orphanages, to help war widows, and the war-maimed."[7]

The Ridgway Letter

When General Matthew Ridgway took command of Eighth Army, he found his troops demoralized by their retreat. On the night of January 21, 1951, he drafted the following message to be distributed to his troops.

In my brief period of command duty here, I have heard from several sources, chiefly from the members of combat units, the questions, "Why are we here? What are we fighting for?" What follows represents my answers to those questions. The answer to the first question is simple and conclusive. We are here because of the decisions of the properly constituted authorities of our respective governments.

The second question is of much greater significance and every member of this command is entitled to a full and reasoned answer. To me the issues are clear. It is not a question of this or that Korean town and village. It is not restricted to the issues of freedom for our South Korean Allies.

The real issues are whether the power of Western civilization will defy and defeat communism; whether the rule of men who shoot their prisoners, enslave their citizens, and deride the dignity of man, shall displace the rule of those to whom the individual and his individual rights are sacred.

This has long since ceased to be a fight for freedom for our Korean allies alone and for their national survival. It has become, and it continues to be, a fight for our own freedom, for our own survival, in an honorable, independent national existence.

In the final analysis, the issue now joined right here in Korea is whether communism or individual freedom shall prevail, and make no mistake, whether the next fight of fear-driven people shall be checked and defeated overseas or permitted, step by step, to close in on our own homeland and at some future time, however distant, to engulf our own loved ones in all its misery and despair.

These are the things for which we fight.[8]

Changing Character of the Army

As the war progressed, it changed. By late 1951, it was a different kind of war, and a different kind of soldier was fighting it. The war, which had begun as a fast moving, mobile confrontation had begun to slow, becoming more and more static, more defensive than aggressive. Those who first manned the battle stations—the old timers, the retreads, the first of the reserves recalled—were now mostly gone. The men of the 40th and 45th National Guard were no longer involved. A high portion of the men now on the front lines, and manning the backup services, were draftees. Many were unskilled. All seemed to be very young. They were new, they were trained but not highly experienced, they were loyal but not professionals; they were just what was expected, temporary soldiers doing their job the best they could.

MYTHS

One of the myths stated that most of the men were physically out of shape. This is not as true as was believed. The military did everything it could to bring the troops up to standard. "Not only had 8th Army been gradually rebuilding its equipment and manpower, but it had embarked on a more vigorous training program in the fact of the reduction of such activities elsewhere in the U.S. Military."[9]

Another popular myth was that the American serviceman was soft. Before long, everyone was getting into the act. Betty Friedan, later to write *The Feminine Mystique,* reported that "millions of American men were psychologically incapable of facing the shock of war, of facing life away from their 'moms.' In an article in the *Saturday Evening Post* an army sergeant was quoted as saying that the behavior of prisoners of war (POWs) was to be explained by the fact that "these spoiled and pampered kinds had no guts—too much mamma." Philip Wylie, a popular author of the period, blamed the "cult of momism" for draining the nation of its manly virtues: "mamma's boys who lacked the emotional and physical toughness that made America great." This was a view also endorsed by such significant recorders as Harold Ickes and Walter Winchell.[10]

Memories of the war including the rather ambiguous conclusions, a cease-fire remarkably close to the same lines, the 38th Parallel, at which the war began, and the lack the decisiveness of previous wars had left most Americans with an uncertain and unsatisfying feeling about the conclusion.

The failure to come up with a decisive victory led to the belief that U.S. servicemen, particularly those who had been POWs, had somehow failed to uphold the highest standards of moral and military resolve. As a result, the attitude of the American public was often skeptical and even occasionally antagonistic, casting the returning veteran as the war's unfortunate scapegoat.

S.L.A. Marshall commented on this in 1954. Though some of his ideas and conclusions have been challenged in recent years, his insight into the life of the fighting man is based on considerable experience and knowledge. It was his position that the American troops with whom he had been dealing for two years were "perhaps the best of all fighting men who served the country." He acknowledged that some statistics suggested that a large percentage of those engaged were not mentally or physically as tough as might be desired. But soft they were not, and when engaged in combat proved themselves as reliable as soldiers involved in combat everywhere.[11]

CONCLUSION

The myths were that the troops were unprepared, unequipped, and unready, and it is hard to say if the myths emerged from reality or the other way around. Evidence shows that these beliefs were only partially, but certainly not extensively, true. Nevertheless, it was not so much the reality of these early concerns that made the difference; part of the difference was made by what the men and women thought about the situation, how the media portrayed it, and what sort of morale the soldiers were able to keep. Having entered the war in the midst of a massive retreat, and been beaten back down the Peninsula a second time, the morale of the Eighth Army was low. It was not until the arrival of General Ridgway and his positive, aggressive approach that morale began to grow, and it stayed reasonably strong until the stalemate years began to drag through the final days of the armistice talks.

S.L.A. Marshall in his *Men Against Fire: The Problem of Battle Command in Future Wars,*[12] states that during World War II, less than 25 percent of the riflemen fired their weapons in combat, an increase in the percentage during World War I . . . Marshall's data remains in question, but provides some additional evidence to support the belief that the American soldier in Korea carried his share of the load. The percentage of captures, of desertions, of self-inflicted wounds, of absence without leave (AWOL) was about the same in this war as in all other wars.

What is not so clear is just how much of a role the media played in forming the myths or altering the morale. The coverage of the Korean War was adequate if not flashy, but never as supportive as the nation had come to expect during World War II. The war was a story to be told, but with some few exceptions, it was not told well, nor were the American people terribly anxious to hear about it.

NOTES

1. Max Hastings, *The Korean War* (New York: Simon & Schuster, 1987), 81.
2. Hastings: 81.
3. Stanley, Sandler (ed.), *The Korean War: An Encyclopedia* (New York: Garland Press, 1995), 24.
4. Addison Terry, *The Battle for Pusan: A Korean War Memoir* (Novato, CA: Presidio Press, 2000), 179.
5. Max Hastings, *The Korean War* (New York: Simon & Schuster, 1987), 174.
6. Hastings: 80.

7. Stanley Sandler, *The Korean War: No Victors, No Vanquished* (Lexington: University Press of Kentucky, 1999), 63–64.

8. 50th Anniversary Committee: www.koreanwar.net

9. Stanley Sandler, *The Korean War: No Victor, No Vanquished* (Lexington: University Press of Kentucky, 1999), 63.

10. Adam J. Zweiback, "The Turncoat GIs: Nonrepatriations and the Political Culture of the Korean War" *The Historian* (Winter, 1998): 2.

11. S. L. A. Marshall, "Combat Stress," paper presented at conference Recent Advances in Medicine and Surgery, Army Medical Service Graduate School, Washington, D.C., April 30, 1954, 2.

12. S. L. A. Marshall, *Men Against Fire: The Problem of Battle Command in Future Wars* (New York: William Morrow and Company, 1961), 9.

11 CARRYING ON

Korea has been a blessing. There had to be a Korea either here or someplace in the world.

—General James Van Fleet

A good deal of effort was expended to keep life as normal as possible. The combat situation made this most difficult but, as far forward as possible, the military tried to meet the basic needs of the soldiers including efforts to meet the needs of religion, relaxation, and entertainment.

RELIGION

There was not a lot of organized religion in Korea during the war. Chaplains of all denominations performed services of their own and other belief systems, and the opportunity to attend religious services, even as one moved close to the front, was there. People in the service, like people everywhere, represented the degrees of belief reflected by their own society, but religious conviction in a combat area is something different from what so often passes for religion. "There are no atheists in foxholes," soldiers are used to hearing, but it is known that is not true. When men and women were away from home, depressed, and frightened, they had a tendency to turn to some higher beliefs, no matter what the faith, to sustain them. Certainly men in danger of death, or suffering from a desperate wound, are inclined to call out the name of God in search of help. But even then, there were soldiers for whom a structure of religious beliefs was missing. Some of the men and women, sensing the desperation and futility of war, any war, blamed God for the situation. "Whatever religion I had going into Korea was lost soon after I arrived. God didn't seem interested in protecting anyone, in keeping anyone alive."[1]

Others, of course, discovered a faith, or found that their faith increased as they faced the hardships of their military commitment. These men and women took their beliefs into battle, calling on the name of the Lord, giving praise, and begging for consideration. Everyone in the military, however, the hostile as well as the deeply religious, were served by men who found the calling of their devotion in the Chaplains Corps. These men went with the troops, providing sacred direction and secular help.

Chaplains

Since the inception of the Army Chaplain Corps on July 29, 1775, more than 200 chaplains have been killed in battle while in service to the men and women of the Armed Forces. Like the other military services, the chaplaincy had been cut during the inter-war period. In addition, the formation of the Air Force Chaplaincy, following the creation of the independent Air Force, had reduced the number of Army chaplains, by July 1950, to 700. When war broke out, a voluntary recalled was initiated but did not provide the number of clergy required, so an involuntary recall was sent out as well as activating Reserve and National Guard units. Sent to Korea, the chaplains soon found themselves involved in every aspect of the effort. Donald F. Carter served with the troops at Pusan and expressed his own fears as "cooks and clerks were pressed into service as riflemen as the situation became desperate."[2]

General MacArthur maintained a strong belief that the spiritual condition of a nation affected its national history and felt the spiritual condition of the American soldier was essential to victory. Chaplain Vernon P. Jaeger, American Baptist, published an article that not only assured the nation of the ultimate victory in Korea, but the conversion to Christianity of the Korean people.[3] U.S. forces were regularly accompanied by chaplains and many openly participated in religious worship. The chaplains came ashore at Inchon, followed the troops north, took part in the retreat. As the talks dragged on, it became easier for chaplains to reach their troops but no less dangerous. One chaplain estimated he traveled between 1,500 and 2,000 miles a month to provide counseling and religious services. Concentrating much of their efforts at aid stations and hospitals, they prayed, read psalms, and sometimes simply held on to men who were desperately afraid. The character of their work was affected by the attitude of the soldier, deeply affected by the debates over the value of their service. The on-again, off-again negotiations continued while blood was shed over the same land over and over again, which made many soldiers feel like political pawns.

One Jewish chaplain wrote of his experience: "I find most of my work with men of Protestant and Catholic faiths. . . . When they bring them in on a litter covered with mud, blood-soaked, with fear and shock in their faces, you can't tell who they are until you look at their dog tags. To serve such men is my privilege."[4]

Chaplain Wendell F. Byrd, 13th Engineers, wrote "To me there is something fascinating about the courage of men who can go out through mines facing enemy fire on dangerous missions and raids, then come back to their tents or foxholes, and stomach a good meal in a cheerful mood."[5]

During the Korean War, thirteen chaplains gave their lives as they worked among the blood and misery they shared with the soldiers. Robert Crane, the last chaplain killed in Korea, died among the men he was there to comfort. During the war, 175 Army chaplains received 218 decorations including 22 Silver Stars. Chaplain William H. Weitzel received the Marine Commendation Medal with "v" for valor in his voluntary work among front-line Marines. Chaplain Cormac A. Walsh, 180th Regiment, received his third Silver Star personally carrying wounded way from intense enemy fire.[6] The dedication of these men who did their job despite the danger, and who lived out lives which portrayed the very best of their beliefs, was a constant source of encouragement and support.

CELEBRATIONS AND ENTERTAINMENT

Celebrations

For those on the line, few holidays were celebrated. The exceptions were Christmas and Thanksgiving. Most other holidays, such as New Year's, presidents' birthdays, and Halloween were ignored, and often passed without notice. The Marines, even those on the line, always managed to celebrated the birthday of the Corps. On November 10, the Marine Corps birthday, they celebrated with turkey and mashed potatoes and cranberry sauce. Those on the line were pulled back out of the trenches and the outpost bunkers to enjoy a couple of hours over the meal and time in a warm-up tent. The experiences on these occasions were vastly different. For those on the line it was generally not much different from other days.

"I don't remember Christmas, I'm sure it passed but if it did no one who was on the line with me remembered it. It was just another day waiting."[7]

In other locations, however, there were the time and resources to engage in some pleasant activities. Many outfits went to considerable trouble to have excellent meals, complete with traditional foods, and with menus and decorations provided. Colonel George B. Sloan, Commanding the 27th Infantry Regiment (Wolfhound), addressed his men at the Christmas dinner, Tuesday December 25, 1951. "Our faith in our cause rests in Him whose birth is celebrated today," he said, and then the headquarters sat down to enjoy a Christmas dinner that consisted of shrimp cocktail, stuffed olives, stuffed celery hearts, assorted pickles, roast young tom turkey with dressing, giblet gravy, cranberry sauce, buttered peas, buttered whole grain corn, snow flake potatoes, candied yams, hot rolls, butter, jelly, jam, coleslaw with dressing, fresh apples, tangerines, oranges, mincemeat pie, fruit cake, and pumpkin pie.[8]

United Service Organization

Over the course of the war, a significant number of United Service Organization (USO) shows came to Korea. They were usually in a rear area, and the number of men in attendance meant that most could hardly see the stage, but they did wonders. For many GIs, it was the first view of an American woman since they arrived in Korea; besides that, the show was a touch of home, a moment of joy away from the routine.

Movies

Movies, both feature films and recorded TV programs, were a popular form of entertainment and, when available, were shown. Westerns, comedies, and occasional World War II movies were the most popular. Unfortunately, the system was not foolproof, and the distribution and availability of films was sometimes a real mess. Lewis Oglethorpe remembers seeing the second reel of *Diamonds Are a Girl's Best Friend* five times as some confusion continued to bring the same reel back to the division rear for showing. Shown against the side of a tent or a draped cloth, with sandbags and ammo boxes for seats, the quality of the projection was poor. Equally poor were the supply and equipment, as were those trained to use it. Many an evening entertainment was ruined for the lack of a bulb. The greater problem, however, seemed to be the synchronization, though some GIs capitalized on it to provide their own commentary.

Newspapers

News was important to the GI, especially those whose assignments kept them primarily isolated from the sources of news. It is true that in combat, unlike in other places, a front row seat is not always the best. Most men and women who were serving on the line received very little news about the larger picture of what was going on. However, when it came to national news, many GIs were very skeptical about what they heard and read. In the main, soldiers fighting for the crest line of a hill known only by its number were always amazed to see headlines about major losses or victories; it is hard to relate what the individual was doing with what journalists saw fit to expound on for the American public.

The most significant newspaper for the troops overseas was the *Stars and Stripes*. It was always hard to find and several days old, but it provided a good deal of information. The service of the Public Information Officer (PIO) was to provide the troops with information, but the PIOs were rarely seen and not often believed. While the news was welcome, the available papers also provided irritants, as stories of the home front showed a lack of knowledge of, or interest in, what was happening in Korea. The third page placement of stories about significant battles, pages behind accounts of economic growth or a change in the dog licensing laws, created some unrest.

On occasion, a man would received his hometown newspaper through the mail and it would make the rounds. The news was often very old and generally more inclined to carry the story of a special farm sale than one about the war in Korea, but these too were enjoyed. Magazines provided the best source of printed news. *Life* magazine seemed to cover the war with more concern and, when it was available, was well received. The only problem was that it tended to sanitize much of the coverage.

There were a lot of journalists in Korea before, and after, the censorship was imposed. Several of them managed to get stories out that conveyed something of the conditions and the hardships of those in on the fighting. Homer Bigart, a highly respected war correspondent from World War II, reported during the early months of the Korean War and received a Pulitzer prize for his efforts. He shared the prize with the young and aggressive Marguerite (Maggie) Higgins from the *Herald*. Higgins was an up-front-and-in-your-face type reporter who managed, first in her news articles and later in her books, to portray the Korean War carefully. However, from what little commentary is found, it would seem that most GIs saw the war correspondents as a pain. There were obvious exceptions to this, and Maggie Higgins was a prime example, but some of that has to be attributed to the fact that she was young, pretty, white, and there. The other exceptions were the few who made an effort to understand the war. This group was seen as being small in number and, after the first six months, when censorship was imposed, what was read in and about Korea tended to be bland, uncritical, and very much alike.

Radio

In most locations in Korea, if there was a radio, it was possible to pick up the Armed Forces Radio Station. The station, which had been started on May 26, 1942, and gained such popularity during World War II, was reactivated. When the war started in 1950, AFFS leased a number of trailers and literally followed the troops as "Radio Vagabond." Later, in 1950, the American Forces Korea Network established itself in Seoul.

Some of the more popular music listened to by the troops—some of it popular even before 1950—included: Cole Porter's "Allez-Vous-En", "Go Away"; Tennessee Ernie Ford's performance of Cliffe Stone's "Anticipation Blues"; John Turner, Eberhard Storch, and John Sexton's "Auf Wiederseh'n, Sweetheart"; Bob Hilliard and Milton De Lugg's "Be My Life's Companion"; Bernie Wayne and Lee Morris's "Blue Velvet"; Betty Hutton singing Frank Loesser's "A Bushel and a Peck"; Patti Page singing Joe Darion and Larry Coleman's "Changing Partners"; Harry Stone and Jack Stapp's "Chattanoogie Shoe Shine Boy"; W. Mack David's "Cherry Pink and Apple Blossom White"; writer and singer Hank Williams' "Cold, Cold, Heart"; Ross Bagdasarian's "Come on-a My House" sung by Rosemary Clooney; Artie Glenn's "Crying in the Chapel"; Slim Willet's "Don't Let the Stars Get in Your Eyes"; Bill Trader's "A Fool Such as I"; Doris Day singing Cole Porter's "From This Moment On"; Jack Rollins and Steve Nelson's "Frosty the Snow Man"; Richard Rodgers and Oscar Hammerstein's "Getting to Know You"; Huddie Leadbelly's "Goodnight Irene"; Sammy Kay's rendition of Jimmy Kennedy's "Harbor Lights"; Hank Williams' "Hey Good Looking!"; Ned Washington's "Do Not Forsake Me"; Richard Rodgers and Oscar Hammerstein's "Hello, Young Lovers"; Harry Noble's "Hold Me, Thrill Me, Kiss Me"; Frank Loewe and Alan Jay Lerner's "I Talk to the Trees"; Johnny Mercer and Hoagy Carmichael's "In the Cool, Cool, Cool of the Evening"; Paul Campbell's "Kisses Sweeter than Wine"; Johnny Ray's "The Little White Cloud that Cried"; Teresa Brewer singing Stephen Weiss's "Music, Music, Music"; Bob Merrill's "My Truly, Truly Fair"; Kay Twomey's "Never Let Her Go"; Irving Berlin's "Play a Simple Melody"; Sid Frank and Ray Getezou's "Please Mr. Sun"; Max C. Freedman's "Rock Around the Clock"; Robert Wright's "Stranger in Paradise"; Al Alberts' "Tell Me Why"; Frank and Loewe and Allen Jay Lerner's "They Call the Wind Maria"; John Warrington and Sidney Prosen's "Till I Waltz Again with You"; Irving Gordon's "Unforgettable"; George Weiss and Bennie Benjamin's "Wheel of Fortune"; Kenny Devine's "Yellow Roses"; singe, composer Hank Williams' "Your Cheating Heart"; Harry Warren, Saul Chaplin and Jack Brooks' "You Wonderful You"; and Harry Warren and Leo Robin's "Zing a Little Zong."

One "disc-jockey" that appeared regularly was a lady called Seoul City Sue. She was really Anne Wallace Suhr, an American who had come to Korea originally as a Methodist missionary, and remained in Seoul after the Communist first captured it. She swore allegiance to the Democratic People's Republic of Korea and began broadcasting in late July 1950. While often listened to, she had very little effect on the morale of the troops.

Public Information Officers

Among those called on to listen to the PIO lectures, there may be some question if these reports should be listed under entertainment. But, while not all that exciting, they were informative and, for many, a break in the routine. The Public Information Officer generally provided an update on the war, something about what was going on at home, and often information about current trends and fads.

Personal Entertainment

The military had little objection to keeping its men and women busy and, in fact, went to some lengths to create work or training whose primary purpose was to prevent there being too much free time. Nevertheless, there was a lot of down time and GIs used it in a vast number of ways. To a large extent, soldiers, whether in a garrison or on the line, provided their own entertainment, learning to kill time in some highly creative

Some soldiers were able to take advantage of a swimming hole set up behind Heart Break Ridge, Korea, 1952. (*Used by permission of the Center for the Study of the Korean War, Graceland University*)

ways. The primary activities included "shooting-the-bull," sleeping, writing letters home, rereading letters received, playing sports (basketball, soccer with the British troops, boxing, skeet shooting, baseball, football, and, sometimes, volleyball), playing cards both in terms of gambling and more sophisticated games like of bridge or cribbage, and playing chess, checkers, and monopoly. They also read, some studied courses either to advance in the military or toward the completion of a degree program. Much time was spent cleaning equipment, and drinking beer. Also a lot of daydreaming, arguing, drawing, religious study, and complaints. Many developed a talent for and skill with crafts, and thousands of things were created out of military scrap. Every outfit seemed to have a man working on a novel.

Cigarettes

It would be untrue say that everyone in the service smoked, because they did not. But it often seemed that way, and the person that did not was a rarity. Cheap and readily available, usually by the cartoon—as well as some old and pretty bad cigarettes were provided in C rations. President Franklin D. Roosevelt, himself a smoker, declared tobacco an essential wartime crop. Army training manuals urged leaders to make their troops smoke, and General MacArthur demanded a better supply of tobacco to be provided in a soldier's daily ration.

The troops managed to get cigarettes when ammo was hard to come by and, when unavailable, it led to whole platoons of men suffering withdrawal. The danger of smoking was, of course, not widely recognized at that time, and the advantage for many was significant. It was something to do with your hands when they were shaking, it was an offer of friendship and a habit shared, it was an immediate substitute for food, it was a way to keep your mouth occupied when you wanted to yell obscenities at the Field First Sergeant, it was a jolt to the system when fatigue was sitting it, it was a pause suggesting relaxation, it was a statement when words were not enough.

Alcohol

For most of the American soldiers in Korea, alcohol was the drug of choice. Hard liquor, at least Western brands, was hard to come by for an enlisted man. What could be purchased was consumed in large quantities, and while there were few documented cases that it "made you blind," there were numerous cases of significant injury. Beer was provided rather routinely for the enlisted men, along with candy and cigarettes, and was available even after some concerned mothers complained about their young sons being provided alcohol.[9]

As a general rule, the chronically addicted were found among enlisted men with long terms of service. The numbers reported contained relatively few officers, but that may be because the officers did the reporting. Those that drank to excess were not as numerous as those who drank in binges, during breaks, on Rest and Recuperation (R & R), and for whom the problem of drink was limited to those occasions. Some, who demanded it, would drink just about anything that had alcohol in it. This was a special problem during the early phase of the war, because of the unavailability of reputed brands of alcohol, and the fact that enterprising and often unscrupulous Koreans developed mixes that contained methyl alcohol as well as other toxic substances.[10]

Other Drugs

There were few drug cases (in comparison to Vietnam) among the combat troops, with the number of addicts increasing the further back the troops got, and the closer they were stationed near cities or dock areas. For example, the 25th Infantry Division reported only twelve cases of drug use during the second year of the war, and the 3rd Infantry Division reported only two in an eight-month period.

Nevertheless, the Department of Defense in 1952 reported that in the Far East Command, the number of men arrested for narcotic abuse had tripled since 1949; from 201 to 715. The amount of heroin seized was about three times the amount. In some cases, usually around the port cities, it was not unheard of for officers to report that 50 percent of their were men involved in drugs, though a large percentage of them were arrested and charged with possession rather than use.

It was during the Korean War, however, and among U.S. Troops, that the earliest intravenous use of amphetamines was reported. Some soldiers stationed in Japan, and later in Korea, had developed the habit of mixing heroin with amphetamines and injecting the combination. There were some deaths from overdoses, usually of heroin. Also, some deaths occurred among those who were caught up in the system, and who were killed in protection of either sources or suppliers. It was estimated that a significant number of servicemen returning from Korea brought the habit with them.[11] Thirty or forty percent of the drug traffickers arrested in Japan and South Korea were pushing drugs that originated in Communist China. The traffic was traced from Communist China through North Korea and Hong Kong to leaders in Japan. From there it was distributed though prostitutes, indigenous night clubs, village stores, and GIs who worked within their own units.

A variety of efforts were used to try and cut down usage, and this included undercover men from the Civilian Intelligence Division (CID), the periodic shakedown, physical examinations for needle scars, and the like. Because it was so small, there was no uniform legal or administrative procedure for dealing with addicts, other than what seems to have been an understanding that discharge only encouraged others to try it, and sending them home was unfair to the civilian population. Most of those caught were dealt with through the military system, with punishments ranging from dead time (time that did not count toward rotation or discharge) to prison time.

There were constant rumors that the Chinese were on drugs. Major Liberian, the commander of a Canadian company, claimed that his men believed that the Chinese were doped before they were committed to battle because they appeared to be oblivious to danger. There is little evidence to support this.

Prostitution

Where there are soldiers, there will be prostitutes. This was as true during the Korean War as any other. Prostitutes were available and they became more readily available the further back from the front line the soldier was. Probably any generalization made about the women would be false, but it appeared that many entered prostitution for economic reasons, simply to make enough to live. This would certainly be true among R-girls, who were available for a four-day companionship during R & R, or some who tied up with men stationed in the cities and large villages. Venereal disease was the constant fear of the military, and many men fell to its ravages. Every effort was made to educate the GI and to provide protection by providing condoms and pro-kits. Inspections were common, and "Peel it back" was a constant command when moving in or out of a station. Many a man hesitated as a WAVE (Women Accepted for Volunteer Emergency Service) Lieutenant issued the order.

There is a harsh and ongoing argument about the degree to which the U.S. military was providing prostitutes for the men, or at the least was behind efforts to do so. Individual officers and enlisted men know the answer to this question better than the historians or researchers. There is no doubt the local authorities, city police and the like, either turned a blind eye, or made a profit on the activities. The South Korean government appears to have made women available for their troops. One account suggests the government standard of performance for such women was to service at least twenty-nine men a day.

For those stationed in Japan, there was always the potential of a long-term relationship with a Japanese girl—often called *Babysan* or *mama-san*—with whom they could take up housekeeping for a few dollars and some GI food. While the Japanese had come a long way since the end of World War II, they still suffered from economic and social poverty. For many, an attachment to a serviceman was salvation for themselves and their family. In addition to romantic relationships, many American servicemen developed close "speak friends," that is friends to talk to.[12]

HUMANITARIAN EFFORTS BY THE U.S. MILITARY AND CIVILIANS

Many American members of the armed forces were deeply hurt by the destruction they witnessed in Korea. They recognized the devastation the war caused to the civilian population and were particularly concerned by the number of children who were orphaned by the fighting. In many cases, there was nothing that could be done but, throughout the war, a surprising number of fighting men went out of their way, spending their own time and money, to help young people in need. A few examples will indicate the diversity of efforts. The 260 "uncles" of the USS *Missouri* "adopted" a Korean child, providing whatever was needed for the care of the infant. The U.S. Marine 1st Marine Aircraft Wing supported an orphanage at Pyongtaek. The 7th Infantry Division donated $36,734 in support of Korean relief charities, as well as supporting Boys Town on Koje-do and conducted "Operation Santa Claus." The U.S. Air Force 18th Fighter-Bomber Wing purchased the land for a home for the elderly in Masan. They also provided clothing and worked with the UN to finance construction of a home to house ninety-two elderly men and women at Wonju, and supported six orphanages with monthly contributions. During 1953, the soldiers of the U.S. Army I Corps donated $385,000 to Korean relief charities. The 45th Infantry Division contributed $300,000 to Korean relief organizations. After returning to the United States, members of the division continued to support the Orphan's home on Cheju-do. The 5th Regimental Combat Team sponsored a Boys Town in Ranje-do, raising money to construct housing and schools for 900 boys. In December 1950, the U.S. Air Force Combat Cargo Command diverted 15 cargo planes to ferry nearly 1,000 war orphans from Inchon to Cheju-do in Operation Little Orphan Annie. They returned the next year with items for the children.

A series of people-to-people programs also offered help to a wide variety of charitable organizations designed to improve the lot of the South Korean people. Most of these were helped in some manner by members of the military. The Save the Children Federation shipped clothing, blankets, and school materials. The Church World Service provided garments knitted by American women. The American Relief for Korea established a number of agencies that also provided knitted garments as well as other clothing.

The Presbyterian Board of Foreign Missions, in cooperation with the Church World Service, established special orthopedic wards and facilities to construct braces and artificial limbs. World Vision, working with the Armed Forces, established the Paik Sun Orphanage that cared for 200 children, The Foster Parents' Plan for War Children operated several programs, one that distributed shoes and food to "adopted" children. The Mennonite Church provided vocational training and academic schooling to about 150 orphaned boys. The Methodist Committee for Overseas Relief lent money to farmers and businessmen to purchase equipment and stock. The Heavenly Light Village in Taejon was supported by American charity and provided care for the family of the blind. The Virginia Milk Kitchen supplied 150 cups of hot food daily. The American-Korean Foundation provided major facilities: buildings, tractors, locomotives, and tenders. The Christian Children's Fund supported an "adoption plan" where American families could support Korean War orphans for $10.00 a month. Women's clubs, CARE, and National Education Association helped finance the American Korean school assistance program. And the Heifers for Relief program supplied bee hives, rabbits, and goats to South Korea.[13]

CONCLUSION

Human beings have a great adaptability. When necessary, they can take root and make a home just about anywhere. And while many GIs during the Korean War found themselves in almost unbelievable circumstances, it is a tribute to them and to those who encouraged them, that they were able to find and to create so much normality. The military did a good job in helping to make this possible, as did civilian outfits like the USO, the Red Cross, and the Salvation Army. Just about everything that the troopers needed, and a lot they just wanted, were provided—from religious services to movies and holiday celebrations. Never the same as being at home, there was, nevertheless, a great deal of comfort provided to offset the otherwise harsh conditions.

NOTES

1. Paul M. Edwards, CSKW GU, A. 001.

2. Roger R. Venzke, "Confidence in Battle, Inspiration in Peace," *The Army Chaplaincy* (Winter/Spring, 2002): 3.

3. Roger R. Venzke, "Remembering our Army at War in Korea" Chapter Three. *The United States Army Chaplaincy 1945–1975*. Washington D. C.: U. S. Army Chaplain Center (1977): 4.

4. Roger R. Venzke, *The United States Army Chaplaincy, 1945–1975* (Washington D.C.: Office of the Chief of Chaplains, 1977), 117.

5. Roger R. Venzke, "Remembering our Army at War in Korea" Chapter Three, *The United States Army Chaplaincy 1945–1975* (Washington, D.C.: U.S. Army Chaplains Center, 1977): 4.

6. Venzke, Remembering: 4.

7. Paul M. Edwards, CSKW, GU A.0001.

8. Menu, 27th Infantry Regiment, CSKW, GU A. 07367.

9. T. R. Fehrenbach, *This Kind of War,* (Washington D.C.: Brassey's, 1963), 158.

10. H. J. Anslinger and W. F. Tompkins, *The Traffic in Narcotics.* (New York: Funk and Wagnalls Co, 1953), 168–169.

11. Cynthia Kuhn, Scott Swartzwelder, Wilkie Wilson, Leigh Heather Wilson, and Jeremy Foster, *Buzzed: The Straight Facts About the Most Used and Abused Drugs from Alcohol to Ecstasy,* 1st ed. (New York: W. W. Norton & Company, 1998).

12. Bill Hume *Babysan, A Private Look at the Japanese Occupation* (Tokyo, Japan: Kasuga Boeki K. K., 1953), 7.

13. Robert H. Mosier and Gerald Kornblau, "The GI and the Kids of Korea," *National Geographic Magazine* 103 (May, 1953): 635–678.

12   COMING HOME

It was very easy to start a war in Korea. It was not so easy to stop it.

—Nikita Khrushchev 1894–1971

When the Demilitarized Zone (DMZ) was established, it was a strip of land slightly more than 2.5 miles in width that stretched across the entire Korean peninsula. It separated the Democratic People's Republic of Korea (DPRK) from the Republic of Korea (ROK). It began at a point just south of the 38th Parallel on the west coast and ran to a point slightly north of the line on the east coast.

Both communist and UN troops continued to fire until 2200 hours, the moment the cease-fire went into effect. At that moment, pretty much all across Korea, the guns stopped, the planes returned to their carriers or bases, and the naval guns grew silent. As command radios delivered the good news to forward commands, some units received the news with appreciative silence, while others celebrated. Bugles were blown by the communists and flares shot into the air. Men stood up along the line, lighting a cigarette without fear. United Nations forces greeted the new day surprised to see the communists moving about in the areas in front of them. Some GIs remembered that a few of the Chinese left gifts hanging on tree limbs and invited the men to join them in some sort of celebration. In some few cases, the soldiers intermingled, coming out of their bunkers and trenches to meet one another. Most were just grateful and thinking of going home.

The going-home process was slow, not like World War II when the effort was made to "get the boys home." In the first place, the war might have reached a cease-fire but there was no peace treaty, and the American military was going to remain in Korea. And, because of the rotation point system that had been initiated, men had to wait out their turn.

The men and women who were heading home were different than when they had left. And so was the country.

GETTING HOME

While some servicemen and women were returned by air, most of the available planes were being used to take home the sick and wounded. The majority returned home by ship, usually taking anywhere from twelve to fifteen days. They landed on the coast, Oakland, California, being one of the ports most used.

On arrival, the GI entered a warehouse like building, was given a shower, disinfected, given a clean uniform, an array of the medals and ribbons owed them, a phone call home, an update on all the paperwork, a good meal, and sent out the other side of the warehouse with travel orders. Usually there was an immediate transfer either to another command or, for those getting out, to a relocation depot close to their home.

Recognition: Awards and Medals

When cleaned up and ready to go, the Army made sure that the new uniform carried the symbols of their service. Those who served and fought in Korea were entitled to a variety of medals and ribbons, each of which reflected the degree of service, periods of service, recognition of courage and commitment, and the branch in which the service was performed. The primary service awards were the following.

The National Defense Service Medal
These were the first medals that were issued during the Korean War. These symbols designated that the serviceperson had performed in active service during a period of normal service between June 27, 1950 and July 27, 1954, inclusively. It is to be noted that this period extends beyond the date of the armistice.

The Korean Service Medal
The Korean Service Medal was created by President Truman when he signed Executive Order No. 10179 on November 8, 1950 to commemorate service in the armed forces during the Korean War. Created by Thomas Jones, it shows a traditional Korean gate on the obverse side and the Taegut (Yin-Yang) symbol of the Korean flag. It was awarded for service in Korea or in adjacent waters between the dates of June 27, 1950 and July 27, 1954.

The United Nations Korean Service Medal
The United Nations Korean Medal (originally called the United Nations Service Medal) was available for all those who were eligible for the Korean Service Medal. It was initiated by Resolution 483 (V) of the U. N. General Assembly on December 12, 1950. Presidential approval for awarding the medal was given by President Truman on November 27, 1951. The ribbon is light blue (officially bluebird) with seventeen vertical stripes (generally accepted as representative of the seventeen nations that served in Korea). A medal very much like it was issued by several nations. This award was also available for all those members of the naval service of the United States who qualified for the Korean Service Medal.

The (Republic of Korea) War Service Medal

The Korean War Medal was first offered on November 15, 1951 by the South Korean Minister of Defense. It was intended for those who participated in the war for thirty consecutive or sixty nonconsecutive days, on or after June 25, 1950. Originally, the United States did not authorize the wearing of the medal. The United States has always been slow to recognize foreign decorations. However, after some years, Francis M. Rush Jr. Principal deputy assistant secretary of the Army, authorized the wearing of the medal on August 20, 1998. Most renditions of the medal have the Taegut (Yin-Yang) woven into the ribbon, a symbolic rendering of the Korean nation, over crossed artillery shells. Individuals, ships, and units of the U.S. Navy, Marines were also entitled to the award.[1]

Combat Infantrymen Badge

Begun in 1943, the Combat Infantryman Badge (CIB) was awarded to men of the armed forces, a colonel or below, with an infantry speciality who had performed his or her duty during ground combat. In 1952, primarily because so many fighting in Korean had already won the CIB during World War II, a star was authorized to indicate a second award. This decoration is only awarded to members of the U.S. Army.

The Medal of Honor

Sometimes identified as the Congressional Medal of Honor, it is awarded by the President of the United States for meritorious action. It always represents courage, but is often given for situations in which the recipient has saved the lives of his companions. During the Korean War, a total of 131 men received the nation's highest honor. Of these, seventy-eight went to members of the U.S. Army, forty-two to the U.S. Marines, seven to the U.S. Navy, and four to the U.S. Air Force.

Silver Star

The Silver Star is awarded for distinguished gallantry in action against an enemy or while serving with friendly forces against an opposing enemy force. While the gallantry required is considered less than that for the Distinguished Service Cross, it nevertheless is only given as the result of marked distinction. Begun in July 1918, it replaced the "Citation Star" in 1932. Despite its name, the cross is made of gold, an inch-and-a-half in diameter with a small silver star imposed in the center. On the reverse is the inscription is "for gallantry in action."

Bronze Star

This award was established by the president in February 1944 and was awarded to men and women of the armed services who distinguished themselves. The decoration is given in recognition of heroic action or meritorious achievement in some action other than an aerial flight, and against on opposing armed force. It was given for both combat action or a service achievement in a noncombat role.

Purple Heart

Began in 1782 as George Washington's "badge of military merit," it was restricted in 1932 as the Purple Heart and was awarded to any person for wounds or death while serving in any of the Armed Forces. To qualify, the wound or death had to be the result of an act of any opposing armed force. For those in the Army or Air Force, a bronze oak-leaf cluster is worn for each additional award. For the Navy, Marines, and Coast Guard, a silver oak-leaf cluster is worn for each additional award. While difficult to imagine, the occasion came up often enough that it was necessary to make a further identification: in the Army: a silver Oak-Leaf Cluster is worn in lieu of five Bronze Stars, and in the Navy, Marines, and Coast Guard, a silver star is worn in lieu of five Gold Stars.

The Republic of Korea Presidential Unit Citation

Issued by the government of South Korea to both Korean and foreign units, it was awarded to several U.S. military units during the war in recognition of either a spectacular act or a period of prolonged service. Later, by order of the Korean government, it was retroactively authorized for every unit of the United States Army that had been deployed to Korea between 1950 and 1964. One Canadian unit (2nd Battalion Princess Patricia's Canadian Light Infantry) and one Australian unit (3rd Battalion of the Royal Australian Regiment) were awarded with this citation.

The United States Presidential Unit Citation

Originally established as the Distinguished Unit Citation in 1942, it was renamed in 1966. The citation is awarded to units of the Armed Forces of the United States for extraordinary heroism in action against an armed enemy occurring on, or after, December 7 1941. The degree of heroism displayed by the unit is the same as would be required for an individual award of the Distinguished Service Cross. Every member of the unit may wear the decoration, but it is considered a permanent award only for those who were in the unit when the award was given.

Navy Cross

During the Korean War, 267 men were awarded the Navy Cross for heroism. Two individuals were awarded two of these decorations. Members of the U.S. Navy awarded 41, the U.S. Marines 221, and the U.S. Army 3. Eighty-four of the awards were given posthumously.

Navy and Marine Corps Presidential Unit Commendation

The Navy citation is the same as that of the Army, but is considered the unit equivalent of a Navy Cross. It was established at the beginning of World War II. Members of the Coast Guard may be awarded either version of the Presidential Unit Citation, depending on which arm of the service they were supporting when the award is given.

Korean War Service Medal (ROK)

In 1998, South Korea renewed an offer that the U.S. had previously declined. In 1951, the Republic of Korea had offered a War Service Medal (Korean War Service Medal) to all UN forces. At the time, American law prohibited U.S. soldiers from receiving foreign decorations. Congress reversed the law three years later but, by that time, most of those eligible had returned to the United States. When the offer was made again, the Department of Defense approved the decoration for approximately 1.8 million soldiers, including the next of kin to those who were deceased. On December 2, 2002, President George W. Bush signed the 2003 Defense Authorization Act extending the grant to include all those who served in Korea from the moment of the cease-fire.

Good Conduct Medal

A fairly common medal that was subject to much barracks humor, the Good Conduct Medal was given to members of the armed forces who had been free of disciplinary action for a period of two years. It was one of those decorations that few coveted, but nevertheless most men and women wanted to be eligible for it.

Determining Who Came Home

In September 1951, a point system was introduced to determine when a serviceman or woman was eligible for rotation home. A soldier received four points for every month served in close combat, two points for rear-echelon duty in Korea, and one point for duty somewhere in the Far East. Three points were available for those in reserve division status. Enlisted men were eligible for rotation when they reached forty-three points. For officers, the requirement was fifty-five points. In June 1952, the requirement was reduced to thirty-six points for enlisted men and thirty-seven for officers. Arriving at the needed points did not guarantee rotation but, in most cases, soldiers were rotated within a brief time after they met the requirement.

For many, this was a system of great hope, for it provided a definitive goal for those to whom the war seemed to go on forever. Typical fronting duty would get a soldier home in a year. It was also very popular with those on the home front who now were able to determine, within a reasonable time, when their loved ones would be home.

The rotation system was also criticized for its failures. There were some significant costs involved in the decision. In the first place, it created a category of men who called themselves "short timers." This designation had the psychological effect of reducing the effectiveness of a good many veterans. As their day of rotation approached, they quite naturally grew increasingly cautious. A second problem was that the constant turnover of men meant that the armed services were replacing from 20,000 to 30,000 trained men per month, thus creating a variety of problems. One was the tremendous strain on the training system, requiring it to produce more and more qualified men for combat duty in Korea. It was also to blame for a continuous drain on skilled manpower, as men who had experience—principally noncommissioned officers (NCOs)—were replaced by green recruits who lacked the necessary skills. By fall 1952, a significant number of the junior officers who had World War II combat experience, had been rotated home and replaced by Reserve Officer Training Corps (ROTC) graduates with little or no experience either in command or combat.

While the effect of this was not known until after the war, it was also the source of a decreased personal or unit loyalty. When men were individually sent in as replacements, and individually rotated home, their opportunity for unit identification was lessened.

The POWs Come Home

Among those who came home at the end of the war—and one of the largest numbers to return in a short space of time—were the men who had been held as prisoners of war. While both the military and the home front were aware that men had been held in captivity during the war, and President Truman had made it a point of the armistice that each man could make his own choice about where he would return, the arrival of the POW at the end of the war had a major impact.

It is generally accepted that the DPRK had not expected America's entry into the war. Therefore, they had made no arrangements for the capture and holding of American POWs. The North Korean People's Army (NKPA) did not have the facilities—or sometimes the inclination—to take care of POWS. This became fairly clear following the UN capture of Taejon, where American troops discovered that the NKPA had killed several thousand South Korean civilians and executed forty-two captured American soldiers. While there is no evidence that the North Korean command either initiated or sanctioned these actions, it is evident that the North Korea had no POW program to prevent it.

Until the entry of the Chinese in the war, the NKPA maintained collection points rather than POW camps. During the early months of the war, the UN prisoners were moved to the rear, usually by foot, during which time the prisoners suffered considerable hardship and death. Prisoners weaned from battle and who could not keep up were often left to die. During the 120-mile march in November 1950, an estimated 130 of the 700 POWs died. Once they arrived somewhere and a camp was established, the lack of food and shelter as well as very limited medical aid led to the deaths of many POWS during the early period of the war. In general, the prisoners were fed what the North Korean peasants lived on, but both the amount and the unaccustomed items proved insufficient to support weakened American prisoners.

After the Chinese entered the war, and the resulting capture of several thousand U.S. soldiers and Marines, the Communist Chinese Forces (CCF) set up a temporary camp called the Valley. The living conditions there were very bad and an estimated 500 to 700 of the 1,000 captured died there. Fairly quickly, however, the Chinese Forces created eight permanent camps that covered a 50-mile sector in North Korea along the Yalu River. Prisoners of war were collected in the valley camps and moved on. The main camp, and headquarters for the administration of POWs, was at Camp 5 at Pyoktong.

When the POWs arrived, they were separated according to rank, race, and nationality. As a rule, the Chinese POW camps were relatively open with little barbed wire, tiger boxes, and only a few guards stationed at strategic points. During their captivity in the Chinese camps, the prisoners–or students as they were sometimes called–were subjected to a program of indoctrination that tested their faith, and considerable efforts were made to change their minds and get them to accept the communist ideal. In fact, in February 1953, the American State Department noted with some concern that the communists might release a huge batch of prisoners who, made soft on communism, might do immeasurable harm.

Unlike the North Koreans, the comments from returning prisoners indicated that the Chinese often showed compassion in their treatment of prisoners, especially the wounded. "The Chinese. . .in some instances put Americans on litters, carried them to the roadside, and then withdrew and held their fire so that UN medics could remove them."[2] They also had fairly strict rules about how prisoners were to be treated. Once in captivity, the prisoners were not to be robbed nor abused and to be given food and provided some limited medical treatment.

Callum A. MacDonald in his work *Korea: The War Before Vietnam,* said that the captors tended to treat many of the POWs as victims who had been taken advantage of by the government. They were often seen as students who were in need of serious education. In this process, they were to be directed in order to understand the true causes for the war as well as the decadent nature of their societies. "After such reeducation, prisoners could be either released at the front to rejoin and demoralize their old units, or held for longer-term indoctrination."[3]

This indoctrination was quickly identified as brainwashing. What has been labeled brainwashing seems, in the main, to be the communist effort at education through a variety of means, but in the main by long and repetitive classes on scientific socialism. The idea was to convert them to Communism. Those who played it cool, did not cause a lot of difficulty, and were willing to listen quietly to the indoctrination lectures were called "Progressives" (those who might have communist sympathy). Those who resisted more by small but still difficult acts of defiance were termed "Reactionaries." Despite the movies and a good deal of myth and accusation, no confirmed cases of brainwashing came out of these camps. Whether the twenty-one men who chose to remain in the communist nation at the end of the war did so as a result of the indoctrination, we do not know.

At the time of their capture, the Chinese assured the Americans that they would treat them well. Discipline was maintained in two ways. All officers and NCOs were sent to different camps, and anyone who demonstrated a leadership role was separated from the rest. Second, compliance was achieved by threats of mistreatment and some cases of torture, but physical abuse was not conducted to the same degree as it was in North Korean camps. Punishment was administered by a variety of means designed to modify behavior; slapping, solitary confinement, deficient diets, forced into uncomfortable positions for long periods of time and, occasionally, a dummy firing squad or threats of exile to Siberia and denial of potential repatriation. Good behavior was rewarded by improved diet and living conditions.

Both the Chinese and the North Koreans considered crimes committed by the prisoners as crimes against the state rather than the individual. To steal food, for example, was considered a crime against the North Korean people.

During the war, some 670 (figures at about 10 percent) of the American servicemen who were held in captivity managed to escape. All of these took place from frontline holding points or aid stations within a few hours of capture. There were some fifty documented escape attempts made by POWs from more permanent camps, but none of these were successful. Several factors account for this failure at escape. Among them was the rough terrain that had to be crossed, the difficulty in blending in with the local population, and that most camps were a great distance from the UN lines.

The International Red Cross (IRC) made several attempts to alleviate the plight of the POWs. North Korea did not cooperate, and an effort to get a list of prisoners and camp inspections failed. China agreed to IRC visitations, but only if accompanied by a representative of the North Korean government and members of the Chinese Red Cross.

There were 7,245 American POWs during the war. Of these, 2,806 died while in captivity and 4,418 were eventually returned to military control. Twenty-one UN soldiers refused repatriation.

For years after the war, former POWs showed higher death rates than other veterans. Complicating a difficult homecoming for POWs were attacks by their own countrymen. Arguing that Americans had become too soft and slack to meet the challenge of communist aggression, energetic charlatans of many stripes spread the legend that American prisoners during the Korean War had been uniquely spiritless, dying without cause, and yielding without reason to enemy pressures. Men who had already suffered much faced an ordeal at the hand of some fellow Americans that contrasted sharply with the lavish care that had attended their release.

Returning by Way of Little Switch

Toward the end of the war, and in response to an agreement reached by the Armistice Commission, Operation Little Switch brought home a significant number of the sick or wounded American and United Nations soldiers. Little Switch took place from April 20 to May 3, 1953 when the UN Command turned over 5,194 North Koreans and 1,030 Chinese soldiers, plus 446 civilian internees. They received 684 sick and wounded. There was little understanding of what sort of adjustment these men were facing. There were far too many to provide individual aid and the two attempts at group therapy did not seem to work.

All those returning in this operation were considered to be medical patients and their reprocessing was accomplished through medical facilities. The first day out of captivity, they were sent to an Army Evacuation Hospital and then airlifted to one of two Tokyo army hospitals. When situated, they were given a limited number of privileges: a free phone call home, radios, and a PX card. But in the main, they were given a great deal of personal attention yet, at the same time, were under enough restriction to remind them that they were still members of the Armed Forces. Usually, within three days, they were air-evacuated to Hawaii and then on the United States. During this period, there was no time for any psychotherapeutic intervention.

Many of those returned were seen as apathetic, and some even exhibited a zombie character about them. Many suffered from a lack of memory about the events of their capture. There was also an underlying thanks for the care received from many of the Chinese, and for the lack of torture. The medical history suggests that many were suspended in time, with little talk of future plans.

There was a rather high rate of what was unprofessionally called "give-up-its." The symptoms were an abstention from any kind of physical activity, the preference being to remain in the confines of a room or building, trouble eating without the presence of a large glass of cold water. Some of these persons had quite simply given up.

Those of lesser rank often expressed resentment against officers and NCOs, who they sometimes blamed for their capture in the first place. The Army was surprised at the lack of cohesiveness and their sense of isolation. Unit identifications were rarely mentioned and when asked about their units they often replied they were Americans. Or, when asked about their original units, the prisoners often gave their imprisonment camp number.

Returning Home by Means of Big Switch

When the War ended, the second and final phase of the POW exchange took place. It was called Operation Big Switch. In Operation Big Switch, only the sick and wounded were regarded as medical patients and those physically able were evacuated through regular channels. The Department of the Army required only the standard medical and physical examination. The psychiatric examination, usually given in the first twenty-four to forty-eight hours after their release, consisted of an hour's interview and a set of psychological tests—Wechsler-Bellevue, Rorschach, TAT, Miole-Holsopple, and DAP—and when there was time, a psychiatric history was conducted.

The sort of questions being asked provided information about both the POW and the conduct of others within the POW compounds. The Army asked details of the capture and the prisoners attitude toward both his own capture and the capture of others. Questions were asked about their attitude toward their captors and their fellow prisoners. There were also limited questions dealing with family, schooling, religion, and siblings.

Among returning POWs, there was a high degree of tolerance toward medical and administrative processing. Some, despite their desire to get home as quickly as possible, talked about a need for time to get it together. Many of those exchanged in Big Switch were guarded and suspicious and expressed some anxiety over how they would be treated when they returned home. In many cases, the communists had told them they would be prosecuted when they returned.

The figure usually agreed on was that 75,823 Communists and 12,773 UN (including 3,597 Americans) were exchanged. Prisoners who expressed the desire not to be repatriated were sent to a temporary camp at Panmunjom. At this camp, a representative of their government was allowed to talk with the individual under the supervision of the five-member Neutral Nations Repatriation Commission. After the interviews, the individual was asked to make a final decision about their desire to return home; at that time, they were free to return home or go to a neutral nation. Twenty-one Americans refused to be repatriated, some 21,000 Chinese and North Koreans made this same decision.

Following their return, usually about the third or fourth day, there was an obvious change in the ex-POW behavior. At first, there was a sense of excitement and activity, but they quickly they began to show a noticeable degree of blandness, retardation, and apathy. Talk was slow, shallow, and vague. Physical activity was slowed.

Retained primarily at the Army Replacement Depot at Inchon, they were identified as returnees and headed home by the usual rotation means. They were well taken care of, with bunk-beds and fresh linen, showers, PX available, and several Red Cross units to provide help. The Red Cross facilitated the release by providing badly need supplies and comfort articles, calls home, and updates on the families of the returnees. In most cases, the military discipline was very lax; there were no retreats or formations. Later it was believed this was not a good idea, in that those who are not treated as soldiers soon fail to act like soldiers. But the replacement depots were not geared up for this additional burden due to shortages of staff.

Once the ex-POWs went on board ship, they received special treatment. They were provided more room and were treated as if they were special. It was determined that all POWs who had been a prisoner for more than six months needed to be involved in some sort of group therapy. These men were taken home by ship and during the 14-day voyage were provided six sessions. The goal of the sessions was an immediate adjustment, to bring the prisoner into the here and now.

In Operation Big Switch, thirty of the returning POWs were considered to be severely neurotic. They were immediately sent to the Neuropsychiatric Center in Korea. Of the remainder, ninety-three were determined to be sufficiently disturbed that they were not allowed to be interviewed by the press at the time. A dozen others, those determined to be emotionally disturbed but not incapable of normal functions, were provided supportive care and allowed to return to the Zone of Interior (ZI-United States).

Initial interviews with POWs provided many charges of collaboration. The Department of Defense investigated more than 500 of these charges, but only a few men were charged or convicted of misconduct by court-martial.[4] There was some concern about the effect that captivity had had in terms of the prisoners' general attitude. In February 1953, the United States Department of Defense had suggested that there might be some concern that released prisoners who had accepted their reeducation would make trouble when they went home.

The problems for the returning POWs were massive. Some were the same difficulties experienced by any veteran and some the product of a considerable misunderstanding on the home front. Among the returning POWs, there was the difficulty of re-integration, for the ex-prisoners tended to think of the nation, their families, and themselves as they were at the time of their imprisonment. In general, they were totally unaware of, and unable to deal with, the changes that had occurred. Communication was often difficult at first. What communication the men had experienced in camps was very stylized and consisted of an "ingroup" language. At home, they felt the lack of communication among persons who did not understand the basis for their means of articulation and felt rejected and frustrated trying to maintain human contact. Prisoners of war often found themselves patronized by persons who either sympathetically, or unsympathetically, provoked the veteran to anger.

Some of the prisoners returned to a disinterested nation. Men who had spent up to thirty-six months of captivity found it difficult to return to such a nation. They often ran into persons who were either not very aware of the war or those who considered them foolish to have taken part in it. Added to this was the underlying suspicion of many that all POWs had been indoctrinated (brainwashed) and were no long trustworthy.

Two years after the armistice, the Army issued a report on POWs after interviewing all returning POWs while they were on their way home. It reported that the Chinese divided prisoners based on their potential for re-education. The incorrigibles were usually housed in separate camps, while those judged to be "potential" were indoctrinated, sometimes as many as five hours a day, sometimes accompanied by torture. It was the Army's findings that a large number had "succumbed" in one degree or the other. Unfortunately, the report supported what was becoming a popular obsession with the idea of brainwashing.[5]

Defectors

The fact that twenty-one Americans refused to return to the United States after their confinement as POWs hit America like a sledgehammer. It was very hard to believe that any American would choose not to live in the United States. The fact added considerable fuel to the fear of communism that was already burning brightly, fanned on the charges of McCarthyism. In this concern, the rational understanding of the events were often ignored. First of all, there have always been defectors in American wars. Human beings act differently under the pressure imposed by capture, and since the American Revolution, soldiers have changed sides. A second, perhaps far more important, reason was that the Korean War was a vastly different war. It was a war in which POWs were not just a military inconvenience, but one in which the POWs became pawns in the ideological cold war that was being waged. The condition of North Korean and Chinese POW camps was so poor that nearly 38 percent of those captured died in captivity. This is ten times as high as the death of American prisoners in World War II camps in Germany.

Despite the concern, it is significant to note that time has shown that the vast majority of Americans held in communist captivity conducted themselves with courage and loyalty, surviving the hazards of their confinement with as little cooperation as possible. Over the half-century since the war, about half of the twenty-one defectors have returned to the United States, after the Supreme Court ruled that they could not be tried for offenses committed while they were POWs or for their initial failure to return.

There is little doubt that the majority of those held as POWs behaved as well as Americans captured in the previous war. Yet all POWs were somehow painted with the brush of betrayal. Perversely, even the men who died while in captivity were somehow blamed for what happened to them. After being raked over the coals by the mass media, the negative stereotype rooted in alleged POW misbehavior rubbed off on all Korean War veterans.

THE HOME FRONT

There is considerable evidence that the only one of the belligerent nations for whom the Korean War came as much of a surprise was the United States. And as much as it surprised the administration, the surprise to the average American was even greater. Nevertheless, when President Truman made the decision to send American troops to Korea, the decision appeared to gain popular acceptance. At first Americans acted in response, many remembering the difficulties of World War II and, among other things, began the hoarding of supplies in case rationing was imposed. But as the war moved on, casualties mounted, and the war degenerated into a weary stalemate, the support lessened. According to most indicators, Americans continued to deal with the war with a kind of sullen resignation. Images of the conflict quickly faded as news of the war moved from the front pages and criticism expanded. For many, there was little to remind them of what was happening in Korea other than a brief death notice in a hometown newspaper.

A lot had happened at home during the years of the war. Just after the war began Julius and Ethel Rosenberg were arrested for espionage as a part of the increasing fear of communism. In October 1950, the comic strip *Peanuts* by Charles Schulz was first published. At about this same time, the Federal Communications Commission issued the first license to broadcast TV in color, the honor going to the CBS. President Truman survived an assassination attempt in November by two Puerto Rican nationalists, Grisello Torresola and Oscar Collazo. Foreshadowing a whole industry, Ralph Schneider organized the Dinner's Club Card, which, at the time, only worked in twenty-seven restaurants in New York. Thor Heyerdahl's *Kon Tiki* was a hit as were the movies *Father of the Bride,* with Spencer Tracy and Elizabeth Taylor, and *Harvey,* starring Jimmy Stewart. The popular program *Your Hit Parade* (a successful show on the radio since 1935) premiered on NBC television in July 1950. Author George Orwell and director Walter Huston died.

During 1951, King Abdullah I of Jordan was assassinated. The United States began to enjoy direct dial coast-to-coast telephones and, in August, the first baseball game was televised in color. The movies *American in Paris* and *The African Queen* were in the theaters and in October *I Love Lucy* appeared for the first times. *Dragnet* aired for the first time on NBC. The author Sinclair Lewis died.

During 1952, Queen Elizabeth II became queen of England on the death of George VI, the Senate ratified a World War II Peace Treaty with Japan, Eisenhower was elected to be president of the United States. In sports, the Summer Olympic Games were held in Helsinki. The *Today Show* premiered on NBC, and the first political advertisement on TV was a 30-minute slot for Adlai Stevenson. Curly Howard of the Three Stooges, and Eva Peron, "Evita," died.

The year 1953 saw the death of Soviet premier Joseph Stalin and the announcement of the first polio vaccine discovered by Jonas Salk. Ian Fleming published his first Bond book, *Casino Royale,* Elvis Presley recorded for the first time and *From Here to Eternity* was a major film production. The big bands began to be replaced by rock and roll.

Attitudes at Home toward the Korean War

For a brief period, the invasion launched by the DPRK united all Americans, but the public mood soon changed. The American people viewed the war with ambivalence, tending to be supportive when they considered things were going well, and hostile when we were losing.

Political sensitivity at home was increasingly attuned to the mounting casualty reports, and the nearly stagnant nature of events. Everyone was aware of the desire not to expose more Americans to danger during the time that negotiations were being carried on. A memorandum prepared for President Dwight D. Eisenhower and released with limited circulation in June 1953 reported that a poll of the American people suggested that 45 percent of those polled believed that an armistice agreement with the Chinese would be considered a success. Yet, given these concerns, 69 percent approved of signing an armistice, with the majority suggesting the war in Korea was no longer worth fighting.[6]

For a good many Americans, the events in Korea were both out-of-sight and out-of-mind. Unless the individual was on active duty, or was a member of the family of an active duty man or woman, very few persons paid it much attention. There was neither organized opposition to the war nor unbridled support for it. There were a few rumblings from members of the Progressive Party and even the Longshoreman's Union, but not many. The writer I. F. Stone was a strong dissenter, but he came from the other side of the political wing.

In early December 1950, David McConnell, a correspondent for the *New York Herald Tribune,* who had witnessed the confusion at the early part of the war and was astonished at what he considered to be American weakness, would write, "There is something wrong with the American boy today. He won't fight. He gladly takes a whipping, thinking only of running away. In my day he might have taken a whipping in a fight or baseball game, but always scrapped back. These boys are weak."[7]

Korean Conflict GI Bill

The Korean veteran, like veterans from earlier wars, sought assistance offered by the government to help in their return to civilian life. Significant among these was the GI Bill. In 1636, the Pilgrims decided that if anyone was sent from the community as a soldier and was hurt, he deserves to be maintained by the colony for the rest of his life. Since that time, America has always taken care of those who serve, especially those who lost a limb or their life. The last surviving dependent from the Revolutionary War era received benefits until 1911.

President Truman approved the Veterans Readjustment Assistance Act of 1952 (Public Law 550) that authorized the GI benefit for the Korean War veteran. The law established the eligibility at ninety days of service between the start of the war on July 27, 1950 and February 1, 1955 and required only something other than a dishonorable discharge. This aid took on many forms and was designed to help the GI in his or her return to civilian life. The needs of wounded veterans were given top priority. Disabled veterans were provided for under the provisions of the Vocational Rehabilitation Act of 1950. An estimated 77,000 veterans used these programs.

Public Law 550, the Veterans Readjustment Assistant Act of 1952, signed on July 16, 1952, provided the ex-GI with 1.5 times his active duty time up to a maximum of 36 months for schooling, having to start within 2 years. The veteran received an educational benefit of up to $110. a month, out of which he or she paid tuition, books, fees, supplies, and other training costs. There was some increase for veterans with dependents. The program ended on January 31, 1965 after 2,391,000 of the 5,509,000 eligible veterans took advantage of it. The percentage of use was about 7 percent lower following the Korean War than after World War II. The breakdown suggests that 1,213,000 took advantage of institutions of higher education, 860,000 received training in other types of schools, 223,000 on the job training, and 95,000 in institutional on-farm training. The total cost of the program was $4.5 billion. Forty-three percent of the veterans took advantage of this bill in some form.

A later bill signed by President Johnson, the Veterans Readjustment Benefits Act of 1966, provided home and farm loans, job counseling, and employment placement services in addition to the categories in the previous bill. This was designed retroactively, providing benefits to post-Korean war veterans who served between February 1, 1955 and August 4, 1964. In addition to education, the veterans were able to get Veterans Adminisatration (VA) home loans to purchase homes for which the VA guaranteed more than $32 billion in mortgage loans. The veteran's preference in federal employment was extended by a bill on July 14, 1952.

As of 1999, the VA provided more than 60,000 headstones in cemeteries other than those managed by them and 9,800 were interred in VA national cemeteries. More than 803,000 veterans maintain a life insurance policy.

CONCLUSION

Because of the rotation policy, men came home from the Korean War during the period of the war, and they often arrived individually or in small groups. There was no grand end when whole divisions marched down Madison Avenue, no huge gatherings of spectators as trainloads of soldiers pulled into the station. There was no point at which it could be said the war was over, and the troops all could come home. The dribbling return did little to encourage much celebration. Most families and some smaller towns made an effort to welcome their local heroes back, but an awful lot of men came home, changed their clothes, and settled back into the society with hardly a ripple.

The dead came home to be buried in family plots or, occasionally, at the national cemeteries. The dead who could be identified were shipped and families worked with to bring some sort of closure. For those who were seriously wounded, it meant a return to military hospitals where they underwent long bouts toward final recovery or where, even today, some still remain.

For many, the journey, from the draft or enlistment, or recall, was marked with milestones of memory that they would later recall, some with horror and some with humor, but all with the uniqueness of their experience. Coming home was the goal of those who went, and it was anticipated with great joy. The experience, however, was not always what was expected, for they were different, made strangers by events that had occurred within the nation as well as the family while they were gone. It was a hard adjustment for all concerned.

NOTES

1. Lawrence H. Borts, *United Nations Medals and Missions: The Medals and the Ribbons of the United Nations* (Fountain Inn, SC: Medals of America Press, 1998).

2. Joseph C. Goulden, *Korea: The Untold Story of the War* (New York: Times Books, 1982), 295–296.

3. Callum A. MacDonald, *The War Before Vietnam* (New York: Freepress, 1986), 147.

4. "POW: The Fight Continues After the Battle" A Report for the Secretary of Defense's Advisory Committee on Prisoners of War," Washington, D.C.: July 29, 1955.

5. "POW: The Fight Continues After the Battle," Report for the Secretary of Defense's Advisory Committee on Prisoners of War, Washington, D.C.: July 29, 1955.

6. Eisenhower, General Dwight D., "Memo on Recent Polls on Korea, June 2, 1953" declassified, Eisenhower Presidential Library. JACKDAW 617-Korean War.

7. S. L. A. Marshall, "Combat Stress" paper presented at conference, Recent Advances in Medicine and Surgery, Army Medical Service Graduate School, Washington D.C. April 30, 1954.

13   REMEMBERING WAR

When I came home from Korea the family welcomed you, and that was it. I never talked about the war. People weren't interested, and wouldn't know where it was even if you told them.

—Fritz Heistermann, ex-Marine

THE QUIET AMERICAN

When the Korean veteran returned home, the events in Korea were still not acknowledged as a war. It was not until the National Defense Authorization Act for Fiscal Year 1999 (section 1067) that the Congress officially changed the title of the events in Korea from the Korean Conflict to the Korean War. Only a fraction of Americans had been affected by the agony of Korea and the society at large remained blissfully unaffected. There was no rationing, very few shortages, no bond drives or scrap metal collections. Rather, Americans at home during this period enjoyed an increase in prosperity. There was little of the passion of previous wars. Unlike World War II, Americans did not generally display flags at their windows marking a serviceman in the war. At one point, an effort was made to get Americans to wear buttons in support of the war but even that failed. The word that seemed to define the situation was indifference.

There was one consolation, wrote *Parade* columnist James Brady: the folks at home did not stage a lot of parades for us, but then "neither did people spit at us." This is true. There was some, but little of the animosity shown servicemen during the Vietnam War. But there had emerged a popular, rather subtle, defamatory image of the American soldier who was soft, and who, when captured, collaborated with the enemy. Even men who died during captivity were tarnished with this brush, suggesting that it was in some way their own fault.

In January 1953, the *Army Times* commented on the poor response shown to the Korean veteran, saying that the men "who fight it are lonesome symbols of a nation too busy or too economy-minded to say thanks in a proper manner."[1]

In the mind of some persons, the Korean War was a fight lost, and the stalemate represented by the armistice was considered a failure by the American military. The American soldier was held up in many cases as the one responsible for this failure.

The idea that Korean War POWs were unusually given to collaboration has remained despite being meticulously debunked both by military and civilian inquirers. The source of the charge arises from a difference in the nature of the captivity, not in an essential difference in those captured. The fact that some men did make broadcasts in favor of their captors results from treatment and conditions which, spurred on by the politics of the Cold War, brought to bear unimaginable pressures on those held and interrogated.

The popular press suggested that the American serviceman lacked courage, pride, discipline, assertiveness, and the traditional American virtues of individualism and toughness. This supported the belief that the veteran could not—or at least did not—uphold the high moral and the military resolve that Americans were supposed to possess. This attitude left many Americans skeptical and, on occasion, antagonistic. Some individuals even suggested that Americans had become weak-willed and dishonorable. This idea was reinforced, albeit without complicity, by films released during the final months and just after the war. In these films, the American veterans were portrayed as suffering psychoneurotics, as in *Niagara* (1953), *Hatful of Rain* (1955), and *Five Against the House* (1955). For some who seemed to find a lack of masculinities and a decline in the spirit of the American soldier, the explanation was often portrayed as "brainwashing." *The Manchurian Candidate* (1962), a popular and critically acclaimed movie, did, in fact, provide a scenario of a Korean War soldier who had been brainwashed to become a political assassin.

The average veteran, on his return, received little recognition. By 1952, the war had pretty much left the front pages as well as the public mind. If a generalization can be made, many veterans appeared to have returned home with a rather profound sense of fatalism. Most of them returned to their jobs, or their families and, keeping a low profile, quickly submerged into the larger community, saying little. As far as can be told, these veterans readjusted to civilian life. Few, however, would forget their experiences there.

A VETERANS ORGANIZATION

For a variety of reasons, the Korean veteran felt no urge to organize. It was nearly thirty years later that the first separate organization appeared. The Chosin Few, made up of veterans, Army and Marines, who were involved in that 1950 battle, was begun on April 22, 1983. The national organization, the Korean War Veterans Association, was founded by William T. Norris of New York on June 25, 1985. That same year, the original nine-member board began the publication of a magazine called The *Graybeards,* a title which reflected the age of the veteran at that time. Meeting in Arlington, they attended a ceremony to recognize the first issue of the United States Post Office's new Korean War veterans stamp. When they returned, forty members signed up. Membership today totals somewhere in the vicinity of 10,000 veterans, about 7 percent of the eligible veterans.

Part of this late organization can perhaps be explained by the very impersonal pipeline system that moved men in and out in rotation, without regard to units, thereby denying them the opportunity to develop a sense of pride in a unit. Being in a command for a shorter period of time, many did not develop the lasting friendships that emerged from World War II. Another reason may well be that sensing that folks at home lacked a great deal of interest in their service, they saw no reason to bring it up, or draw attention to it.

Another phenomenon of the still misunderstood war is the fact that "retreads"—those who were called back to fight in Korea after having served in World War II–often prefer to identify themselves with the "big war" or, as it has come to be called, "the good war."

It has been estimated that at least 20 percent of the Korean War veterans were adversely affected by their experiences in the war. This ignores the obvious fact that, in one way or another, all those who were involved in the fighting of the Korean War were affected by the experience. But today, men who are now in their seventies, still report suffering negative psychological effects associated with long-term and distressing memories that have been allowed to fester.

THE WAR REMEMBERED

Paul G. Pierpali Jr. suggests that the Korean War is unavoidably compared with and subsumed by the myth and memory of World War II. It seems to have "emerged like an unwanted mutation from a linear, Darwinian-like process that seamlessly linked World War II with the Cold War (*sic*) and its early evolutionary process." It thus became a "prisoner of the rigid mentality and ideology of the early cold war and, while it inherited too much myth from World War II" it has not managed to develop enough myths of its own.[2]

There is not a great deal to remind America of the Korean War. The simplest of tests given to those old enough to remember the war might indicate some knowledge of a few place names: Jane Russell Hill, Pork Chop Hill, or even the invasion at Inchon in 1950. But little else would be recalled. The Korean names, hard to pronounce and remember in the first place, are now lost forever: Wonju for example has been referred to by historians as the "Gettysburg of the Korean War," but would strike little memory among Americans. What has been done is limited and, at least for the Korean War veteran, leaves a great deal to be desired.

Lyndon Johnson, then a Democrat senator from Texas, described much of the American feeling, when he called the cease-fire a fraud that only allowed the enemy to release its aggressive armies somewhere else. There is little doubt that the end of the war—an armistice rather than a victory—had a good deal to do with the memory of the war. The cease-fire was just that, it did not solve the original problems nor provide any potential results. Americans were not accustomed to wars ending unfinished. It was a situation in which Americans "preferred amnesia to self-doubt or introspection."[3] The fact that it took half a century to construct a memorial is some evidence that this was true.

Memorials

Most Korean veterans, visiting the memorial in Washington, D.C., would agree that it is a fitting and realistic tribute to their companions, living and dead, who shared this experience with them. As it should, it evokes many memories. One memory, however, is that it was a long time coming.

The Korean War Veterans Memorial in Washington, D.C. (© *Wally McNamee / Corbis*)

The Korean War Memorial was authorized by Public Law 99-572 on October 28, 1996, fifty-three years after the armistice. The order established a board of twelve veterans appointed by the president. The site that was selected in Washington D.C was adjacent to the Lincoln Memorial and directly across the reflecting pool from the Vietnam Veterans Memorial.

The memorial consists of nineteen stainless statues, wearing parkas and moving through rough terrain. It is reflected off a 164-foot long black granite wall. On the wall are carved more than 2,500 images of men, women, and equipment. There is an area of remembrance, consisting of a circular reflecting pool at the apex of a grove of 40 Linden trees. On the part of the wall that extends into the pool area is engraved "Freedom Is Not Free." The Pool of Remembrance has the inscription: "Our nation honors her sons and daughters who answered the call to defend a country they never knew and a people they never met."

The American Battle Monuments Commission managed the project and the U.S. Army Corps of Engineers provided assistance. The architect of record is Cooper Lecky Architects. The completed monument was dedicated on July 27, 1995 by President Bill Clinton and South Korean President Kim Young Sam. There has been some reconstruction, primarily the provision of a kiosk, and lighting. The statues were sculpted by Frank Gaylord and cast by Tallix Foundries of Beacon, New York. They represent an ethnic cross section of Americans: twelve Caucasians, three African American, two Hispanic, one Oriental, one Native American. Fourteen represent the Army, one the Navy, three the Marines, and one the Air Force. The names of the twenty-two UN nations that responded to the call are engraved on the curb stone along the north entrance.

When it was dedicated in July 1995, an estimated 50,000 were on hand to share in the event. It is interesting to note, however, that the event was somewhat overshadowed by the conflict in Bosnia and the O. J. Simpson trial. It did not receive the attention that was given to the Vietnam memorial after its opening in 1982.[4]

More than a half century after the hostilities ended, many states are erecting monuments. Spurred on by aging veterans, these community-based expressions have appeared in large numbers in the last decade.

The Unknown Soldier

On August 3, 1956, the 84th Congress enacted Public Law 975, sponsored by Congressman Price of Illinois, authorizing the burial of an unknown serviceman from the Korean War at Arlington National Cemetery. It was signed by President Eisenhower. The unknown soldier from World War I had been interned on November 11, 1921. The bodies of four, unknown Americans who had died in the Korean War were selected for the final ceremony, placed inside identical caskets and draped with the American flag. They were escorted by the Hawaii Service Police to the Army's mortuary at Kapalama Base where a final check was made to be sure there was still no clue as to their identity. Then were brought to Washington, D.C. There, on May 15, 1958, they were placed on hearses and transported to the cemetery. The invocation was given by Chaplain Colonel F. B. Henry. Lieutenant General Robert M. Cannon gave a brief address. Then Sergeant Ned Lyle placed a wreath of blue and white carnations, representing the Korean Service Medal, on one of the caskets, thereby identifying which would be buried. The caskets lay in the Capital Rotunda until May 30, and on Memorial Day, 1958, the Unknown Soldiers of World War II and Korea were laid to rest in a national ceremony at Arlington Cemetery. The words on the sculpted panel read "Here Rests in Honored Glory an American Soldier Known But to God."

Commemorations

On July 27, 2003, a stamp honoring the 50th anniversary of the Korean War was issued by the United States Post Office. The first stamp was issued at the Korean War Veterans Memorial in Washington. The statuary troop patrol consisted of fourteen soldiers, one sailor, one airman, and three marines, moving through a field of snow. The picture, taken from the Korean Memorial, represented a cross-section of Americans – white, African American, Asian Americans, Native Americans, and Hispanics. John W. Alli of Catonsville, Maryland, took the photograph on the stamp just before a snowstorm in January 1996. There had been other stamps issued earlier. A 33-cent stamp was issued as a part of the Celebrate the Century in 1999. In 1985, a 22-cent Korean Veterans stamp was issued.

Literary and Cinematic Versions of the Korean War

There is evidence available to suggest that the Korean War has never received the self-reflection through literature or films that are necessary to understand what happened. The literary response to the war was, at best, limited in both quality and quantity and, thus, has left little impact on the American memory. For nearly thirty years, few if any articles about the Korean War or its veterans were published in a popular periodical.

Novels

There have been few Korean War novels of merit and those that have appeared have tended to reflect the serviceman as detached from the larger issues. These soldiers in literature tend to an air of professionalism, fighting men just doing a job while waiting to go home, resigned, if not fatalistic, and stoically accepting their fate. To this day, only a handful of works have delved into the innermost feelings of the Korean GI. It could be argued that this is the most realistic portrayal of the Korean veteran, but to many critics the works fail to do what the war novel is designed to do, to portray the human spirit under crisis. Perhaps that was the point the poet Wilfred Owens was trying to make with his World War I poems. Maybe all the language with which to deal with war has been exhausted.

Poetry

Even more than the novel, the poetry of the Korean War has lapsed into oblivion, if it has ever amounted to anything in the first place. Recognizing that the verse written by the average GI is intensely individual and usually highly emotional, we are looking beyond verse to the more sophisticated and universal poetry, which has previously emerged from the poet-soldiers of other wars.

The few written by the Korean poets, and poems about Korea, tend to deal more with colonial experience and a variety of caustic insights into military dictatorships, what Ji Moon-Suh of the Korea University calls a conflict between brotherhood and patriotism. These poems consider the unspeakable horrors caused by the war in such a manner as to avoid expressing hatred toward the enemy. The best being written allows us to better understand the tragedy as it occurred to the Korean people and certainly is one reason for the enduring effect the war has had in the Republic of Korea.

This is not true for that written by Americans. While the war produced more than its share of verse written by the lonely or frustrated GI, there was little in terms of serious poetry that either describes or provides analysis to what was happening to the men and women fighting the war. There is no Korean War poetry included in Fussell's *Norton Book of Modern War* nor is any included in Carolyn Forche *Against Forgetting: Twentieth Century: Poetry of Witness*. The *Hermit Kingdom* was the first anthology of Korean War poems and it was not until W. D. Ehrhart and Philip K. Jason produced *Retrieving Bones* in 1999 that any serious study came out.

Plays

There have been a few plays based on the Korean War, most of them written and performed in the years immediately following the war. A high percentage of the plays produced have been based on court-room situations dealing with "brainwashing" and other conflicts that emerged from the plight of the prisoners of war. Perhaps the most significant of these was *Time Limit* by Henry Denker and Ralph Berkey. In total, there are fewer than a dozen that can be located and, among these, few that will outlast the immediacy of the events they depict. Certainly there is the argument that it is difficult to represent the conditions of war on the stage, but that did not prevent some remarkable plays about earlier wars. Koreans, both North and South, have produced several plays which, as one would expect, tend to be more reflective of political attitude than they do the lives of those involved in the war.

Movies

There have been an estimated 2,800 films made about World War II and approximately 800 about the Vietnam War. It depends on what is considered a "war movie." The best count on the Korean War is 110. In these relatively few films, Hollywood has dealt with the ambiguities of the Korean War by avoiding the primary issues. Other than a few attempts at propaganda—the production of *I Want You* for example—the Korean War film avoids the big picture and focuses instead on small groups of fighting men often isolated behind enemy lines. There has been nothing of the scope of *The Longest Day* or the made-for-television series *Band of Brothers*. The films that have come out in the half century since the armistice have created an image of the veteran that is very imprecise, and borrows heavily on the individuals and experiences of other wars. The primary difference being that the typical melting pot—the squad portrayed—now often includes an African American, and one of Japanese ancestry, to acknowledge a more modern understanding.

The films are most definitely a continuation of films made about World War II. There were few battles, as Hollywood defines them, and thus the action focuses on a hill, or an outpost, or a patrol. The themes of these films reflect fears of disloyalty and domestic subversions which, at times, seems to reach almost hysterical proportions. Hollywood films routinely suggest that soldiers collaborated with the communists, perhaps contributing to the war's uncertain end. They also expressed "a cynicism and uncertainty about the reasons for the war and its eventual outcome."[5] The films of the Korean War rather consistently carry a theme that questioned the military leadership. One of the most remembered films dealing with the Korean War, the *Manchurian Candidate,* portrayed the Korean War veteran as weak-minded and psychologically unbalanced. It came to symbolize the war for many Americans, and anticipated the public perception of the Vietnam vet.

Among the movies generally considered to be the most reflective of the war, and participation in it, are *The Bridges at Toko-ri* (1954), *Porkchop Hill* (1959), *Retreat Hell!* (1952) and *The Steel Helmet* (1951). Of these, the last, a film produced in only twelve days and completed within six months of the beginning of the war, is one of the best in terms of depicting the early conflict and disillusionment.

Perhaps the best known movie associated with the Korean War is the feature film *M*A*S*H* and the long term tv series that followed. This story takes place in Korea during the Korean War and for that fact alone is credited with giving the American people some aid in remembering the war itself. However, the movie, and even less the series, are not good depictions of the war in Korea. It was written and produced as a protest against Vietnam and reflects disagreement against distinctly Vietnam era concerns; authority, military blunders, efficiency placing persons above the law. Those were not the issues in Korea and the humor and sarcasm, however well done, addresses more universal problems.

Hollywood is primarily motivated by economics and one reason to explain the lack of Korean War films can be found in the lack of interest among Americans. The viewing public was not buying the war that the Korean War movies portrayed. It was a hard sell, for the movie goer did not come into the theater—as they did with World War II films—with a preconceived notion of the legitimacy of it all.

THE LEGACY

When the Korean War veteran returned home, he came home to a different world. In the first place, the war had altered much of what might normally have been the progress of these years. Among other things, it diverted the nation from the curse of racism and delayed attention to the problems caused by segregation and poverty.

The anticommunist hysteria kicked in and, supported by men like Joseph McCarthy, grew to engage a good deal of the public attention. The National Association of Manufactures began to crack down on labor at home, weakening the power of the unions. The popular culture had changed as well. As one GI put it, "we left to the sounds of Glenn Miller and returned to Elvis Presley." In the immediacy, a great deal had changed in the daily lives of the citizens, and much was seen as different. The immediate legacy was confused, but it is the long-term legacy that has affected most citizens.

The goals of the war have never been clear. Perhaps the intent, as well as the expectations of the various nations involved, can be seen in how they identified the war. In the Republic of Korea where the war is fiercely remembered, it is identified by the day—"June 25th War." In the People's Republic of China, a rough translation of the event is "The Anti-American War in Support of North Korea." The North Koreans called it the "Fatherland Liberation War." The United States did not settle on a name for a long time, calling it a Police Action, Mr. Truman's War, the Forgotten War, The Proxy War and other euphuisms, until it was finally identified as the Korean War in the National Defense Authorization Act for 1999.

Costs of the War

In the long term, there is no way to ever total up the costs of a war, either to the nations involved, or to the world at large. But the cost for the nations involved may at least be suggested. Both North and South Korea were devastated during the war. Their buildings were destroyed and the urban areas were nearly flattened. The existing hydro-electric systems were ruined, tunnels had been collapsed, rail lines separated and broken, ports destroyed, and hundreds of thousands of civilians dispossessed. In both cases, the economy was in utter ruin. UN forces claim to have destroyed 11,000 railway engines and cars as well as cutting rail lines more than 28,000 times. It is estimated that more than 80 percent of the industrial and public facilities, including transportation and the infrastructures, were destroyed. And, despite the intentions of both sides, it left the peninsula permanently divided.

Apart from the smaller hamlets or isolated farms, much of what had been Korea did not exist. The nation suffered enormous casualties on both sides of the 38th Parallel. After the war, an estimated 10 million families had been separated, not only separated physically, but totally lacking any means of communication. The chance for the unification of the nation, never very good before, was now nearly impossible. The war had intensified the distrust between the communist and anticommunist camps in Korea, and the presence of United States was a continuing agitation to the North Koreans. The casualties of the war must be counted in the millions, the financial costs in the billions.

For South Korea, the casualties in the war totaled 238,656, about 47,000 killed and 183,000 wounded. An additional 8,656 were taken prisoners of war. The civilian casualties far exceeded this, with an estimated one million civilians either killed or hurt. As is usually the case, civilians were caught up in the fighting and died in large numbers through no fault of their own. North Korea suffered an estimated 630,723 casualties, including 520,000 killed or wounded. The civilian deaths in the north were about the same as in the south; one million. The unknown deaths as well as those that resulted from long-term exposure and stress can never be known.

The People's Republic of China suffered an estimated 390,000 military casualties, about 110,000 killed, 21,600 died of wounds, 13,000 died of disease, and 21, 374 were taken as prisoners of war. The outcome of the war may well have been less than they anticipated, but considering the political advantages—defying of the power of the United States and holding them at some sort of a stalemate—it was highly advantageous to the Chinese and acknowledged Red China as a great power in the east. It needs to be noted, as well, that China took no advantage of the North Korean situation. They took no assets as a result of their involvement, nor did they demand any repayment via territorial advantages. Chinese troops were pulled out in 1958.

While the situation was very complex, the war must have contributed to the decline in Sino-Soviet relations. Both the Soviet's stringent interpretation of help, and China's ability to hold its own again the U.S., contributed to this decline.

On the other hand, the Korean War may well have saved the Republic of Taiwan. Every evidence shows that the United States was cooling in its support of the Nationalist government. But Truman, fearing that a two-front war would be to the advantage of the Chinese, agreed to protective action that not only gave the Nationalist government new life, it greatly angered the Communist China.

Perhaps the nation that came out ahead as a result of the war was Japan. The war hurried the settlement of the peace ending World War II. As well, the $3.5 billion dollars spent with Japanese companies went a long way to expand the economy. The war put Japan in the position of functioning as a huge war supplier and rear support base for the Americans. This led to the speedy economic recovery, which was witnessed in its most extreme case in the 1980. The Japanese aided the UN cause in a variety of ways, some considered—by the Chinese Communist at least—as illegal in terms of Japan's position. Japanese LSTs(Landing Ship, Tank), some even crewed by Japanese sailors, were used during the invasion of Inchon.

Effects on the United Nations

There is still some discussion about the effect of the war on the United Nations. Many see that the UN willingness to take action gave it a new sense of authority in the world. Others will argue that the UN did not do enough and that what it tried to do in terms of political intervention accomplished nothing. The fact that the war was fought under the pale blue of the UN flag did not disguise the fact that it was a war in which the United States carried the brunt of the involvement, and was a major factor in UN decisions about the war.

Effects on the United States

One of the most obvious outcomes of the Korean War was the transformation of the cold war into a military activity. Up to this time, the cold war had been fought politically and economically. And in this transformation, Americans took the fight against the communist in Korea to be a general fight against communist aggression everywhere. The war caused the Truman administration to totally reassess its foreign policy and move toward defense commitments all around the world. It changed America's view of the Third World, most obviously Indochina, where Americans had originally been critical of the French action there. After Korea, they began to heavily support the French, slowly committing itself to the slippery slope toward involvement in Indochina.

The Korean War was the first military action of the cold war and as such it did much to set the model for conflicts that would appear later. It introduced the idea of a limited war in which two superpowers could fight over an issue without taking on the devastation of an all-out war involving nuclear weapons. It also gave the United States the perfect excuse for militarizing NATO by the reinforcing of American troop deployment in Europe and naming General Dwight D. Eisenhower, in December 1950, as the Supreme Allied Commander, setting the stage for the rearming of West German.

Emerging from the Korean War was the baptism of the national security state that has grown ever since. It was during this war that we began to understand—though not quickly enough—that the government's inability to communicate any passionate or moral reason for wars of containment would result in the loss of support, even repudiation at the polls. It could be argued that the Korean War provided the media a powerful 20th century trend, the estrangement of the government from the governed. This trend is seen in the appearance of the man or woman defined as an expert, and the emergence of the professional administrator who assumed positions of power within the bureaucracy and, at the same time, became makers of American policy, though they became less and responsible to the electorate. The national security advisor and the council are but one example of this. National security provided a means for decisions to be made behind closed doors by persons who were accountable to no one but the person who hired them. Pierpaoli describes it as "annihilation without representation."[6]

Perhaps the least obvious effect, but the one that has hit America the deepest and the longest, was a change in fiscal ideology. Prior to the war, the process had been to determine the extent of the budget and then adjust military expenditures to meet it. But, during and following the war—certainly by 1952—the concept of budget had changed, and it was quickly decided that spending on national security can only be determined by what was seen as the threats to national security. The government was no longer in a position to enjoy the luxury of making decisions about military expenditures on the basis of the normal concept of the "ability to pay." The post-Korean War policy was to build a cold-war deterrence, and worry about paying for it later. Other characteristics of this mood can be noted, for example, in the 1951 decision to redirect the payment in the Marshall Plan from political and economic recovery to military rearmament.

The Korean War brought us face to face with not one, but three, highly significant constitutional challenges. The first was the somewhat precedented, but vastly over-used, action by President Truman to enlist the United States in a large-scale war without any congressional discussion or mandate. Strangely, this misuse of presidential power, and its threat to the rights of Congress, went primarily unchallenged. The war established a "precedent" that has been central to administrative policy ever since.

A second challenge came in 1952, when President Truman nationalized the steel mills in order to prevent a strike. While many agreed with him—it was the longest and costliest strike in history at that time and unforgivably denied 105 artillery shells to the men on the battlefield—citing the national emergency and the possibility of delaying equipment to the men in Korea—it was beyond presidential power. Later challenged by the courts and overturned, what remains surprising is the degree to which it was accepted by those who saw the need for tighter control in a national security state.

The third of these challenges was launched by General MacArthur and again, while prevented by presidential action, it nevertheless called into question the long tradition of civilian control of the military. What is so astonishing is not that General MacArthur questioned his civilian orders—that was in the nature of the man—but the degree to which both the military and some elements of the government sided with MacArthur.

Part of the loss of innocence that occurred in Korea was the realization—but not the acceptance—of the fact that what America needed to fight such wars was not a militia, but rather a national legion. The war needed professional military men and women, for the war was becoming too complicated to be fought by a militia. Professor T.R. Fehrenbach, in his classic work *This Kind of War* says it so well.

> However repugnant the idea is to liberal societies, the man who will willingly defend the free world in the fringe areas is not the responsible citizen-soldier. The man who will go where his colors go, without asking, who will fight a phantom foe in jungle and mountain range, without counting, and who will suffer and die in the midst of incredible hardship, without complaint, is still what he has always been, from Imperial Rome to sceptered Britain to democratic America. He is the stuff of which legions are made; he does the job—the utterly necessary job—no militia is wiling to do. His task is moral or immoral according to the orders that send him forth. It is inevitable, since men compete.[7]

Some historians suggest that the coming down of the Berlin Wall began with the war in Korea. Others suggest that the heated-up war simply increased the Soviet determination. Either way, a note about the confrontation between the Soviets and the United States is in order here. The war illustrated, if it did not establish, a realism that might have been considered impossible somewhat earlier. Both the United States and the Soviet Union involved themselves in this war, but both powers took great pains to avoid an expansion of the war. An expansion of the conflict was to the advantage of neither side. While the truce talks dragged on, the Chinese and Soviets, as well as the UN Command, took care to limit their reaction. The UN declined to use Chinese Nationalist forces, Chinese took no action to threaten Taiwan, and our staging bases in Japan were never threatened. In Korea, the ambitions of both sides were slowed, but they were not deterred. It was less than a year before the same scenario was being played out in another Asian country, Vietnam.

Certainly as a by-product, even if not as an immediate result, was the decline in Sino-Soviet relations during and following the Korean War. Several factors were involved: the Soviet failure to provide promised air cover for the Chinese intervention, the fact that the Soviet government required the Chinese to pay for arms out of money loaned for economic development, and the growing power that China was gaining in the international community.

Military historian Richard Rovere suggests that the goals established for Korea were accomplished and the United Nations demonstrated the value of collective security. He, and others, has suggested that it was the turning point in the struggle against communism. On the other hand, Korean combatant, and one of America's most respected heroes, the Marine Corps' Chesty Puller, was highly critical, "Stalemate, hell! We lost the first war in our history, and it's time someone told the American people the truth about it." Eric Sevareid, the war correspondent and respected long-time anchor man, concluded in 1953 that the behavior of GIs in Korea "outmatches the behavior of those who fought our wars of certainty and victory this is something new in American society. This is something to be recorded with respect and humility."[8] Every evidence today is that the Americans who fought in Korea did so with as much courage and determination as any group of young American men and women have done. One hundred and thirty-one Medals of Honor were awarded to Korean servicemen, 53 percent of these posthumously.

ATROCITIES

War is an atrocity. How can there be a war without them? Certainly there are documented accounts of North Korean and Chinese troops torturing and executing prisoners. There are some accusations that this was also true of United Nations troops. There are recently declassified documents that show American troops were under orders to consider unidentified persons in the battle area as enemies, and there are numerous accounts of communist infiltrators hidden among the refugees. There are many accusations that civilians were shot at, and killed, by UN aircraft strafing. Most have been denied, few have been proved. But there is no doubt that in this war, as in most wars since gunpowder appeared on the scene, civilians have been severely and routinely killed by all the warring parties involved.

While no one condones this, it is important to keep in mind that this war, like so many wars, was fought by young men and women under unbelievable stress. It was a war that was fought without lines, and thus without real safety. With an enemy who believed in encirclement, and with enemy and friend looking very much alike, every unidentified individual appeared as a target. The wonder, perhaps, is that men and women, from the calm of their home or office, can be so surprised that war is brutal, and that many innocents are killed, not because anyone wants that, but because that is the nature of war.

CONCLUSION

Wars tend to grow respectable with age. In the last decade or so, the Korean War has begun to draw the attention of scholars as well as the popular press. The creation and dedication of the Korean War Memorial in Washington, D.C. did a great deal to acknowledge the contribution of the Korean veteran. However, in the larger perspective, the war still remains unrecognized, perhaps more honestly ignored than forgotten.

NOTES

1. Richard Kolb, "Korea's Invisible Veterans' Return to an Ambivalent America," *VFW Magazine* (November, 1997): 24–31.

2. Paul G. Pierpaoli, Jr., "Beyond Collective Amnesia: A Korean War Retrospective," *Military History* 14 (Spring, 2000): 1

3. Paul G. Pierpaoli, Jr., "Beyond Collective Amnesia: A Korean War Retrospective," *Military History* 14 (Spring, 2000): 2

4. Lester H. Brune, "Recent Scholarship and Findings about the Korean War," *American Studies International* 36 (October, 1998): 4–14

5. D. McCann, "Review of Philip West and Shu Ji Moon *Remembering the Forgotten War: The Korean War through Literature and Art*," *Korean Studies Review* 4 (2001): 2.

6. Paul G. Pierpaoli, Jr., "Beyond Collective Amnesia: A Korean War Retrospective," *Military History* 14 (Spring, 2000): 7

7. T. R. Fehrenbach, *This Kind of War* (Washington, D.C.: Brassey's, 1963), 455.

8. Richard Kolb, "Korea's Invisible Veterans' Return to an Ambivalent America," *VFW Magazine* (November, 1997): 3–4.

14 CONCLUSION: INHERITANCES AND MYTHS

To the men and women who participate, no war is a forgotten war.

The acknowledgment of the Korean War as the "forgotten war" tells us a great deal about America in the late 1950s, but not very much about the young men and women who fought this war, who died in it, or who have carried its memories with them for more than half a century.

In the American memory, in its commemoration, as in the popular and scholarly works designed to recount it, the role of the serviceman or woman has been discredited, not out of any desire to do so, but in the rush to explain. There is considerable difference between the history of a war that is attempting to provide causes and excuses, to foster nationalism or save patriotic pride, and the history of being at war. The Korean War has been studied more from the first of these positions than from the second. In the effort to understand, to place the war into a context that has some meaning for us and our history, there is the tendency to assume that all wars are alike, and that in presenting the military situation we have somehow come to understand those who make up the military.

When it comes to the veterans of the Korean War, we know both a great deal and very little about them. They gathered from all over the United States, represented nearly every ethnic group, came from every class, and were forged together both by training and action into a body of fighting men who fought the war they were asked to fight. As illustrated throughout this book, they answered the call of the nation, fought when necessary, and maintained as much of their lives and goals while learning to live and to function in the military establishment. And when it was over, they returned home with little thanks, less fanfare than they might have expected, and set about returning to their civilian lives with little comment and few criticisms. And, for many, it is sufficient to leave it like this.

Chris Hedges in his significant work *War Is a Force that Gives us Meaning* (New York: Public Affairs, 2002), suggests that most societies are never able to recover from the wounds inflicted on them during wartime. For what the war leaves behind, and what is commemorated, is not memory but amnesia. What men and women do when the war is over is to return as quickly as possible to the pre-war concerns. Perhaps this is why the wall of names on the Korean and Vietnam memorials have been so powerful, for it is these persons who are calling upon us to remember, in a way that the institutional monument—designed to remember only that it is past—cannot do.

Yes, why have we forgotten this relatively recent war and those who participated in it? Perhaps one reason is that these silent veterans are the product of a silent generation. While no one seems to pay much attention to this generation—what, for lack of a better name, is called the "bumper generation"—it is worth noting that these were the young persons born too late to participate in World War II and too early to be identified with the "boomers." They were members of a transition generation who had been raised with, and had held on to, much of the traditions of an earlier America, even as they entered and experienced adulthood through the sweeping changes of the 1950s, 60s, and 70s. They were less the participants in these decades than they were the observers. While as a nation we have been quite vocal about the young persons of these decades, the men and women of America who had, in this period, moved into their thirties, forties, and fifties, were also greatly affected, caught between two highly articulate generations. Many of them, having lost their innocence in a war considered to be traditional, came home to a vastly untraditional world. Born too late for the patriotic fervor of American emergence and too late to enjoy such trends as the sexual revolution, they were mostly silent. Like the awkward teenager at the neighborhood dance, there was not much to say to either the younger or the older ones.

There is another reason, of course, shared with all veterans from all wars. And this is illustrated by the word itself. Veteran comes from *vetus,* meaning old, ripe, worn, belonging to the past. The fact that the war had been fought places those that fought it in the past, the often forgotten past. What they did is old, what is being done today is new. And as society, we find it better to remember them collectively rather than individually for, individually, they tell a variety of stories that we do not wish to hear.

THE MYTHS

The myths that are often created about war, and this one in particular, are themselves much of the source of collective forgetfulness. The power of the myth is to be found in the fact that it provides a means to give meaning to the mayhem, and justification for the cruelty and violent death, without forcing us to face the truth. And, in doing so, removes the necessity to look carefully at what happened, who was affected, and what are the lasting effects, not so much on the nation's political identity as on the lives of those who carry the war with them in their memory. These myths, among other, are that Americans lost the war, that the troops were not as brave as they needed to be, that our men were brainwashed, that those who returned home were free of the effects of their service, that the war was unnecessary.

It is not possible to address these myths in any detail, nor to argue them one way or the other. But the evidence is fairly clear about many of them and, as they apply to the individual soldier, sailor, marine or airman, they have answers. One of these myths is that America lost the Korean War. Such a position is far more political than it is military. America did not lose the Korean War. But it is also true that they did not win it in the manner America was accustomed to winning. American troops were called upon to defeat the North Koreans and drive them from the Republic of Korea as the United Nations had determined. This they did. The American forces were called upon to drive the North Koreans to the Manchurian border in an effort to unite all of Korea under a single government. This they did. When the war changed, and the mission became one of survival, they did this as well.

Another of the myths is that American troops were not brave and did not fight with distinction. This is simply not true, and any comparison with the behavior of the men and women in Korea to troops in any other war—from the American Revolution to Iraq—will provide the evidence needed. There is no doubt that the performance of the U.S. military during the early phases of the war was less than effective. Certainly the fatal neglect that occurred between World War II and Korea can explain a good deal of it. But once in line, and having heroically and narrowly saved themselves from potential disaster, they responded, and in the following periods made themselves far more effective and, above all, became a self-confident, fighting force. Historian Max Hastings suggests that one senior military commander had remarked, "We went into Korea with a very poor army and came out with a pretty good one. We went into Vietnam with a pretty good army and came out with a terrible one."[1] For the men and women who defended the line, who climbed the hills, who flew the missions, who hunted the mines, and who faced two distinctive and efficient enemies, the performance was remarkable successful. Certainly the fact that Americans awarded their combat troops 131 Medals of Honor should indicate that at least those involved were aware of acts of supreme courage and humanitarian effort.

Another of the myths emerges from the overworked American fear of communism at the time, and the concern over the manner in which prisoners of war were treated and responded. There is no doubt, at least statistically, that the number of POWs who cooperated with the enemy was very small, and that Americans who had been captured and held captive by the communists, behaved as well during the Korean War as during any other war in which Americans have been involved. There is no evidence that Americans held captive accepted the enemy's beliefs and returned home with them, planning to corrupt the democratic society. Yet, there appears to have been an irresistible urge to clear the American conscience of any blame for not preventing so many prisoners being taken; and in doing so, the high death rate and collapse of the POWs was sometimes blamed on the character of the American soldier, not on the appalling anguishes they suffered. POWs were even blamed for the fact of their own deaths, and those who survived were considered with suspicion. And yet, in all the efforts to prove collaboration, very few were ever documented, and fewer still ever found guilty of the crimes that some wanted to blame them for.

There is also the significant misconception, most likely brought on by the fact that most Korean veterans have not called attention to themselves, that they returned from the war primarily unaffected by it. Part of this is because there are few ways to explain what happened to them if they have not been willing to talk about it a lot themselves. There are very few novels, poems, or even anti-war movies that are able to recreate the horror of war, and of this war in particular. These fictional representations, like the events they try and portray, are easily seduced by the war-machine, and sometimes give in too easily to the romance of events preferably seen in the global scale than in the lives of the victims.

German authors, writing after World War I, often talked of the *automatisme anesthesiant,* that situation in which prolonged combat turns the soul into an entity that has lost its feeling for things. There are no studies in which to support this, but there are such studies to suggest that no one can experience those things experienced in war and come out the same. Among the other casualties of war is the identity of "the same." And, significantly, it must be noted that the veteran who returned did so with none of the help he or she had been given as they were going to war. One would think that the civilization would note the need for a *rite d'entree,* like boot camp, to aid the veteran to re-enter society. One returning veteran reported that when coming home, the Army gave him a new uniform, some back pay, a thirty-minute lecture on using toilet paper and not saying the "F" work at the dinner table, and let him go. It took the military eighteen weeks to teach him to kill and then provided only seven hours to forget it.

One thought that plagues the veteran is that the war was unnecessary. This idea will be argued for years and never settled. The question of necessity is more a political one than military, for the necessity of any war—for those who fight it—is that the individual has been sent to fight it. It appears now, however, fifty years after it began, that the war was not only necessary but vitally important to American interests at the time, and that those impacts remain significant even today.

Korea is a beautiful country with a long and proud history and culture. But it is not a very good place to fight a modern war. Underdeveloped at the time, with few roads or railways, and subject to extremes of climate, it was not the kind of environment that war planners would want. But that is where the war was, and that is where the United States sent its young men and women to fight it. That they did. For the average Korean War veteran there is no single memory.

NOTE

1. Max Hastings, *The Korean War* (New York: Simon & Schuster, 1987), 333.

BIBLIOGRAPHY

PRIMARY

Documents and Manuscripts

Army Regulations 350–90, June 1957
Boston Globe, 1950–1953

Alan Millet Semper Fidelis: The Story of the United States Marine Corps. New York: Macmillan, 1980.
Coakley, Robert W. "Highlights of Mobilization, Korean War." Office of the Chief of Military History, Department of the Army (March 10, 1959). Historical Manuscript Collection 2–3. 7AF.C
DA PAM 3051. *Handbook on the Chinese Communist Armies*, September 1952: 75–76
Eisenhower, General Dwight D. "Memo on Recent Polls on Korea, June 2, 1953", declassified November 6, 1953. Eisenhower Presidential Library. JACKDAW 617-Korean War
50th Anniversary Committee, National Salute to Korean Veterans, Department of Defense, (July 9, 2003).
Guidebook for Marines, 1945 edition.
Korea: General File. Harry S. Truman Presidential Museum & Library, Independence, Missouri
Marshall, Irvine H. *Malaria in Korea*. Paper presented 29 April 1954, Army Medial Service Graduate School, Walter Reed Army Medical Center, Washington, D.C.
Marshall, S. L. A. "Combat Stress." Paper presented at conference, Recent Advances in Medicine and Surgery, Army Medical Service Graduate School, Washington, D.C., April 30, 1954.
"Menu" 27th Infantry Regiment. Center for the Study of the Korean War, GU. A. 07367.
National Security Resources Board, 1952, Record Group 304, box 3, "Safe File" National Archives
"POW: The Fight Continues After the Battle" A report for the Secretary of Defense's Advisory Committee on Prisoners of War, Washington, D.C.: 29 July 1955.
"Primary Conclusions of Battle Experience of Unsan" in *Tearing up U.S. Paper Tiger in Korea, Part II. The Strategy of the People's War*. Revolutionary Worker # 1060, June 25, 2000.

Pugh, Lamont. Paper presented before the Association of Military Surgeons of the United States, November 17, 1952.
Special Regulations, Nol. 32-20-2. Department of the Army.

Memoirs

Brown, Rex. Center for the Study of the Korean War, GU. RG 1 A.2100
Crum, Bill: Koreanwar-educator.org/memoirs/crum_bill
Edwards, Paul M. Center for the Study of the Korean War, GU. A.0001
Halverson, Roger. Center for the Study of the Korean War, GU. A. 0076
Hampshire, Oliver. Center for the Study of the Korean War, GU. RG1 A0178
Johnstone, Robert. Center for the Study of the Korean War, GU. RG 9 A.0005
Oglethorpe, David. Center for the Study of the Korean War, GU. A. 1076
Richter, John: www.rt66.com/~koreteng/smal/army/gyrendoc.htm
Schultz, Alexander. Center for the Study of the Korean War, GU. RG 1. 009
Secor, Harold: www. Koreanwar-educator.org/memoirs/secor_harold
Sonley, John. http://www.korean-war.com/Archives/ 2003/12/msg 00082.html
Wathlers, Jimmy James. Center for the Study of the Korean War, GU. RG 7. B. 0016
Wilson, David. Center for the Study of the Korean War, A.8977

SECONDARY

General

Air University Research Web: research.maxwell.af.mil. Excellent and user friendly source of materials, primarily concerning the U.S. Air Force.
The American War Library: members.aol.com/veterans/warkib6k. Source of art, photographs, maps, book, and articles.
Army Quartermaster: qmmuseum.let.army.mil/korea. Covers the logistical concerns of the services during the Korean War.
Center for the Study of the Korean War: koreanwarcenter.org/new_page_9. Library and archives with an excellent collection of oral histories.
China: centrychina.com/history/faq5. Good source for the Chinese Communist side of the question.
Coast Guard: uscg.mil/hq/g-cp/history/h_womm. Deals primarily with women in the Coast Guard.
Eisenhower Presidential Library: eisenhower.archives.gov. Primary source for presidential records dealing with the later part of the Korean War.
Food: gmmusemlle.army.mil/korea/food_UN_korean. All about how the United Nations fed its troops during the Korean War.
Grunt's Military Site: gruntsmilitary.com. Details on military rank, insignia, medals, ribbons, and glossary.
Hamburger, Kenneth E. *Leadership in the Crucible*. College Station, TX.: Texas A & M University Press, 2003.
Ji Moon-Suh. "Portfolio." *The Korean Society Quarterly* (Summer, 2000):12.
Korean War Educator: koreanwar-educator.org/best/k. Site where veterans can discuss and read about particular outfits. Information diverse and subjective.
Korean War 50 year Commemoration: korea50.army.mil/ Maps, images, quotes concerning the Korean War.
Korean War: Net:koreanwar.net/. One of the best broad coverages of details of the war.
Korean War Veterans: kwva.org/. Topics of interest to veterans as well as members of the Korean War Veterans Association.
Korean War Veterans Memorial Home Page: nps.gov/kwvm/home/.

Marshall, S. L. A. "Messages Between the Joint Chiefs of Staff and General Headquarters in Tokyo." *Foreign Relations of the United States*, Vol. 7, (1951).

Meerloo, Joost. A. *The Rape of the Mind.* New York: World Publishing Company. (Out of print).

Mines: 2id.org/minewar. Broad information concerning mine warfare.

National Archives and Records Administration, Central Plains Region, Kansas City, Missouri: archives.gov/central_plains/kansas-city/index. Invaluable source of U.S. Military information.

Paschall, Rod. *A Study in Command and Control: Special Operations in Korea, 1951–1953.* Carlisle Barracks, Pa: U.S. Army Military History Institute, 1988.

Truman Presidential Museum and Library: trumanlibrary.org/ Primary location for all presidential documents related to the war.

University of Missouri at Kansas City (Library): ukc.edu/lib. Primary source of government documents.

U.S. Army Center of Military History: army.mil/cil-pg/ Basic source for military subjects, has good collection of after action reports.

U.S. Army Chaplain Center and School. Remembering Our Army at War in Korea. usachcs.armyu.mil/Korea/Battleforkorea1. Provides an overview of the work of U.S. Chaplains in the Korean War.

U.S. Army Military History Institute: carlisle-www.army.mil/usamhi/ Database concerning manuscript collections and photographs.

U.S. Naval Historical Center: history.navy.mil/ Basic source of information about the Navy during the Korean War, has some excellent maps and chronologies.

Overview

Appleman, Roy E. *Ridgway Duels for Korea.* College Station, Texas: Texas A&M University Press, 1990.

Appleman, Roy E. *U.S. Army in the Korean War: South to the Naktong, North to the Yalu.* Washington, D.C.: Government Printing Office, 1961.

Bajanov, Evgueni. "The Origins of the Korean War: An Interpretation from the Soviet Archives." Conference Paper "The Korean War, An Assessment of the Historical Record" Georgetown University, July 24–25, 1995.

Cagle, Malcolm and Frank Manson. *The Sea War in Korea.* Annapolis, Md.: Naval Institute Press, 1957.

Catchpole, Brian. *The Korean War 1950–1953.* New York: Carroll and Graf Publishers, Inc. 2000.

Coleman, J. D. *Wonju: The Gettysburg of the Korean War.* Washington, D.C.: Brassey's 2000.

Cowdrey, Albert E. *United States Army in the Korean War: The Medics' War.* Washington, D.C.: Center of Military History, United States Army, 1987.

Cumings, Bruce. *The Origins of the Korean War.* 2 volumes. New Jersey: Princeton University Press,1981, 1990.

Fehrenbach, T. R. *This Kind of War.* Washington, D.C.: Brassey's, 1963.

Futrell, Robert F. *The United States Air Force in Korea, 1950–1953.* New York: Duell, Sloan and Pearce, 1983.

Geer, Andrew. *The New Breed: The Story of the U.S. Marines in Korea.* New York: Harper and Brothers, 1962.

Giangreco, Dennis M. *War in Korea: A Pictorial History.* Novato, CA.: Presidio Press, 1990.

Goulden, Joseph C. *Korea: The Untold Story of the War.* New York: Times Books, 1982.

Hallion, Richard P. *The Naval Air War in Korea.* Baltimore, Md.: The Nautical and Aviation Publishing Company of America, 1986.

Hastings, Max. *The Korean War.* New York: Simon & Schuster, 1987.

Hermes, Walter O. *United States Army in the Korean War: Truce Tent and Fighting Front.* Washington, D.C.: Office of the Chief of Military History, 1988.

Higgins, Marguerite. *War in Korea.* Garden City, NY: Doubleday and Company, Inc. 1951.

Korean Institute of Military History. *The Korean War.* Three Volumes. Lincoln: Nebraska: University of Nebraska, 2000.

MacDonald, Callum A. *Korea: The War Before Vietnam.* New York: Freepress, 1986.

Matray, James I. *Historical Dictionary of the Korean War.* Westport, Conn.: Greenwood Press, 1991.

Mossman, Billy C. *Ebb and Flow: November 1950–July 1951, 5, United States Army in the Korean War*, Vol. 5, Washington, D.C.: Department of the Army, Center of Military History, 1990.

Russell, William C. *Stalemate & Standoff: The Bloody Outpost War.* DeLeon Springs, FL.: W. Russell, 1993.

Sandler, Stanley (ed.). *The Korean War: An Encyclopedia.* New York and London: Garland Publishing, Inc., 1995.

Sandler, Stanley. *The Korean War: No Victors, No Vanquished.* Lexington, KY.: University Press of Kentucky, 1999.

Schnable, James. Policy and Direction: The First Year, United States Army in the Korean War. Washington, D.C.: Office of the Chief of Military History, 1972.

Smith, Thomas W. Jr. *Alpha* Brovo* and Delta* Guide to the Korean War.* Indianapolis, Indiana: Alpha Books, 2004.

Stanton, Shelby L. *America's Tenth Legion: X Corps in Korea.* Novato, CA.: Presidio Press, 1989.

Stokesbury, James L. *A Short History of the Korean War.* New York: William Morrow, 1988.

Moving Toward War

Chen, Jian. *China's Road to the Korean War.* New York: Columbia University Press, 1994.

"Letters: Stalin, Kim, and Korean War Origins." *Cold War International History Project (CWHP) Bulletin*, Fall, 1994.

Pierpaoli, Paul G., Jr. *Truman and Korea: The Political Culture of the Early Cold War.* Columbia: University of Missouri Press, 1999.

Rose, Lisle A. *The Cold War Comes to Main Street: America in 1950.* Lawrence: University of Kansas Press, 1999.

Weathersby, Kathryn. "To Attack, or Not to Attack? Stalin, Kim Il Sung and the Prelude to War" *Cold War International History Project (CWHP) Bulletin*, Spring 1995.

Raising the Military

Bailey, C., et al. *Battle Analysis, Wonsan, Rear Area Operation, Rear Area Security, 3rd Infantry Division, Korea, November 1950.* U.S. Army Command and General Staff College, 1984.

Berebitsky, William. *A Very Long Weekend: The Army National Guard in Korea 1950–1953.* Shippensburg, PA.: White Mane Publishing, 1996.

Breuer, William B. *Shadow Warriors: The Covert War in Korea.* New York: Wiley, 1996.

Currie, James T. and Richard B. Crossland. *Twice the Citizen: A History of the U.S. Army Reserves, 1908–1995.* Washington, D.C.: Government Printing Office 1977.

Dalfiume, Richard M. *Desegregation of the Armed Forces: Fighting on Two Fronts, 1939–1953.* Columbia: University of Missouri Press, 1969.

Evanhoe, E. *Dark Moon: Eighth Army Special Operations in the Korean War.* Annapolis, MD: Naval Institute Press, 1995.

Goodspeed, Hill. "Minutemen of Naval Aviation: The Naval Air Reserve in Korea." *Naval Aviation News.* (September–October, 2001): 2.

Hall, Thomas A. "KMAG and the 7th ROK Division." *Infantry,* 79 November–December, 1989.

Holm, Jeanne. *Women in the Military: An Unfinished Revolution.* Novato, CA.: Presidio Press, 1992.

Mosier, Robert H. and Gerald Kornblau. "The GI and the Kinds of Korea." *National Geographic Magazine*, Vol. 103, No. 5 (May, 1953): 635–78.

Price, Scott T. *The Forgotten Service in the Forgotten War: The U.S. Coast Guard's Role in the Korean Conflict*. Annapolis, Md.: Naval Institute Press, 2000.

Rottman, Gordon L. *Korean War Order of Battle*. Westport, CT.: Praeger, 2002.

Schafer, Elizabeth. "Cavalry Units, U.S. Army" in Stanley Sandler *The Korean War: An Encyclopedia*. Garland Publishing, Inc, New York and London, 1995: 63–64.

Stemlow, Mary V. *A History of the Woman Marines, 1946–1977*. Washington, D.C.: U.S. Marine History and Museums Division, 1986.

Turbak, Gary. "Engineers in Combat." *VFW Magazine*, (November, 2002).

Westover, John G. *Combat Support in Korea*. U.S. Army in Action Series, Washington D.C.: Center of Military History, 1987.

Logistics and Weapons

Anything, Anywhere, Anytime: Illustrated History of the Military Airlift Command, 1941–1991. Headquarters Military Airlift Command, Scott Air Force Base, Illinois. May 1991.

Donnelly, William M. "Thunderbirds in Korea: The U.S. 45th Infantry Division, 1950–1952." *Journal of Military History* 64, (October, 2000):1131–1139.

Huston, James A. *Guns and Butter, Powder and Rice: U.S. Army Logistics in the Korean War*. Selingrove: Susquehanna University Press, Associated University Presses, London, 1989.

Marshall, S. L. A. "Commentary on Infantry Operations and Weapons Usage in Korea, Winter of 1950–1951." West Chester, Ohio. Nafziger Collection, Inc., 2002.

Orgokiewics, Richard M. *Armoured Forces and their Vehicles*. New York: Arco Publishing Company, Inc., 1970.

Owen, J. I. H. (ed.). *Brassey's Infantry Weapons of the World 1950–1975*. New York: Bonanza Books, 1979.

Stanton, Shelby L. *U.S. Army Uniforms of the Korean War*. Harrisburg, PA.: Stockpile Books, 1992.

Uzal, W. Ent. "War on a Shoestring" *Military History*, Vol. 17, No 38 (July, 2000): 7.

Communist Forces

Bradbury, William Chapman. *Mass Behavior in Battle and Captivity: The Communists in Battle and Captivity. The Communist Soldier in the Korean War: An Explanatory Study*. Samuel Meyers and Albert D. Biderman, (eds.) Washington, D.C.: Georgetown University, 1968.

Chen, Jian. "China's Changing Aims During the Korean War, 1950–1953." *The Journal of American-East Asian Relations*, Vol. 1, No.1 (Spring, 1992): 8.

Cohen, Eliot A. "The Chinese Intervention in Korea 1950." *Studies in Intelligence*. Volume 32, No. 3, (Fall, 1988): 56.

"Communist Camouflage and Deception." *Air University Quarterly Review*, No. 6, (Spring, 1953).

Gittings, John. *The Role of the Chinese Army*. London: Oxford University Press, 1967.

Goncharov, Sergei, John W. Lewis, and Xue Litai. *Uncertain Partners: Stalin, Mao and the Korean War*. Stanford CA.: University Press, 1993.

Griffith, Samuel B. *The Chinese People's Liberation Army*. New York: McGraw-Hill, 1967.

O'Neill, Mark. "Soviet Involvement in the Korean War: A New View from the Soviet-era Archives." *Magazine of History: Korean War*, Vol. XIV, No. 3: 20–23.

"U.S. Prisoners of War in the Korean Operation: A Study of Their Treatment and Handling by the North Korean Army and the Chinese Communist Forces." 1954.

Weathersby, Kathryn. "The Soviet Role in the Early Phase of the Korean War," *Journal of American-East Asian Relations* 2:4 Winter 1993; 425–450.

Weathersby, Kathryn. *Cold War International History Project Bulletins*, (Fall, 1993).

Whiting, Allen. *China Crosses the Yalu: The Decision to Enter the Korean War*. New York: MacMillan, 1960.

The UN Armies

Barris, Ted. *Deadlock in Korea.* Toronto, Canada: Macmillian, 1999.

Cunningham-Boothe, Ashley, and Peter Farrar. *British Forces in the Korean War.* London: The British Korean Veterans Association, 1988.

Grey, Jeffrey. *The Commonwealth Armies and the Korean War: An Alliance Study.* New York: Manchester University Press, 1988.

Landsdown, John R. P. *With the Carriers in Korea: The Sea and Air War in Southeast Asia, 1950–1953.* Wilmslow Cheshire, United Kingdom: Crely, 1997.

Meyers, Edward. *Thunder in the Morning Calm: The Royal Navy in Korea 1950–1955.* St. Catharines, Ontario: Vanwell, 1991.

Morale, Media, and Myths

Esposito, David M. "Rotation System." in Sandler, Stanley. *The Korean War Encyclopedia.* New York: Garland Publishing, Inc. 1995: 310–311.

Grossman, David. *On Killing: The Psychological Cost of Learning to Kill, in War and Society.* New York: Little Brown and Company, 1995.

Haeges, Chris. *War is the Force that Gives Us Meaning.* New York: Public Affairs, 2002.

Hoare, J. E. "British Public Opinion and the Korean War." Papers of the British Association for Korean Studies, No. 2, 1992.

Kolb, Richard. "Korea's Invisible Veterans' Return to an Ambivalent America."*VFW Magazine* (November, 1997):1.

Kolb, Richard. "The First Moral Crusade." *VFW Magazine* (June, 1988).

Life. "Life on the Newsfronts of the World." *Life Magazine*, Vol. 34, (January 19, 1953): 33.

Marshall, S. L. A. *Men Against Fire: The Problem of Battle Command in Future Wars*, New York: William Morrow and Co, 1961.

Matray, James. "Revisiting Korea: Exposing Myths of the Forgotten War. Part 2. *Prologue Magazine,* Vol. 34, No. 2 (Summer, 2002):1–8.

Moeller, Susan D. *Shooting War: Photography and the American Combat Experience.* New York: Basic Books, 1991.

Perkins, Dexter. "Dissent in Time of War" *Virginia Quarterly Review*, Vol. 47 (Spring, 1974).

Pierpaoli, Paul G., Jr. "Portfolio," *The Korean Society Quarterly,* (Summer, 2000): 12 *Prologue Magazine.* Vol. 34, No. 2. (Summer, 2002) 1–8.

Rose, P. K. "Perceptions and Reality: Two Strategic Intelligence Mistakes in Korea, 1950." *International Social Science Review.* (Fall-Winter, 2001).

Solomon, Normon. *War Made Easy.* New York: John Wiley & Sons, Inc. 2005.

Time. "American Fighting Man: Destiny's Draftee" (January 1, 1951).

Thomas, Charles S. as quoted in *MSTS Magazine* (October, 1954).

"World War II, Korea, and Vietnam." *Public Opinion and the Military Establishment*, ed. Charles C. Moskos, Jr. (1971).

Carrying On

Borts, Lawrence H. *United Nations Medals and Missions: The Medals and the Ribbons of the United Nations.* Fountain Inn, SC.: Medals of America Press,1998.

Coakley, R. W., P. J. Scheips, E. J. Wright, with G. Horne. "Antiwar Sentiment in the Korean War, 1950–1953" in Sandler, Stanley (ed.). *The Korean War: An Encyclopedia.* New York: Garland Publishing, Inc. 1955: 24.

Hume, Bill. *Babysan: A Private Look at the Japanese Occupation.* Tokyo, Japan: Kasuga Boeki K.K., 1953.

Schafer, Elizabeth. "Geneva Conference of 1954." in Stanley Sandler, *The Korean War: An Encyclopedia.* Garland Publishing, Inc. New York and London, 1995:120–123.

Venzke, Roger R. "Confidence in Battle, Inspiration in Peace." *The Army Chaplaincy* (Winter/Spring, 2002).

Venzke, Roger R. *The United States Army Chaplaincy, 1945–1975.* Washington, D.C.: Office of the Chief of Chaplains, Department of the Army, 1977.

Coming Home

Blumenson, Martin. "Lessons Learned: Reviewing the Korean War." *Army Magazine* (May, 1997): 6.

Pierpaoli, Paul G., Jr. "Truman's Other War: The Battle for the American Homefront, 1950–1953." *Magazine of History*, Vol. 14, No. 3 (Spring, 2002).

Zweiback, Adam J. "The Turncoat GIs: Nonrepatriotes and the Political Culture of the Korean War." *The Historian* (Winter, 1998): 1–13.

Wounded and Dead

Chappell, Richard G. and Gerald E. Chappell. *Corpsmen: Letters from Korea.* Kent, Ohio: The Ken State University Press, 2000.

Elder, Glen and Elizabeth Clipp. "Combat Experience (in WWII and the Korean War) and Emotional Health: Impairment and Resilience in Later Life." *Journal of Personality*, Vol. 57 (June, 1989): 311–341.

Omori, Frances. *Quiet Heroes: Navy Nurses of the Korean War 1950-1953, Far East Command.* St. Paul, MN.: Smith House Press, 2000.

Segal, Henry A. "Observations on Prisoners of War Immediately Following Their Release." Paper presented to Army Medical Service Graduate School, Walter Reed Army Medical Center 30 April 1954.

Smith, Robert B. "Disaffection, Delegitimation, and Consequences: Aggregate Trends for Treatment." Department of the Army, Office of the Assistant Chief of Staff, G-2.

Varhola, Michael. *Fire and Ice: The Korean War, 1950–1953.* Madison City, Iowa: Sava Publishing Company, 2000.

Remembering War

Berry, Henry. *Hey, Mac, Where Ya Been: Living Memories of the U.S. Marines in the Korean War.* New York: St. Martins Press, 1988.

Bodnar, John. *Remaking America: Public Memory, Commemoration and Patriotism in the Twentieth Century.* Princeton, N.J.: Princeton University Press, 1996.

Brune, Lester H. "Recent Scholarship and Findings about the Korean War." *American Studies International.* Washington, D.C., Vol. 36, No. 3 (Oct, 1998): 4–17.

Brune, Lester H. *The Korean War: Handbook of the Literature and Research.* Westport, Conn.: Greenwood Press, 1996.

Day, William W., IV. *The Running Wounded.* Riverton, Wyoming: Big Bend Press, 1990.

DeWeerd, Harvey A. "Lessons of the Korean War," *Yale Review*, 40 (Summer, 1951): 592–603.

Edwards, Paul M. *To Acknowledge a War: The Korean War in American Memory.* Westport, Conn.: Greenwood Press, 2000.

Epstein, Stephen R. "Review of Dan McCann and Barry S. Strauss War and Democracy: A comparative Study of the Korean War and the Peloponnesian War." *Korean Studies Review*, No. 15, (2002).

Ehrhart, W. D. and Philip K. Jason, eds. *Retrieving Bones: Stories and Poems of the Korean War.* New Brunswick, N.J.: Rutgers University Press, 1999.

History Book Club. *Remembering the Forgotten War: 1950–1953.* History Book Club, New York, 2000.

McCann, D. "Review of Philip West and Shu Ji Moon *Remembering the Forgotten War: The Korean War through Literature and Art*" *Korean Studies Review*, No. 4 (2001).

Pierpaoli, Paul G., Jr. "Beyond Collective Amnesia: A Korean War Retrospective" *Military History*. Vol. 14, No. 3 (Spring, 2000): 1–4.

Venzke, Roger R. "Remembering our Army at War in Korea" Chapter Three. *The United States Army Chaplaincy 1945–1975* Office of the Chief of Chaplains, U.S. Army Chaplain Center, Fort Jackson South Carolina Washington, D.C. 1977.

Weintraub, Stanley. "How to Remember the Forgotten War" *American Heritage*, New York, Vol. 51, No. 3 (May/June, 2000):100.

West, Philip. "Interpreting the Korean War." *American Historical Review* (February, 1988): 4.

West, Philip and Suh Ji-moon (eds.). *Remembering the Forgotten War: The Korean War through Literature and Art*. Armonk, NY: M. E. Sharpe, 2000.

Oral History and Memoirs

Knox, Donald. *The Korean War: Pusan to Chosin; An Oral History*. New York: Harcourt, Brace, Jovanovich, 1985.

Smith, Theodore H. *The Double 1* . New York: Xlibris Corporation, 2002.

Strait, Sandy. *What Was It Like in the Korean War?* New York: Royal Fireworks Press, 1999.

Terry, Addison. *The Battle for Pusan: A Korean War Memoir*. Novato, CA.: Presidio Press, 2000.

U.S. Naval Historical Center. "Special Series Interviews," Volume 3, pp 217–218 as quoted in Howarth, Stephen. *To Shining Sea: A History of the United States Navy*. New York: Random House, 1991: 489.

INDEX

Germ warfare, xxiv
GIs, xiii, 7, 9, 17, 55, 61, 68, 87, 114, 118,
    121, 122, 124, 128, 143, 152, 156, 158,
    159, 160, 170, 178, 180
Gloster Hill, 28
Gloucester Battalion, 28
Goguryeo Kingdom, 9
Go-Joseon Kingdom, 9
Goncharov, 4
Good Conduct Medal, 163
Goryeo Dynasty, 9
Graceland University, xv, xvi
Grand Alliance, 12
Graves Registration, 110, 117
Graybeards, xii, 174
Gray Ladies, 122
Great Britain, including military, xxi, 6, 8,
    12, 15, 22, 75, 76, 80, 83, 103, 127,
    129, 133, 136, 144, 155
Greater East Asian Co-Prosperity Sphere, 3
"Great Seabee Train Robbery," 121
Greeks, xxi, xxii, 52, 83, 127
Gregory, Captain Oree, 102
Grenade, 59, 72, 78, 92, 138
Grunt, xii, 77
Guard duty, 61
Guerillas, xxiii, 24, 133, 135

Hagaru-ri, xvi
Haile Selassie, Emperor, 128
Halazon tablets, 99
Hamgyong Province, 8
Hamhung, xxii, 9,23, 24
Hampshire, Oliver, 86
Han River, xx, 8, 26, 28, 50
Hangul, xv
Hansen, LeRoy, 142
Harrington and Richardson, 71
Harvey, 169
Hastings, Max, 23, 187
Hatful of Rain, 174
Haven, USS, 103, 104
Hawaii, 34
Heartbreak Ridge, xxiii, 29
Heat, as in climate, 92
Hedges, Chris, 185
Helicopters, xiv, xxiii, 37, 48, 100, 101,
    102, 104, 109, 111, 115
Hemorrhagic fever, 105
Henry, Colonel F. B., 177
Hermit Kingdom, xiii
Hermit Kingdom, The, 178

Hershey, Lewis B., 45
Heyerdahl, Thor, 169
Hickman Air Force Base, 104, 110
Higgins, Marguerite, 98, 143, 152
High Speed Transports, 121
Hill 111, 32
Hill 119, 32
Hill 180, 26, 73
Hill 234, 32
Hill 235, 28
Hill 303, xx, xxi
Hill 355, 106, 137
Hill 773, 29
Hill 940, 29
Hill 983, 29
Hill War, 18, 29
Hispanics, 49, 176, 177
Historiography, 3
Hodge, Lieutenant General John R., 12, 13
Hodong, 20
Hoengsong, 26
Homefront, 169–170
Homesickness, 3
Hongchon, 26
Hong Kong, 22, 156
Hook, battle of the, xxiv, 38
Hope, Bob, 123
Horace A. Bass, USS, 121
Hospitals, 52, 98, 100, 104, 105, 107,
    122, 128
Hospital ships, 52, 103–104, 111, 120, 128
"Hostilities only," 3
Houston, Walter, 169
Howitzers, 67, 76, 78
Humanitarian efforts, 157–158
Hungnam, xxii, 3, 24, 35, 38, 39
Hwachon Reservoir, 9, 27
Hwanghae Province, 133
Hydroelectric plants, 17, 37

Ickes, Harold, 145
Imjin River, 25, 27
Inactive reserves, 46
Inchon, xxii, 7, 12, 17, 22, 23, 25, 26, 35,
    37, 39, 47, 52, 92, 99, 103 111, 121,
    150, 167
India, 12, 17, 39, 128
Indiana, 10
Indochina, 128, 181
Innovations, 10–8
Insulated footwear, 108
Integration, 49–51, 51

ABOUT THE AUTHOR

PAUL M. EDWARDS is Professor Emeritus and the Senior Fellow at the Center for the Study of the Korean War on Graceland University's Independence, Missouri, campus. Among his publications are *The Hill Wasrs of the Korean Conflict* (2006); *A to Z of the Korean War* (2005); *The Korean War: A Historical Dictionary* (2003); *The Korean War: A Documentary History* (1999); *A Guide to Films of the Korean War* (1997); and *The Inchon Landing, Korea* (1994). Dr. Edwards is a veteran of the Korean War.